high note 1

Student's Book

CONTENTS

WELCOME! About me

VOCABULARY Countries and nationalities
GRAMMAR Subject pronouns, *to be*
SPEAKING Greetings, giving and asking for personal information, asking for spelling

Kathy	Welcome to 'Let's talk!' English video chat. I'm your teacher, Kathy. I'm from Scotland and I'm twenty-five.
Carlos	Good morning, Kathy! I'm Carlos and I'm Argentinian.
Kathy	Hello Carlos. Nice to meet you! How old are you?
Carlos	I'm eighteen.
Fatma	Hi guys! My name's Fatma and I'm seventeen.
Kathy	Sorry, can you spell your name, please?
Fatma	Yes, it's F-a-t-m-a.
Kathy	Welcome, Fatma! Where are you from?
Fatma	I'm from Istanbul. I'm Turkish.
Sanjit	Hello everyone! Pleased to meet you! I'm Sanjit. That's S-a-n-j-i-t. It's an Indian name.
Kathy	Hello Sanjit. Are you from India?
Sanjit	No, I'm not. I'm French, but my parents are from India.
Carlos	Kathy, what's your email address?
Kathy	Good question! It's kathyclaire@letstalk.co.uk.

1 SPEAKING **In pairs, ask and answer the questions.**

1 Do you use video chats?
2 Which ones? Who with? What for?

2 *1.2* **Read and listen to the video chat. Answer the questions.**

1 What's the teacher's name?
2 Where's Carlos from?
3 How old is Fatma?
4 What nationality is Sanjit?
5 Where are his parents from?
6 What's Kathy's email address?

Subject pronouns, *to be*

3 **Study the Grammar box and complete the rules.**

1. In affirmative sentences we put subject pronouns *before* / *after* the verb.
2. In negative sentences we add 'not' *before* / *after* the verb.
3. In questions we put subject pronouns *before* / *after* the verb.

Subject pronouns, *to be*

	I	He • She • It	We • You • They
+	**I am ('m)** Brazilian.	**He is** Brazilian.	**We are** Brazilian.
-	**I am not ('m not)** from Poland.	**She is not (isn't)** from Poland.	**You are not (aren't)** from Poland.
?	**Am I** a student? Yes, **I am.**/No, **I am not ('m not).**	**Is it** your address? Yes, **it is.**/No, **it is not (isn't).**	**Are they** students? Yes, **they are.**/ No, **they are not (aren't).**

Grammar Reference and Practice > page 160

4 **Correct the sentences and rewrite them with the correct subject pronouns.**

1. Carlos, Fatma and Sanjit are on the Face-to-face app. (Let's talk!)
   No, they aren't. They're on the Let's talk! app.
2. My family and I are from Brazil. (France)
3. Carlos is American. (Argentinian)
4. Kathy's phone number is 07756759941. (0775679888)
5. Sanjit is a Greek name. (Indian)
6. You and your friend are sixteen. (fifteen)
7. I'm a teacher. (student)

5 **Complete the conversation with the correct form of *to be*.**

Kathy Let's welcome our new student: Hi! What [1]*is* your name?
Ariadne It [2]_________ Ariadne.
Kathy Can you spell it, please?
Ariadne Yes, it [3]_________ A-r-i-a-d-n-e.
Kathy What a lovely name! [4]_________ it Italian?
Ariadne No, it [5]_________. It [6]_________ Greek.
Kathy [7]_________ you from Greece?
Ariadne Yes, I [8]_________.
Kathy How old [9]_________ you, Ariadne?
Ariadne I [10]_________ sixteen.

6 **SPEAKING In pairs, ask and answer the questions from Exercise 5.**

7 **1.3 Complete the table with the missing words. Listen and check.**

Country	Nationality	Country	Nationality
Argentina	Argentinian		Scottish
Brazil		Spain	
	Egyptian		Turkish
Hungary		China	
	Indian		Japanese
Italy		Vietnam	
	Moroccan		French
Romania		Greece	
	English		New Zealander
Poland		The USA	

8 **1.4 Listen and complete the student cards.**

1
NAME: [1]*Mito*
AGE:
COUNTRY:

2
NAME:
AGE:
COUNTRY:

3
NAME:
AGE:
COUNTRY:

9 **SPEAKING Work in pairs. Take turns to talk about famous people from the box. Ask questions to guess who your partner is talking about.**

Adele (1988) Alice Braga (1983) Andy Murray (1987) Donatella Versace (1955) Kendall Jenner (1995) Lana Condor (1997) Lionel Messi (1987) Mark Zuckerberg (1984) J.K. Rowling (1965) Paloma Picasso (1949) Rafael Nadal (1986)

A *Is it a man?* **B** *No, it's a woman.*
A *Where is she from?* **B** *She's English.*
A *How old is she?* **B** *She is thirty-one.*
A *Is it Adele?* **B** *Yes, she is!*

10 **Write a short online profile about yourself. In your profile include:**

- your name.
- your age.
- your nationality.

0B About my stuff

VOCABULARY Personal possessions, basic adjectives
GRAMMAR Plural nouns, articles, *this/that/these/those*
SPEAKING Describing things

1 **SPEAKING Which of the things in the pictures 1–12 are with you in class right now?**

2 ***1.5*** **Match the words with the pictures. Listen and check.**

bag books headphones diary skateboard keys scarf smartphone sunglasses tablet wallet ~~watch~~

3 **Read the posts. Answer the questions.**

1 What's **long**?
2 What's **cool**?
3 What's **expensive**?
4 What's **old**?
5 What's **gold**?
6 What's **new**?
7 What's **orange**?
8 What's **small**?

1 skateboard

Plural nouns, articles

4 **Study the Grammar box on page 7 and complete the rules.**

Plural nouns

1 We add ________ to make the plural of regular nouns.
2 We add ________ to make the plural of nouns ending in *-ch*, *-s*, *-sh*, *-ss* or *-x*.
3 We delete ________ and add ________ to make the plural of nouns ending in *-y*.

Articles

4 We use ________ or ________ to talk about single objects in general.
5 We use ________ to talk about specific objects.
6 We don't use ________ or ________ to talk about plural objects in general.

@myfavouritethings

followers: 304 following: 321

Here are my favourite things:

That's my bag.
And those are my favourite books.
This is a wallet with no money in it!
That's a mini tablet – it's very small!
This isn't just a phone – it's a gold smartphone!
Those are my cool sunglasses.
This is my secret diary!
These are the keys to a new scooter. Yay!
These are very expensive headphones!
That's an old watch from Dad.
That's an orange scarf.
Oh! And that's a really long skateboard!

1 *watch*

2 ________

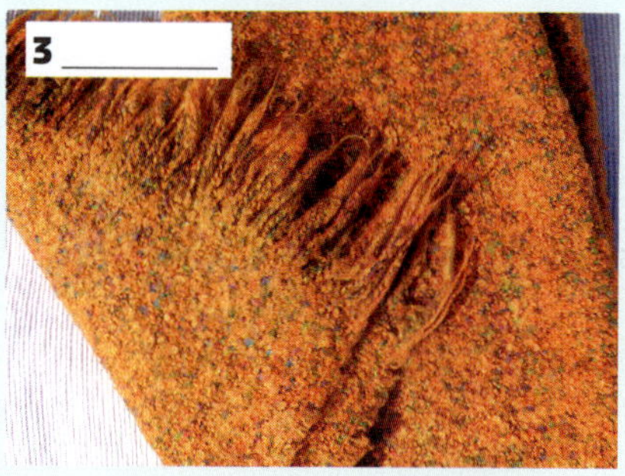
3 ________

4 ________

5 ________

6 ________

7 ________

8 ________

9 ________

10 ________

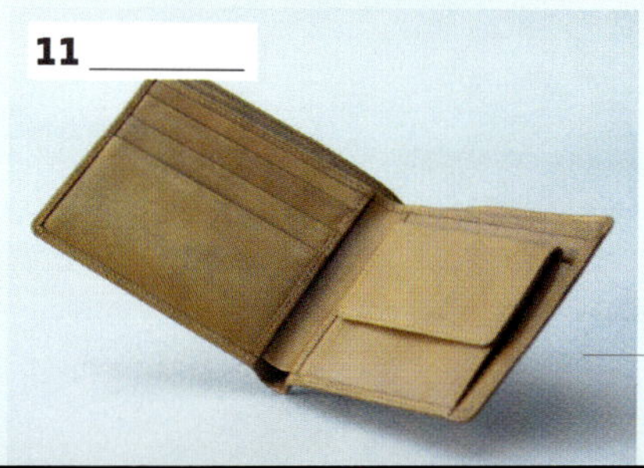
11 ________

12 ________

Plural nouns, articles

Plural nouns

Regular	key-**keys**, smartphone-**smartphones**, wallet-**wallets**
-ch, -s, -sh, -ss or -x	watch-**watches**, bus-**buses**, brush-**brushes** class-**classes**, box-**boxes**
Consonant +y	country-**countries**, diary-**diaries**
Irregular	child-**children**, man-**men**, mouse-**mice**, person-**people**, scarf-**scarves**

Articles

a/an	It's **a** watch. It's **an** old watch.
the	It's **the** watch from my father. They are **the** keys to the house.
No article	They are old watches.

Grammar Reference and Practice > page 160

This/that/these/those

This is my wallet.

That is my schoolbag.

These are my headphones.

Those are my sunglasses.

Grammar Reference and Practice > page 160

5 Write the plural forms of these words.

1 bag *bags*
2 tablet ________
3 baby ________
4 class ________
5 woman ________
6 bus ________

6 Look at the picture and complete the description with a, an, the or no article.

It's [1]*a* picture of [2]________ young woman. In her hand are [3]________ two shopping bags: [4]________ yellow bag and [5]________ red bag. [6]________ woman is happy. It's [7]________ nice day!

This/that/these/those

7 Study the Grammar box and complete the rules.

1 We use ________ for singular objects near us.
2 We use ________ for singular objects not near us.
3 We use ________ for plural objects near us.
4 We use ________ for plural objects not near us.

8 *1.6* **Read the conversation and choose the correct words. Listen and check.**

Paula Look! [1]*This / These* is my new smartphone.
John [2]*This / That* phone on the table over there?
Paula No, [3]*this / that* phone here in my hand!
John [4]*These / Those* modern phones are good but they're big! I prefer [5]*that / those* old, small phones!
Paula No way!

9 Rewrite the sentences in their plural form.

1 That's a big wallet!
Those are big wallets!
2 Where's the key?
3 'What's that?' 'It's just an old box.'
4 Keep out! A diary is secret!
5 Look at this new scarf – it's beautiful!
6 It's a game for a child.

10 *1.7* **Listen and match each person with their favourite thing. There are two extra things.**

1 ☐ Javier
2 ☐ Sofia
3 ☐ Greta
4 ☐ Parvez

a bag
b diary
c football
d headphones
e smartphone
f sunglasses

11 *1.7* **Complete the missing information. Then listen again to check your answers.**

1 *This* is my favourite thing – my smartphone. It's really ________!
2 My favourite thing is ________ yellow and red bag – it's ________ birthday present.
3 What? I can't hear you! ________ new headphones are fantastic!
4 ________ old football in ________ photo is my favourite object!

12 Write your own post about your favourite things. Then tell your partner about them.

This new sports watch is my favourite thing. It's big and black and from ...

0C About my family

VOCABULARY Family, jobs
GRAMMAR Possessive adjectives, possessive *'s*, *have got*
SPEAKING Describing family

MY FAMILY

Hi, I'm Julia and I'm sixteen. I haven't got a very big family, just my mum, my dad, my brother Aden (he's fourteen) and me.
My mother's name is Suzanne – she's thirty-eight and she's an office worker. My father's name is Daniel. He's forty and he's a nurse.
My parents haven't got brothers or sisters, so I haven't got uncles or aunts or cousins. But I've got cool grandparents. Their names are: Sam and Alice (on the bikes) – mum's parents, and Ben and Trudy (in the sports car) – dad's parents. My grandfather Sam is sixty and he's a doctor and his wife, Alice, is fifty-eight and she's a science teacher. My other grandmother, Trudy is an actor and her husband, Ben is a pilot. They're great!

1 *1.8* **Read and listen. Decide if statements 1–6 are true or false.**

1. Julia's brother is 14.
2. Her sister is called Suzanne.
3. Her father has got two brothers.
4. Her grandmother, Alice, is a doctor.
5. Ben and Trudy are her father's parents.

Possessive adjectives, possessive 's

2 **Study the grammar box and complete the rules.**

1. We use possessive adjectives or possessive *'s/s'* to say who *does / has* something.
2. We put the apostrophe *before / after* the *-s* for singular nouns.
3. We put the apostrophe *before / after* the *-s* for plural nouns.

Possessive adjectives, possessive 's

Possessive adjectives

My • Your • His • Her • Its • Our • Your • Their
My family is big.

Whose* and possessive *'s/s'

Singular	Plural
Whose friend is she?	**Whose** friends are they?
She's my sister**'s** friend.	They're my parent**s'** friends.
Whose toy is it?	**Whose** house is it?
It's the baby**'s** toy.	It's my cousin**s'** house.

Grammar Reference and Practice > page 160

3 **Read about Dan's family and choose the correct words.**

Hi! [1]*My / Your* name's Dan. I've got one brother, [2]*her / his* name is Alex, and a sister, [3]*his / her* name is Liz. [4]*Our / Your* parents are both busy doctors, and we've got lovely grandparents. We've also got two cats – [5]*his / their* names are Laurel and Hardy!
Tell me about [6]*our / your* family.

4 **SPEAKING In pairs, ask and answer questions about the photos above.**

A *What colour is Julia's grandparents' car?*
B *It's blue.*

5 **Write *'s* or *s'* to complete the sentences.**

1. This is Tom<u>'s</u> tablet.
2. My two brother ________ bikes are new.
3. My grandparent ________ house is very big. They live in the country.
4. Is your dad ________ name Alastair?
5. That's Aden ________ ball. Don't touch it!
6. Our cousin ________ house is in America. Their names are Paul and Anne.

6 **SPEAKING Work in pairs. Ask and answer questions about things in your classroom.**

A *Whose bag is that?*
B *It's Hanna's.*
A *Whose books are those?*
B *They are Andy's.*

7 🔊 ***1.9*** **Complete the table with the words from the box. Listen and check.**

aunt brother children cousins father grandfather grandmother grandparents mother parents sister uncle

Male	*brother*			
Female				
Male or female				

8 Complete the definitions.

1 Your mother's mother is your *grandmother*.
2 Your aunt's child is your __________.
3 Your father's brother is your __________.
4 Your mother and father are your __________.
5 Your parents' parents are your __________.
6 You, your brother and sister are your parents' __________.

9 🔊 ***1.10*** **Match photos 1–12 with the words from the box. Listen and check.**

☐ actor ☐ doctor ☐ factory worker ☐ farmer
☐ nurse ☐ office worker ☐ pilot ☐ police officer
☐ scientist ☐ teacher ☐ server ☐ vet

10 SPEAKING In pairs, ask and answer questions about your family's jobs.

A *What's your father's job?*
B *He's an office worker. What's your mother's job?*
A *She is a pilot.*

Have got

11 Study the grammar box and complete the rule.

We use *have got* to talk about *actions / possessions*.

Have got		
	I • You • We • They	He • She • It
+	I **have ('ve) got** a car.	He **has ('s) got** a big family.
-	You **have not (haven't) got** pets.	She **has not (hasn't) got** a brother.
?	**Have** they **got** grandparents? Yes, they **have**./No, they **have not (haven't)**.	**Has** she **got** a sister? Yes, she **has**./No, **she has not (hasn't)**.

Grammar Reference and Practice > page 160

12 Complete the conversation with the correct forms of *have got*.

Amy [1]*Have* you *got* a big family?
Mark Yes, I [2]__________. What about you?
Amy I [3]__________ a brother or a sister, but I [4]__________ three cousins. [5]__________ you __________ a brother or a sister?
Mark Yes, I [6]__________. I [7]__________ two brothers and three sisters!
Amy Wow! [8]__________ your mother __________ a job?
Mark Yes, she [9]__________. She's a French teacher.

13 SPEAKING In pairs, use the questions in Exercise 12 to help you talk about your family.

14 Write a short blog post about your family. Use the text in Exercise 3 as a model.

My family is very big ...

1

2

3

4

5

6

7

8

9

10

11

12

0D About my class

VOCABULARY Classrom instructions
GRAMMAR Imperatives, object pronouns
SPEAKING Giving instructions

1

2

1 🔊 ***1.11*** **Read and listen. Check you understand the instructions. Which instructions match the photos 1–2.**

ask and answer questions   copy it from the board
don't disturb the lesson   listen to the teacher
make notes in your exercise book   read the instructions
speak English   use a dictionary   work in groups

Imperatives

2 **Study the Grammar box and complete the rules.**

1. We use the imperative to say we want *to do something / somebody to do* something.
2. There are no *subject pronouns / verbs* in imperative sentences.

Imperatives

Finish the exercises!
Don't speak Italian!
Listen to me/you/him/her/it/us/them!

Grammar Reference and Practice > page161

3 🔊 ***1.12*** **Complete the instructions with the correct forms of the verbs from the box. Then listen and check.**

~~ask~~   find   not forget   not leave   read   use   write

How to do your homework

[1]*Ask* your teacher if you don't understand your homework.
[2]______ to do it! [3]______ it to the last minute!
[4]______ a quiet place to study.
[5]______ your homework in your exercise book.
[6]______ a dictionary to check your spelling and
[7]______ your homework again to check for mistakes.

Object pronouns

4 **Study the Grammar box and complete the rule.**

Object pronouns go *after / before* the verb or preposition.

Object pronouns

Ask **me** questions.
Work with **him**.
Talk to **her**.
Copy **it** from the board.
Tell **us** about your holiday.
I can help **you**.
Meet **them** in class.

Grammar Reference and Practice > page 161

5 **Choose the correct words to complete the instructions about how to relax.**

1. A nice hot bath – have *it / you* just before you go to bed!
2. Lights – don't forget to switch *him / them* off!
3. A good friend – spend time with *her / us*!
4. Find a good book – and read *him / it*!
5. Computers or tablets – don't use *me / them* all the time!
6. The dog – take *him / you* for a long walk!

6 **In pairs, write your own instructions for one of the following situations. Then give them to another pair.**

how to learn English songs   how to pass exams
how to remember new vocabulary
how to watch English films

How to learn English songs:
- *find a song on the internet.*
- *listen to it four or five times.*
- *read ...*

About my time

VOCABULARY Days of the week, months, seasons, times, dates
GRAMMAR Ordinal numbers
SPEAKING Saying what date it is, asking about birthdays, telling the time

1 *1.13* **Look at Alice's diary and answer the questions. Listen and check.**

MONDAY 1.10	
5 p.m.	hairdresser's appointment
TUESDAY 2.10	
8 a.m.	start of autumn term
WEDNESDAY 3.10	
3 p.m.	piano lesson
THURSDAY 4.10	
8 a.m.	dentist's
FRIDAY 5.10	
3 p.m.	shopping for books
SATURDAY 6.10	
8 a.m.	my birthday
8 p.m.	my party
SUNDAY 7.10	
1 p.m.	Grandma's

1 What day is it today? *Monday*
2 What's the date?
3 Which month is next?
4 Which season is it now?
5 When is Alice's birthday?
6 What time is her party?

2 *1.14* **Complete the table with the words from the box. Then listen and check.**

January July March May November Saturday September summer Thursday ~~Tuesday~~ winter

Days of the week	**Monday,** *Tuesday*, **Wednesday,** ______, **Friday,** ______, **Sunday**
Months	______, **February,** ______, **April,** ______, **June,** ______, **August,** ______, **October,** ______, **December**
Seasons	**Spring,** ______, **autumn,** ______

WATCH OUT!

You write *4th September*, but you say: *'the fourth of September'*.

You write *2019*, but you say: *'twenty nineteen, two thousand and nineteen'*.

3 *1.15* **Say the following dates in pairs. Listen and check your answers.**

1 31/3/1992
2 24th July
3 12/11/2015
4 22nd April
5 5/2/2004
6 9/6/1978
7 13th July

The thirty-first of March nineteen ninety-two.

4 SPEAKING **In pairs, study the expressions. Then look at the clocks and ask and answer questions about the time.**

What' the time?/What time is it?

6.00	**It's six o'clock.**
3.15	**It's a quarter past three.**
2.30	**It's half past two.**
3.45	**It's a quarter to four.**
12.50	**It's ten to one.**
24.00	**It's midnight.**

1

2

3

4
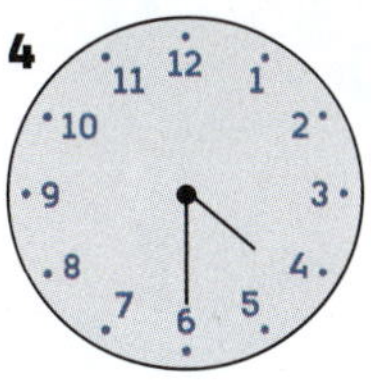
5
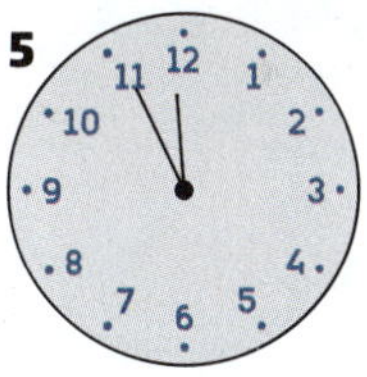
6

7
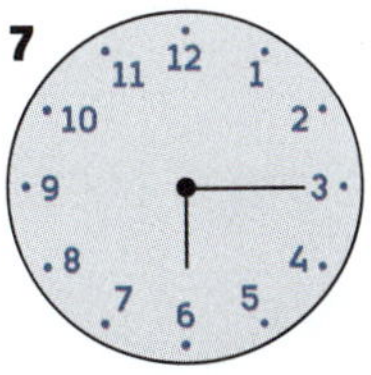
8

1 What's the time?
It's ten o'clock.

5 SPEAKING **In pairs, use the prompts to ask and answer questions.**

When/birthday?
What/time ...?
What/day ...?
Which month/Christmas day?
What/date ...?
Which season ...?

A *When's your birthday?*
B *It's on ...*

01 The things we do

VOCABULARY Daily routines, free-time activities and frequency expressions

GRAMMAR Present Simple affirmative and negative, adverbs of frequency and Present Simple questions **Use of English** > page 172

SPEAKING Talking about likes and dislikes

WRITING A personal profile

VIDEO Grammar ▷ Documentary ▷ Communication ▷

Different countries, **different routines**

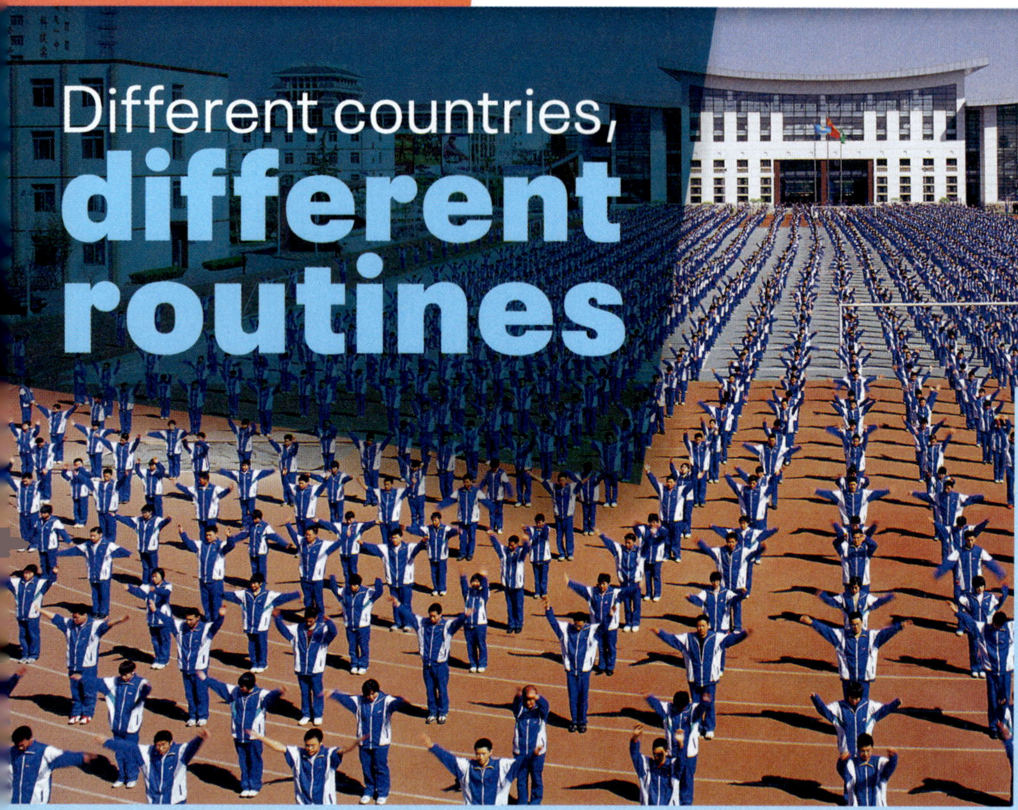

A

Lan-Fen In China, we do exercise before school starts. #differentworlds
Lily Wow! Are all those people students at your school?
Lan-Fen Yes. We've got 5,000.
Lily That's amazing! Our school's got 600 students.

B

Yuna I get up at 6 a.m. I'm at school until 5 p.m. and then I have extra lessons. I get home at 9 p.m. This isn't unusual in Japan. #differentworlds
Josie 😮 That's a LONG day!
Yuna I know. And then I do my homework!

C

Luis We have dinner at 9.30 in the evening. It isn't unusual in Spain. #differentworlds
Gemma That's really late! We eat at about 6.30 p.m. in the UK. Or maybe 7 p.m. at weekends. I go to bed at 10!

D

Khalid The weekend starts on Friday in the United Arab Emirates. I don't go to school and my dad doesn't go to work. We play chess. #differentworlds
Ellis Three days without school! You're lucky!
Khalid We don't have three days. Our weekend is Friday and Saturday. School starts on Sunday morning again.

1A GRAMMAR AND VOCABULARY

Present Simple: affirmative and negative

1 **Look at the photos and read posts A–D. In pairs, decide which post is about:**

1 ☒ D free time?
2 ☐ a meal?
3 ☐ a morning activity?
4 ☐ a typical schoolday?

2 **Match sentences 1–2 with rules a–b.**

1 ☐ The weekend starts on Friday in the United Arab Emirates.
2 ☐ We have dinner at 9.30 in the evening.

a We use the Present Simple to talk about a regular/repeated action/activity.
b We use the Present Simple to talk about a fact.

3 **Study the Grammar box and find more examples of the Present Simple in the text.**

Present Simple: affirmative and negative

	I • You • We • They	He • She • It
+	I **go** out with my friends on Saturdays. We **get up** at 10 a.m. at weekends.	My cousin **lives** in the UK. My mum **goes** to work at 7.30 a.m.
–	They **don't have** lessons on Sundays.	He **doesn't go** to my school.

Spelling rules for third person he/she/it:
Most verbs: **live** → **lives**, **play** → **plays**
Verb ends in *-o*, *-ch*, *-sh*, *-s*, *-x*: **watch** → **watches**
Verb ends in a consonant + *y*: **study** → **studies**

Grammar Reference and Practice > page 162

4 **Read the posts again and choose the correct words.**

1 Lan-Fen *goes / doesn't go* to a very big school.
2 Yuna *starts / doesn't start* school at 6 a.m.
3 Gemma *has / doesn't have* dinner before 7 p.m.
4 Khalid *plays / doesn't play* chess on Sundays.

5 **SPEAKING In pairs, talk about how your life is different from the people's in the posts.**

I don't get up at 6 a.m. I'm at school until 3 p.m.

6 **Complete the table with these words. Which activities are in the photos in Exercise 1?**

do get go ~~go to~~ have

1 *go to* school/work/bed
2 ________ exercise/homework/housework
3 ________ a shower/lessons/breakfast/lunch/dinner
4 ________ home/out with friends/shopping
5 ________ home/dressed/up

7 **1.16 Complete the text with the correct forms of the verbs in brackets. Then listen and check.**

For Yuna, in Japan, the schoolday [1] *starts* (start) at 8.30 so on weekdays she [2] ________ (get up) at about 6 a.m. 'I [3] ________ (have) a shower and I [4] ________ (get) dressed – we wear a uniform. I [5] ________ (not like) it!'
She [6] ________ (have) lessons until 3.30 p.m. Then after school she goes to clubs. Yuna [7] ________ (not like) sport. She [8] ________ (go) to a homework club. Then she and her friends [9] ________ (go) to extra English lessons at a private school. 'Our teacher [10] ________ (come) from London, in England. He [11] ________ (not speak) any Japanese so we [12] ________ (speak) English all the time.'
Yuna [13] ________ (get) home at about 9 p.m. She [14] ________ (study) for another hour. Then it's time for bed.

8 **1.17 PRONUNCIATION How do we say the final 's' in the verbs in the table? Put the verbs from the box in the correct column. Listen and check your answers. Practise saying these verbs.**

~~eats~~ goes likes lives studies watches

/s/	/z/	/ɪz/
starts *eats*	plays	teaches

9 **Complete the table with these time expressions. Then write six sentences using the verb phrases from Exercise 6 and these time expressions.**

6 a.m. ~~Friday~~ January Saturday morning the evening weekends

on	Wednesday afternoon, weekdays, [1] *Friday*, [2] ________
in	the morning, August, [3] ________, [4] ________
at	eight o'clock, midnight, [5] ________, [6] ________

I do homework in the evening.

10 **SPEAKING In pairs, talk about what you do on Saturdays. Then tell the class.**

On Saturdays I get up at 8. Sally gets up at 10!

1 Read the sentence below and watch the video. Say what the speakers answer. Then in pairs, talk about your typical Sunday.

Tell me about your typical Sunday.

GRAMMAR VIDEO

☐ **I can use the Present Simple to talk about daily routines.**

1 **Match verbs 1–12 with activities a–d. Which of the activities can you see in the photos?**

1	☒c hang out	**a**	shopping
2	☐ go	**b**	computer games
3	☐ go to	**c**	with friends
4	☐ play	**d**	a friend's house
5	☐ play	**a**	to music
6	☐ listen	**b**	books
7	☐ read	**c**	to the cinema
8	☐ go	**d**	games on your mobile phone
9	☐ play	**a**	sport
10	☐ go	**b**	a blog
11	☐ write	**c**	to parties
12	☐ watch	**d**	TV or films

2 ***1.18*** **Listen to six people and check your answers to Exercise 1.**

3 **Complete the text with the verbs from Exercise 1.**

I love weekends. On Saturdays I [1]*hang* out with my friends. We [2]_________ to the cinema or we [3]_________ shopping in the city. Every month we [4]_________ to a party or a concert – we [5]_________ to music a lot.

On Sunday mornings I get up late and I [6]_________ a book in bed. I spend the rest of the day with my family. My brother and I [7]_________ computer games or we all [8]_________ sport together. My parents love sport. On Sunday evenings we [9]_________ a film.

4 **Look at Felix's diary. Complete the sentences.**

1 He *has a guitar lesson* on Tuesday and Sunday evenings.
2 He ____________ on Mondays, Thursdays and Saturdays.
3 He ____________ on Friday and Saturday evenings.
4 He ____________ on Mondays, Tuesdays, Wednesdays, Thursdays and Sundays.
5 He ____________ on Saturday afternoons.
6 He ____________ on Wednesday and Fridays.

Monday	5.30 p.m.	football
	8 p.m.	homework
Tuesday	6 p.m.	guitar lesson
	8.30 p.m.	homework
Wednesday	4 p.m.	art club
	5.30 p.m.	homework
Thursday	5.30 p.m.	football
	8 p.m.	homework
Friday	4 p.m.	art club
	7 p.m.	go out with friends
Saturday	10.30 a.m.	football
	2 p.m.	go shopping
	7 p.m.	go out with friends
Sunday	3 p.m.	homework
	6 p.m.	guitar lesson

WATCH OUT!

We use frequency expressions to talk about how often we do things:

I have a party ***once a year****.*
I go the cinema ***twice a month****.*
I play sport ***three/four times a week****.*

Grammar Reference and Practice > 162

5 **Rewrite the sentences in Exercise 4 with the expressions from the box.**

once a week   twice a week   three times a week   five times a week

1 He has a guitar lesson twice a week.

6 **SPEAKING Use a word or phrase from each column to talk about how often you do these activities.**

have English lessons	once	a day
make dinner for my parents	twice	a week
do exercise	three times	a month
go to the cinema	four times	a year
go to parties		
have a shower		

I have English lessons three times a week.

☐ **I can talk about free-time activities and hobbies.**

5 SIGNS YOU ARE A PHONE ADDICT

01

1 You **always** check your phone before you get up.
2 Your phone battery **usually** dies before you get home.
3 You **often** check your phone for new messages.
4 You are **never** without your phone.
5 You **sometimes** feel nervous when your phone doesn't get a signal.

1C GRAMMAR

Adverbs of frequency

1 **Read *5 signs you are a phone addict*. Which sentences are true for you?**

2 **Study the Grammar box and put the adverbs in brackets in the correct place in the sentences below.**

Your phone is with you. (always)
You check your phone after each lesson. (usually)

Adverbs of frequency

We often use adverbs of frequency with the Present Simple:
never < *hardly ever* < *sometimes* < *often* < *usually* < *always*
0% 100%

We put **adverbs of frequency**:
- before the main verb
- after the verb *be*

Grammar Reference and Practice > page 162

3 **1.19 Read the conversation and choose the correct words to complete the sentences. Then listen and check.**

Rachel Do you want to have lunch, Tom? Tom?
Tom Lunch? Yes, I do. Sorry.
Rachel On your phone again!
Tom It's a quiz: *Five signs you are a mobile phone addict*.
Rachel Well, the answer for you is 'Yes'.
Tom You're the same!
Rachel No way! I [1]*hardly ever use / use hardly ever* my phone.
Tom Let's see, One: How often do you check your phone before you get up?
Rachel Well, I [2]*always do / do always* that. I [3]*get sometimes / sometimes get* important messages.
Tom So that's 'True'. Two: How often does your phone die before you get home?
Rachel Never. It [4]*usually has / has usually* about 50% left.
Tom Three: How often do you check your phone for new messages?
Rachel Only when I hear the sound for a new message.
Tom OK. Four: Do you ever go out without your phone?
Rachel No, I don't. It [5]*always is / 's always* in my pocket.
Tom Another 'True'. And five: How do you feel when your phone doesn't get a signal? Bad, maybe?
Rachel Bad? Never. But I [6]*feel often / often feel* bad when I miss lunch! Let's eat!

Present Simple: questions

4 **Read the questions. Choose the correct words to complete the rules.**

Do you want to have lunch, Tom?
How often does your phone die before you get home?

1 We use *do / does* to form Present Simple questions with I/you/we/they.
2 We use *do / does* to form Present Simple questions with he/she/it.
3 In questions with *does*, the main verb *has / doesn't have* an *-s* ending.

5 **Study the Grammar box and check your answers to Exercise 4.**

Present Simple: questions

	I • You • We • They	He • She • It
?	**Do** you **go out** on Saturdays? Yes, I **do**./No, I **don't**.	**Does** he **work** at weekends? Yes, he **does**./No, he **doesn't**.
Wh-?	What time **do** you **get up** on Sundays?	How **does** your dad **go** to work?

Grammar Reference and Practice > page 162

6 **Put the words in the correct order to make questions. Then, in pairs, ask and answer the questions.**

1 games / Does / on / your / her / mum / phone? / play / mobile
Does your mum play games on her mobile phone?
2 does / often / How / sport? / play / dad / your
3 write / you / a / blog? / Do
4 shopping? / often / do / you / go / How
5 friends? / with / you / hang / out / do / your / Where
6 text / you? / often / best friend / How / your / does

7 **SPEAKING In pairs, ask and answer the questions.**

1 Do you ever switch your phone off?
2 How often do you check emails on your phone?
3 How many songs have you got on your phone?
4 How often do you take photos on your phone?

☐ **I can ask and answer questions about everyday life and use adverbs of frequency.**

STEREOTYPES! ARE THEY TRUE?

1.20

1 ☐ **EMILY**

My dad often says this about me. It's true that I hardly ever read newspapers. But I read the news online every day. And it isn't all stuff about celebrities or my favourite bands! At school, we also talk about important events or problems. They're important to us. And we often look up more information about them online.

2 ☐ **OLIVER**

Do people really think this is true? It's a really old and boring stereotype. I love all kinds of music: from 1970s music to modern electronic pop. My brother is only thirteen and he's the same. When my parents put on their favourite songs in the car, we usually love them.

3 ☐ **HARRY**

The problem is teenagers don't have the experience of adults. I don't always think before I do things. I sometimes go out with my friends until late and we often forget to send our parents a message. Hey, we're sixteen! We forget! But they worry about me. And when I get back, they're sometimes angry.

4 ☐ **EVIE**

I think teenagers and adults do this. My mum loves games. And my dad never puts his mobile down. He often checks his emails at dinner. He reads the news and he plays games as well. I never play games. They're a waste of time. OK, I read a lot of social network stuff on my phone and that isn't very useful. But I also use it for homework, take photos and listen to music and podcasts.

5 ☐ **GRACE**

This isn't true! I play sports at school twice a week. I get up at eight on Saturdays and I play football in a team. I usually cycle to school and when I go out, I hardly ever eat fast food. Of course, some teenagers stay in all the time and their only hobby is TV or computer games. Adults don't help much. Parents hardly ever go out and play games with their children.

1D READING AND VOCABULARY

1 SPEAKING Read the stereotypes about teenagers. Who usually says these things about teenagers?

a 'They often make bad decisions.'
b 'They are hardly ever interested in the real world.'
c 'They wear terrible clothes.'
d 'They don't do any exercise.'
e 'They're always on their phones.'
f 'They always listen to terrible music.'

2 Do you agree or disagree with the stereotypes in Exercise 1? Use the phrases below.

I don't agree!
This is often true.
This is sometimes true.
I agree.

3 Study Active Reading and match quotes a-f from Exercise 1 with comments 1-5 on page 16. There is one extra stereotype.

ACTIVE READING | Understanding the main idea of a paragraph

- Read the text quickly.
- Don't worry about new words.
- Find important words or phrases in each paragraph.

4 Read comments 1–5 again and choose the correct answers.

1 Emily thinks that teenagers
a prefer talking about news to reading news.
b are only interested in celebrity news.
c care about the real world.

2 What do we know about Oliver's taste in music?
a It's often similar to his parents'.
b It's very different from his brother's.
c It's mainly modern.

3 Harry thinks that teenagers
a are often angry.
b often forget things.
c worry all the time.

4 What does Evie say about mobile phones?
a She only uses her phone for useful activities.
b Her parents sometimes waste time on their phones.
c Her dad takes photos on his phone.

5 Grace says she
a often eats unhealthy food.
b loves computer games.
c does a lot of sport.

5 Complete the questions with the highlighted phrasal verbs in the comments on page 16. Then in pairs, ask and answer these questions.

1 When you go out, do you ever *get back* after midnight?
2 Do you ever ________ on Saturday night?
3 How often do you ________ a favourite song when you get up?
4 What kind of information do you often ________ on your phone?
5 Why is it not a good idea to ________ your phone ________ on the table in a café?

6 REFLECT | Society Read the quotes. Which group of people are they about? Do you agree with the quotes? Discuss in groups.

“*They never listen to young people.*”

“They work all the time and they don't have fun.”

“They always talk about boring subjects.”

“They always watch TV in the evenings.”

7 SPEAKING In groups, think of other stereotypical views teenagers have of adults. Are they always true?

2 WATCH AND REFLECT Go to page 150. Watch the documentary *Free time on an island* and do the exercises.

☐ **I can understand the main idea of a paragraph and talk about stereotypes.**

1E SPEAKING

1 **In pairs, ask and answer the questions.**

1 How often do you buy presents for your friends on their birthdays or on other special days?
2 What kind of presents do you usually buy?
3 What kind of presents do you like?

2 *3* *1.21* **Phoebe wants to buy a present for Finlay. Watch or listen and decide who suggests each idea – Mum (M) or Phoebe (P)?**

1 a computer game
2 a fantasy book
3 two cinema tickets

3 **Study the Speaking box and tick the sentences that are in the dialogue.**

Phoebe What's that?
Mum It's a new lamp for Finlay. It's his birthday on Saturday. Have you got a present for him?
Phoebe No, I haven't.
Mum He enjoys playing computer games. What about a game?
Phoebe They're expensive! And anyway, I can't stand playing computer games.
Mum OK, but this is a present for Finlay, not ...
Phoebe What kind of books does he like reading? Does he enjoy reading fantasy books?
Mum Phoebe, I know you like fantasy books, but remember, it's Finlay's ...
Phoebe Yes, sure.
Mum I know, he loves going to the cinema. What about two tickets to see a film?
Phoebe Cinema tickets? Actually, that's a good idea. I quite like watching films at the cinema.
Mum Um, yes ... But Finlay has other friends, Phoebe. Remember, it's his birthday.
Phoebe Yeah, but I don't like staying in on Saturdays. The cinema's a great idea. Thanks, Mum!
Mum You're welcome.

SPEAKING | Talking about likes and dislikes

Asking about likes and dislikes
☐ **What's your favourite** film?
☐ What kind of books **does he like reading**?
☐ Does he **enjoy reading** fantasy books?

Like/enjoy/love
☐ You **like reading** fantasy books (a lot).
☐ He **enjoys playing** computer games.
☐ He **loves going** to the cinema.

Quite like/don't mind
☐ I **quite like watching** films at the cinema.
☐ I **don't mind staying** in on Saturdays.

Don't like/can't stand/hate
☐ I **don't like staying** in on Saturdays.
☐ I **can't stand playing** computer games.
☐ I **hate doing** exercise.

4 **Study *Watch out!* and complete the conversations with the correct forms of the verbs from the box. Then, in pairs, ask and answer the questions.**

do ~~go~~ hang out play stay in watch x 2

A Do you like watching films at the cinema or on TV?
B I quite like [1]*going* to the cinema but I don't mind [2]__________ films at home.

A Do you go out on Saturday nights?
B Always! I hate [3]__________ on Saturdays.

A What's your favourite free-time activity?
B I enjoy [4]__________ with my friends. We listen to music, play football and we talk.

A Does your dad like [5]__________ exercise?
B No. He loves [6]__________ football on TV but he never plays.

A What kind of computer games do you like [7]__________?
B I enjoy sports games.

WATCH OUT!

After the verbs and phrases *like*, *love*, *enjoy*, *hate*, *can't stand*, *don't mind* we use the *-ing* form of the verb.

5 **In groups of three, ask and answer questions to find activities:**

- only one person loves/hates doing
- two people love/hate doing
- all three people love/hate doing

6 **In pairs, role play the situation below.**

It is your friend's birthday next week and you want to buy him/her a present. Discuss the things he/she likes/loves, can't stand/hates doing. Decide on a suitable present.

A *It's Jacob's birthday next week. We haven't got a present.*
B *Does he like watching films?*
A *Not really. He ...*

☐ **I can talk about likes and dislikes.**

1F LISTENING AND VOCABULARY

1 **SPEAKING In pairs, discuss the activities. Which ones do you like, love or can't stand doing?**

dancing in front of the mirror
reading celebrity magazines
singing in the shower   sleeping late
watching children's cartoons
watching reality TV

2 **In pairs, read the podcast summary and discuss the questions.**

1 What is a 'guilty pleasure'?
2 Are any of the activities in Exercise 1 your guilty pleasures?

What is your guilty pleasure? What things do you like doing but you never tell anyone about? Today some of my friends and family members tell me about their guilty pleasures.

3 **1.22 Listen to Zoe's conversation with her three friends about their guilty pleasures. Which activity from Exercise 1 does each person enjoy doing? In pairs, check your answers.**

1 Jen ________
2 Owen ________
3 Jack ________

4 **1.23 Read the questions. Then listen again and choose the correct pictures.**

1 Where does Jen read celebrity magazines?

2 Where is Owen's mum on Saturday mornings?

3 In which situation does Jack watch reality TV?

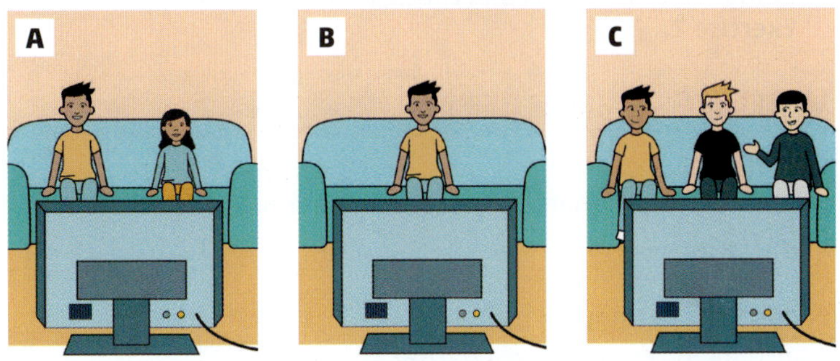

5 **1.24 Dictation. Listen to Zoe talking about her guilty pleasure. Then write down exactly what you hear.**

6 **1.25 Complete the sentences with the prepositions from the box. You can use some prepositions more than once. Then listen and check.**

~~about~~   about   at   for   with

1 I look at the pictures and **dream** *about* the homes, clothes and lifestyles.
2 I never read them with friends. They **laugh** ________ me!
3 I never **tell anyone** ________ my extra sleep.
4 My sister doesn't **agree** ________ me.
5 I **wait** ________ my parents to go to work.

7 **Write five sentences using the verbs and the prepositions in Exercise 6.**

I dream about having a holiday in Australia.

8 **SPEAKING Do you ever tell anyone about your guilty pleasures? Discuss in pairs.**

☐ **I can understand a simple personal podcast and talk about guilty pleasures.**

I'M ALEX

1 **I'm 15 and I'm from the UK.** I live with my parents and my sister in Liverpool. We've also got a cat, Louis.

2 **On schooldays I get up at 7.30 a.m.** I usually get home at 6 p.m. because I go to clubs after school. My favourite club is Spanish but I'm not very good at it.

3 **I enjoy doing different things in my free time but I don't like being alone.** On Saturdays I go out with friends. We usually go shopping and to the cinema. I also love playing computer games. My best friend has a lot of games so I often go to his house.

1G WRITING | A personal profile

1 **Read the profile. Which paragraph does the photo match?**

2 **Match paragraphs 1–3 in the profile with topics a–c.**

a ☐ free-time activities
b ☐ personal information
c ☐ daily routine

3 **Study the Writing box and check your answers to Exercise 2.**

WRITING | A personal profile

Paragraph 1
Introduce yourself (name, age, country/nationality, family):
I'm Alex.
I'm 15 and I'm from the UK.
I live with my parents and my sister.

Paragraph 2
Talk about your daily life:
On schooldays I get up at 7.30 a.m.

Paragraph 3
Talk about your free time – use *like/enjoy/love/can't stand/hate* + *-ing*:
I enjoy doing different things in my free time.

WATCH OUT!

We link information in sentences with *and*, *but*, *so*, *because*. We use:

- *and* to connect similar information:
  I'm 15 ***and*** *I'm from the UK.*
- *but* to contrast information:
  My favourite club is Spanish ***but*** *I'm not very good at it.*
- *so* to talk about a result:
  My best friend has a lot of games ***so*** *I often go to his house.*
- *because* to give a reason for something:
  I usually get home at 6 p.m. ***because*** *I go to clubs after school.*

☐ **I can write a personal profile.**

4 **Choose the correct words to complete the sentences.**

1 I like watching films on TV *but / because* I love watching them in the cinema.
2 I go to school at 7 a.m. *and / so* I get home at 4.30 p.m.
3 It's Tom's birthday *so / because* I need to buy a present.
4 I never play computer games *so / because* I think they're a waste of time.
5 I buy things online *because / but* I don't enjoy busy shops.
6 She plays the guitar *but / and* she plays the piano.
7 I love playing sport *but / so* I can't stand doing exercise.
8 We don't live near a cinema *because / so* I watch films at home.

5 **Complete Carrie's profile with the phrases from the box.**

going shopping | he doesn't live with us | I get up very early | ~~I live in Boston, in the USA~~ | I love clothes | then I have two hours of sports training

My name's Carrie. I'm 16 and [1]*I live in Boston, in the USA*. I have got a brother but [2]________. He's at college, in San Francisco.
School starts at 7.30 a.m. so [3]________. I'm always really tired in my first class. Classes finish at about 2 p.m. but [4]________.
I get home at about 5 p.m. I do homework every night.
In my free time, I spend a lot of time online.
I write a blog about fashion because [5]________.
I also enjoy reading and [6]________.

6 **WRITING TASK Write your personal profile.**

- Use the Writing box as a guide.
- Use linking words: *and*, *but*, so and *because*.

1A GRAMMAR AND VOCABULARY 5.1

activity (n) /æk'tɪvəti/

amazing (adj) /ə'meɪzɪŋ/

before/after school /bɪˌfɔː/ˌɑːftə 'skuːl/

come from sth /'kʌm frəm ˌsʌmθɪŋ/

do exercise /ˌduː 'eksəsaɪz/

do homework /ˌduː 'həʊmwɜːk/

do housework /ˌduː 'haʊswɜːk/

extra lessons /ˌekstrə 'lesənz/

free time (n) /ˌfriː 'taɪm/

get dressed /ˌget 'drest/

get home /ˌget 'həʊm/

get up /ˌget 'ʌp/

go home /ˌgəʊ 'həʊm/

go out with friends /ˌgəʊ aʊt wɪð 'frendz/

go shopping /ˌgəʊ 'ʃɒpɪŋ/

go to a club /ˌgəʊ tə ə 'klʌb/

go to bed /ˌgəʊ tə 'bed/

go to school/work /ˌgəʊ tə 'skuːl/'wɜːk/

have a shower /ˌhæv ə 'ʃaʊə/

have breakfast/lunch/dinner /ˌhæv 'brekfəst/ 'lʌntʃ/'dɪnə/

have lessons /ˌhæv 'lesənz/

life (n) /laɪf/

meal (n) /miːl/

play chess /ˌpleɪ 'tʃes/

routine (n) /ruː'tiːn/

schoolday (n) /'skuːldeɪ/

start (v) /stɑːt/

study (v) /'stʌdi/

unusual (adj) /ʌn'juːʒuəl/

wear a uniform /ˌweər ə 'juːnəfɔːm/

world (n) /wɜːld/

1B VOCABULARY 5.2

every month (adv) /ˌevri 'mʌnθ/

go to a friend's house/the cinema/a party/ a concert /ˌgəʊ tə ə 'frendz haʊs/ðə 'sɪnəmə/ ə 'pɑːti/ə 'kɒnsət/

hang out with friends /ˌhæŋ aʊt wɪð 'frendz/

have a guitar lesson /ˌhæv ə gɪ'tɑː ˌlesən/

late (adv) /leɪt/

listen to music /ˌlɪsən tə 'mjuːzɪk/

once/twice/three times a week (adv) /ˌwʌns/ ˌtwaɪs/ˌθriː taɪmz ə 'wiːk/

play computer games /ˌpleɪ kəm'pjuːtə geɪmz/

play games on your mobile phone /ˌpleɪ ˌgeɪmz ɒn jə ˌməʊbaɪl 'fəʊn/

play sport/tennis/football /ˌpleɪ 'spɔːt/'tenɪs/ 'fʊtbɔːl/

read a book /ˌriːd ə 'bʊk/

spend (v) /spend/

watch TV/a film /ˌwɒtʃ ˌtiː 'viː/ə 'fɪlm/

write a blog /ˌraɪt ə 'blɒg/

1C GRAMMAR 5.3

addict (n) /'ædɪkt/

answer (n) /'ɑːnsə/

check your phone (for new messages) /ˌtʃek jə 'fəʊn (fə ˌnjuː 'mesɪdʒɪz)/

die (v) /daɪ/

feel bad /ˌfiːl 'bæd/

feel nervous /ˌfiːl 'nɜːvəs/

get a signal /ˌget ə 'sɪgnəl/

miss (v) /mɪs/

phone battery (n) /'fəʊn ˌbætəri/

quiz (n) /kwɪz/

sign (n) /saɪn/

sound (n) /saʊnd/

switch off (v) /ˌswɪtʃ 'ɒf/

take photos /ˌteɪk 'fəʊtəʊz/

text (n, v) /tekst/

true (adj) /truː/

1D READING AND VOCABULARY 5.4

adult (n) /'ædʌlt/

be interested in sth /ˌbi 'ɪntrɪstɪd ɪn ˌsʌmθɪŋ/

be on the phone /ˌbi ɒn ðə 'fəʊn/

boring (adj) /'bɔːrɪŋ/

care about sth (v) /'keər əˌbaʊt ˌsʌmθɪŋ/

celebrity (n) /sə'lebrəti/

clothes (n) /kləʊðz/

cycle (v) /'saɪkəl/

do sport /ˌduː 'spɔːt/

event (n) /ɪ'vent/

experience (n) /ɪk'spɪəriəns/

forget (v) /fə'get/

get back /ˌget 'bæk/

have fun /ˌhæv 'fʌn/

hobby (n) /'hɒbi/

kind of music /ˌkaɪnd əv 'mjuːzɪk/

look up /ˌlʊk 'ʌp/

make a decision /ˌmeɪk ə dɪ'sɪʒən/

modern (adj) /'mɒdn/

newspaper (n) /'njuːsˌpeɪpə/

online (adv) /ˌɒn'laɪn/

put down /ˌpʊt 'daʊn/

put on (a song) (v) /ˌpʊt ɒn (ə 'sɒŋ)/

real world /ˌrɪəl 'wɜːld/

send a message /ˌsend ə 'mesɪdʒ/

similar (adj) /'sɪmələ/

social network (n) /ˌsəʊʃəl 'netwɜːk/

stay in /ˌsteɪ 'ɪn/

stereotype (n) /'steriətaɪp/

stuff (n) /stʌf/

subject (n) /'sʌbdʒɪkt/

taste in music /ˌteɪst ɪn 'mjuːzɪk/

team (n) /tiːm/

teenager (n) /'tiːneɪdʒə/

terrible (adj) /'terəbəl/

the news (n) /ðə 'njuːz/

unhealthy food /ʌnˌhelθi 'fuːd/

useful (adj) /'juːsfəl/

waste (n, v) /weɪst/

worry about sth (v) /'wʌri əˌbaʊt ˌsʌmθɪŋ/

1E SPEAKING 5.5

cinema ticket (n) /'sɪnəmə ˌtɪkɪt/

enjoy (v) /ɪn'dʒɔɪ/

expensive (adj) /ɪk'spensɪv/

fantasy book (n) /'fæntəsi bʊk/

good idea /ˌgʊd aɪ'dɪə/

next week (adv) /ˌnekst 'wiːk/

present for sb (n) /'prezənt fə ˌsʌmbɒdi /

1F LISTENING AND VOCABULARY 5.6

agree with sb (v) /ə'griː wɪð ˌsʌmbɒdi/

dream about sth (v) /'driːm əˌbaʊt ˌsʌmθɪŋ/

family member (n) /'fæməli ˌmembə/

guilty pleasure (n) /ˌgɪlti 'pleʒə/

laugh at sth /'lɑːf ət ˌsʌmθɪŋ/

lifestyle (n) /'laɪfstaɪl/

tell sb about sth (v) /'tel ˌsʌmbɒdi əˌbaʊt ˌsʌmθɪŋ/

wait for sb (v) /'weɪt fə ˌsʌmbɒdi/

1G WRITING 5.7

at college /ət 'kɒlɪdʒ/

fashion (n) /'fæʃən/

finish (v) /'fɪnɪʃ/

good at sth (adj) /'gʊd ət ˌsʌmθɪŋ/

personal information (n) /ˌpɜːsənəl ˌɪnfə'meɪʃən/

sports training (n) /'spɔːts ˌtreɪnɪŋ/

Remember More > page 174

VOCABULARY AND GRAMMAR

1 Complete the expressions with the words from the box.

a shower bed ~~computer games~~ dinner films home homework housework out with friends school sport TV

1 play *computer games*, ________
2 go ________, ________
3 do ________, ________
4 go to ________, ________
5 have ________, ________
6 watch ________, ________

2 Complete the sentences with the verbs from the box.

dream about ~~get back~~ laugh at look up put on stay in

1 My parents usually *get back* from work at 7 p.m.
2 I often ________ facts online for homework projects.
3 My friends and I never ________ animal videos on the internet. They're just not funny!
4 I always ________ on school nights.
5 I often ________ being famous one day.
6 I usually ________ the local radio station in the morning.

3 Choose the correct words to complete the sentences.

1 British students *doesn't go* / *don't go* to school on Saturdays or Sundays.
2 I *haven't* / *don't have* breakfast before school because I'm never hungry.
3 My little brother *don't read* / *doesn't read* books – he prefers computer games.
4 My best friend and I usually *hang out* / *hangs out* after school because we *lives* / *live* close to each other.
5 Julia and her sister, Anna, *goes* / *go* to bed at ten o'clock on weekdays. Julia *gets up* / *get up* at seven, but Anna *doesn't get up* / *don't get up* until nine.
6 Charlie *write* / *writes* a blog about sport, but he *don't do* / *doesn't do* it every day.

4 Complete the conversation with the correct forms of the verbs in brackets.

Hayley So, what [1]*do you do* (you/do) in your free time, Elena?
Elena Well, I [2]________ (go) to the cinema quite often.
Hayley Cool! What type of films [3]________ (you/like) watching?
Elena I [4]________ (love) fantasy and horror films.
Hayley Really? Me too! My brother [5]________ (not like) horror films at all!
Elena So what [6]________ (your brother/do) in his free time?
Hayley He [7]________ (listen) to music or [8]________ (read) books. He [9]________ (not enjoy) reading scary books!

5 Put the adverbs of frequency a–f into the correct order.

always hardly ever ~~never~~ often sometimes usually

a [1] never
b ☐ often
c ☐ hardly ever
d ☐ always
e ☐ sometimes
f ☐ usually

6 Add adverbs of frequency to these sentences to make them true for you.

1 I listen to really loud music in my bedroom.
2 My family and I watch TV on Saturday night.
3 My mum helps me do my homework.
4 My brother does the housework.
5 It rains in my country.
6 Our teachers give us a lot of homework.

USE OF ENGLISH

7 Choose the correct words a–c to complete the texts.

STRATEGY | Multiple choice – short texts

Read each text first and try to understand the general idea. Look at the words before and after the gap and choose the right answer.

1 If you and your friends like __ to the cinema, this 2 for 1 offer on tickets is perfect for you!

a go b goes c going

2 Come and __ your homework at after-school club 4–6 p.m., Monday to Friday.

a do b have c put

3 The football team meets __ a week for training.

a one b once c one time

4 DO YOU FIND IT HARD TO GET __ IN THE MORNING? THEN MAYBE YOU NEED MORE SLEEP?

a over b to c up

5 This is an invitation to my birthday party __ 7 p.m., on Friday, 25th June.

a at b in c on

6 RUBY, PLEASE MAKE DINNER __ YOURSELF AND BEN. I NEED TO WORK LATE TONIGHT. XXX MUM

a for b in c with

Use of English > page 172

READING

8 **Read texts 1–5 and choose the correct answers: a, b or c.**

1

PHOTOGRAPHY CLUB
ON WEDNESDAYS AND FRIDAYS
3.30 P.M.–5.00 P.M.
IN THE ART ROOM (H35)
LEARN TO TAKE ***BETTER PHOTOS!***

a They have a photography club in the music room on Wednesdays.
b They have a photography club at school twice a week.
c They have a photography club at school every day.

2

Hi Sam
I live in Manchester in the north of England. In my free time I like playing computer games and watching TV series with my friends. We sometimes play football in the park after school.
Jack

a Jack likes playing football at the weekends.
b Jack loves playing games on his mobile phone.
c Jack enjoys watching television with his friends.

3

FILM AT ODEON CINEMA, OXFORD
FILM TIME: 7.45 p.m.
LENGTH OF FILM: 2 hours, 30 minutes
TICKETS: adults £10.50, children £7.95

a The film finishes at a quarter to eight.
b The film is two and a half hours long.
c The film is the same price for adults and children.

4

Hi Amy
I've got two tickets for the FREE TIME concert on Saturday. Do you want to come with me? I know they're one of your favourite bands. Let me know if you want to come.
Love
Becky

a Amy's got two tickets for a FREE TIME concert.
b Becky wants to give Amy her ticket to a FREE TIME concert.
c Amy likes FREE TIME very much.

5

University Student
BASKETBALL CLUB
needs new players for its men's team
Training: 8.00 p.m. on Monday, Wednesday and Friday evenings
Matches: Saturday afternoons: 4 p.m.
Phone: Luke on 07799 123123

a The team needs men and women.
b The team plays matches at weekends.
c The team trains every Saturday.

SPEAKING

9 **In pairs, take turns to ask and answer the questions.**

1 What do you usually do after school?
2 How many hours of homework do you do on weekdays?
3 How often do you play sport?
4 What do you usually do at weekends?
5 How many hours do you spend online every day?

WRITING

10 **Read part of an email from Pablo.**

I'm Pablo from Barcelona. Please write and tell me about yourself, your family and your friends. Tell me about your school and what you do on a typical day. What do you like doing in your free time?

Write an email to Pablo telling him about yourself and your life.

02 No place like home

VOCABULARY House, household chores, prepositions of place
GRAMMAR *There is/There are, some* and *any, can/can't*, **Use of English** > page 172
SPEAKING Asking for information
WRITING A description of a place
VIDEO Grammar ▷ Documentary ▷ Communication ▷

1

2

3

HOW WE LIVE
HOBBY HOUSES

What are your hobbies? How much time do you spend on your hobby? One, two or three hours a day? In special hobby houses all around the world people practise their hobbies at home 24/7!

A A SKATEBOARDER'S DREAM

This Californian house is a skateboarder's dream! There aren't any straight walls in it so it's possible to skate along the floor and up the walls. You get around the house on four wheels: from the living room, dining room and kitchen area to the bedroom and bathroom area. Then go outside and practise some new moves on the skate terrace.

B A CLIMBER'S PARADISE

This house in Osaka is perfect for free climbers – there aren't any stairs! You use your hands and feet to climb up the high walls to the bedrooms upstairs. There are only two floors, and there isn't an attic, but it is possible to climb up to the roof. Then climb down to the balcony and to the front of the house and start all over again!

C A HOME MUSIC STUDIO

But what if music is your hobby? Are there any hobby houses for music lovers? Yes, of course there are. In this London house there's a music studio in the cellar under the hall. In the studio there are some speakers and some musical instruments. There's a microphone, a computer and a keyboard too.

2A GRAMMAR AND VOCABULARY

1 SPEAKING In pairs, ask and answer the questions.

1. Where do you live and who do you live with?
2. What is your family home like? Is it a flat or a house?
3. Do you like the place where you live? Say why.

2 Match photos 1–3 with texts A–C. Then say which of the things below you can see in the photos.

attic balcony bathroom bedroom ceiling cellar dining room door floor garage hall kitchen living room roof stairs study terrace wall window

3 Add the words from Exercise 2 to the vocabulary map.

HOUSE

Rooms
bathroom, ________, ________, ________, ________, ________

Parts of a room
ceiling, ________, ________, ________, ________

Parts of a house
attic, ________, ________, ________, ________, ________, ________, ________

4 Read the text and match houses A–C with sentences 1-5. Which house:

1. ☐ has a special place under the hall
2. ☐ hasn't got any stairs
3. ☐ has a special terrace to practise a hobby
4. ☐ hasn't got any straight walls
5. ☐ has got a balcony

There is/There are with *some* and *any*

5 Look at the examples and complete the rules.

There are some musical instruments in the studio.
There aren't any straight walls.
Are there any hobby houses for music lovers?

We use *some* / *any* in affirmative sentences.
We use *some* / *any* in negative sentences and questions.

6 Study the Grammar box and check your answers to Exercise 5.

There is/There are* with *some* and *any

	Singular	Plural
+	**There is ('s)** an attic.	**There are ('re) some** stairs.
–	**There is not (isn't)** a garden.	**There are not (aren't) any** pictures.
?	**Is there** a cellar? Yes, **there is.** No, **there isn't.**	**Are there any** flats here? Yes, **there are (some).** No, **there aren't (any).**

Grammar Reference and Practice > page 162

7 Complete the text about an artist with *there is/there isn't* or *there are/there aren't*.

My sister Lily is a great artist. On the walls in her bedroom 1*there are* some fantastic drawings. In my favourite drawing 2________ a wonderful white horse running across a river. 3________ a house behind the horse and 4________ some trees next to the house. But 5________ a person on the horse's back. In fact, 6________ any people in Lily's drawings because she only likes drawing horses.

8 ▷ *1.26* Complete the conversation with *a/an*, *some* or *any*. Listen and check.

Tom In my dream house there's 1*a* swimming pool and a cinema and in the cellar there are 2________ games to play, lots of games. Are there 3________ games in your dream house?
Lily No, there aren't. There aren't 4________ games or TVs but there's 5________ art studio and on the walls there are 6________ paintings by famous artists.
Tom Is there 7________ garden?
Lily Yes, there is.
Tom Are there 8________ animals in your dream house – cats or dogs?
Lily There aren't 9________ cats or dogs but there are 10________ horses!

9 SPEAKING Work in pairs. Which house in this lesson do you like and why?

I like the music house because there's a studio for my band there.

10 SPEAKING Work in pairs. Describe your dream house to your partner. Use *there is/there are*.

There are three bedrooms, a bathroom, a kitchen and a living room in my flat.

▷ 4 Read the questions and watch the video. Say what the speakers answer. Then in pairs, ask and answer the questions.

1. What's your favourite room in your house? Why?
2. What is there in your favourite room?

☐ **I can use *there is/there are* and *some* and *any* to talk about my home.**

2B VOCABULARY | Rooms and furniture

1 SPEAKING **In pairs, look at the website and answer the questions.**

1. Is there a flat or house for rent?
2. Where is it?
3. How many rooms are there?
4. Is there a garage?

Make a move

One-bedroom flat for rent : ***£725*** *per month*

Birmingham
General information:
Modern 1-bedroom flat, with living room, kitchen and bathroom. 10-minute walk from the city centre and the shops.
Click here for more details.

2 1.27 **Listen and add the words from the box to the vocabulary map. Which thing is not in the flat? In pairs, decide what other rooms some of the items can go in.**

armchair bath bed ~~breakfast bar~~ carpet cooker cupboard dishwasher fireplace fridge microwave mirror (LED) TV rug shelf sink shower sofa toilet washbasin washing machine wardrobe

HOUSE

Kitchen
breakfast bar, ________, ________, ________, ________, ________, ________, ________

Bedroom
________, ________

Bathroom
________, ________, ________, ________, ________

Living room
________, ________, ________, ________, ________, ________

3 **Study the pictures below and say where the guinea pig is.**

1 *The guinea pig is between the plants.*

Prepositions of place

4 **Look at the picture of the living room in Exercise 1 again. Complete the text with prepositions of place in Exercise 3.**

The living room has got a lovely black and white rug [1]*on* the floor and there are big windows [2]________ the sofa, so it's very light. [3]________ the sofa there's an armchair. And the little table [4]________ the sofa is perfect for a drink or a snack when you relax and watch your favourite TV programmes. There is another sofa [5]________ the wall with the TV. A cupboard [6]________ the TV is a good place for your favourite CDs. There's also a lovely fireplace [7]________ the TV and some shelves.

5 **What's important for you in a home? Choose four things from the list and write sentences. Then read them to your partner. Do you both agree?**

a beautiful view a big bedroom a big garden a fireplace a games room a swimming pool a TV in every room an attic extra bathrooms

It's important there's a games room for me and my friends.
I'd really like a swimming pool in the garden.

6 SPEAKING **In pairs, role play the situations. Student A go to page 175. Student B, go to page 176.**

☐ **I can talk about rooms, furniture and the location of things in a house.**

CAMPUS LIFE

Are you ready to leave home?

Congratulations on your student place at the Metropolitan University! University is an exciting new time in your life, but are you really ready to leave home? Life on a university campus is not just about parties and fun, you also need to do some chores. So answer these simple questions:

- Can you **keep your room tidy**?
- Can you **sweep the floor** and **vacuum the carpets**?
- Can you **wash and dry your clothes** and not turn them grey or pink?
- Can you **iron your clothes** and not burn them or yourself?
- Can you **cook a simple meal** and **do the washing-up** after?

Are three to five of your answers 'Yes, I can.'? You are probably ready to leave home and there's nothing to worry about. Are three to five of your answers 'No, I can't.'? Maybe it's time to practise some chores around the house before you leave home?

Good luck and remember the Metropolitan University Student Advice Service is here to help you!

1 **Read the article. Who is it for? Which of the chores in bold from the text is in the photo?**

2 **1.28 Listen to Ruby talking to her big brother, Theo, a new university student. Complete the sentences with the words from the box.**

~~cook~~ do the washing-up iron keep our rooms tidy sweep vacuum wash and dry

1. Mum and Dad can *cook* really well.
2. I can definitely __________.
3. That doesn't mean I can't __________ clothes.
4. Anybody can __________ the floor or __________ the carpet!
5. Mum always complains we can't __________.
6. I can't __________ very well.

Can/can't

3 **Look at the examples and tick the correct sentence.**

Mum and Dad can cook very well!
I can't iron very well.
What chores can you do?

1. ☐ Can has the same form for all persons.
2. ☐ Can has different forms for different persons.

Can/can't	
We use ***can*** and ***can't*** to talk about ability.	
I • You • He • She • It • We • They	
+	I **can** run five kilometres.
–	He **can't** play tennis.
?	**Can** you tidy the house? Yes, I **can**./No, I **can't**.

Grammar Reference and Practice > page 163

4 **1.29 PRONUNCIATION Listen and circle the words you hear: *can* or *can't*.**

1. I *can / can't* definitely do the washing-up!
2. You *can / can't* do that!
3. That doesn't mean I *can / can't* wash and dry clothes!
4. Anybody *can / can't* sweep the floor.
5. I can / can't iron very well.

5 **Complete the conversation with *can* or *can't*.**

Luke What's up, Emily?
Emily I [1]*can't* use this microwave!
Luke Really? It's easy!
Emily I never use it! I [2]__________ work it out.
Luke No problem! My mum [3]__________ make a whole meal in it.
Emily I'm sure she [4]__________ do that but I only want to heat some hot chocolate!
Luke Here is your hot chocolate!
Emily Oh, thanks!
Luke You're welcome.

6 **SPEAKING Are you ready to leave home? In pairs, ask and answer questions from the article in Exercise 1.**

A *Can you keep your room tidy?*
B *Yes, I can.*

☐ **I can use *can* and *can't* to talk about household chores.**

2D READING AND VOCABULARY

1 **SPEAKING What do you miss when you are away from home?**

the food   your bedroom   your family
your favourite TV programmes   your friends
your pets   your routines   your things

I miss my dog and all my things.
I miss my favourite TV programmes and the food!

2 **Study Active Reading and answer the questions.**

1 What can you see in the photos?
2 Read the title. Can you guess what the text is about?

ACTIVE READING | Predicting

Before you read, look at the title and the photo. This can help you guess what the text is about.

3 **Read the article and decide if statements 1–6 are true or false.**

1 ☐ 'House' and 'home' have the same meaning in English.
2 ☐ Joy's family hasn't got a pet.
3 ☐ Joy's family doesn't have favourite rooms.
4 ☐ She misses everyday family activities when she's not at home.
5 ☐ She doesn't know her neighbours.
6 ☐ There's a party in her street every year.

4 **Read the text again and answer the questions.**

1 According to the author, what do people usually do in the living room?
2 Where does Joy like to be in her house?
3 Which is Joy's mother's favourite place in the house?
4 Why is the ironing in Joy's sister's room?
5 Who usually makes the meals in Joy's house?
6 What does Jasper do when Joy comes back home?
7 Who looks after Jasper when the family is away?
8 When is the street party?

5 **Work in pairs. Look at the adjectives highlighted in the text and try to work out their meaning. Then match them with the opposites in the table.**

Adjective	Opposite
1 traditional	
2 empty	
3 uncomfortable	
4 cold	
5 tidy	
6 quiet	
7 clean	
8 terrible	
9 normal	
10 light	

6 **Complete the blog post with some adjectives from Exercise 5.**

I live in an apartment in New York City. In America it's [1]*normal* to call flats apartments. There are only two bedrooms, but it's really [2]________ because it's on the top floor where it's often sunny. It's also very [3]________ because we're right in the city centre, where you can hear traffic all the time and the streets are always [4]________ of people. It's quite a [5]________ home, not like my grandparents' traditional house in the UK. But it isn't [6]________ – we are quite messy! I really love our home because it's ours!

7 **In pairs, read sentences 1–5. Which ones do you think are true for Joy? Which ones are true for you? Say why.**

1 I have nice neighbours. I always say 'Hello' when I see them.
2 I don't know my neighbours' names or what they do.
3 I can never ask my neighbours for help.
4 I can talk to my neighbours about any problem, e.g. a noisy dog or a dangerous tree.
5 I often help my neighbours.

8 **REFLECT | Society In pairs, answer the questions.**

1 What makes a good neighbour? Are you one? What about your neighbours?
2 Do you think a street party is a good idea to get to know your neighbours? Say why.

5 WATCH AND REFLECT Go to page 151. Watch the documentary *Micro-living* and do the exercises.

What makes your HOUSE A HOME?

1.30

The words 'house' and 'home' don't mean the same in English. A modern house in towns and cities is a building with four walls and a roof above it, usually in a street with lots of other houses around it. In most houses there are rooms for different activities. So people can eat in the kitchen, sleep in the bedrooms, wash in the bathroom and relax in the living room.

But a home is a house full of people with their favourite rooms. For example, my favourite room is my bedroom. It has all my stuff in it so it's a bit messy but I love it. My mum loves reading in the comfortable armchair in the living room. Jasper, the cat, lies under her feet by the hot fireplace. My younger sister spends a lot of time in the garden – she loves playing there with her friends! My big sister is away at university so her bedroom is the room for ironing. And my dad can cook really well so he's usually in the kitchen.

When I'm away from home I sometimes feel homesick. Of course, I miss all my music, my games, my books and my photographs, but I also miss family routines. Our house is noisy in the morning before work or school. Then, when I get back in the evening, Jasper jumps on me with his dirty cat feet and there is the fantastic smell of my dad's cooking.

So home is the people and animals who live in a house, and the objects in the rooms that are special to us. It's the activities we do, our feelings and the familiar atmosphere around us. But home is also the community we are part of. I often take our neighbours' dog, Milo, out and they look after Jasper when we're away. And every summer, when it's not dark in the evenings, there's a big party in our street with all the neighbours. That's what home is for me.

by Joy Cassidy, student and future journalist

☐ **I can predict what the text is about and talk about houses.**

2E LISTENING AND VOCABULARY

ROOMMATE

In many universities in the USA, students in their first year live with roommates. This means they share a room with one (or sometimes two) other students. Roommates usually sleep and study in the same room.

1 **Look at the photo and read the text. Where do university students live in your country?**

2 **SPEAKING Work in pairs. What qualities in a roommate are important to you? Number the qualities 1 to 5 (1 = very important). Compare your list with a partner.**

a ☐ a clean and tidy person
b ☐ a quiet person
c ☐ a person with the same interests
d ☐ a person with healthy habits
e ☐ a generous person, e.g. they share food/clothes

A *Number 1 for me is 'a clean and tidy person'. I can't stand messy rooms.*

B *The most important one for me is 'a person with the same interests'. It's easy to become friends when you like similar things.*

3 **1.31 Listen to the interview. What is the topic?**

a The types of problems roommates have.
b How universities match roommates.
c Advice for new roommates.

4 **1.31 Read the questions. Then listen again and choose the correct answers.**

1 Christina thinks that it's very important to match students
  a with the same interests.
  b with similar daily routines.
  c who study the same subjects.
2 Older students sometimes help Christina match roommates because
  a they have experience of sharing a room.
  b the computer programme makes mistakes.
  c there are over 1,000 questionnaires every year.
3 At Harris University, they don't usually match people
  a with friends from school.
  b from the same part of the country.
  c with different nationalities.
4 Before university starts, Harris University usually sends students
  a the address of their roommate.
  b a list of furniture to bring.
  c the name and phone number of their roommate.

5 **1.32 Complete the sentences with *do* or *make*. Then listen and check.**

1 At Harris, students *do* **a questionnaire** before they start.
2 Do you ________ **a lot of mess** in your room or is it always tidy?
3 We also ________ **our best** to match people with some similar interests but this isn't necessary.
4 We ask some second or third year students to ________ **suggestions** of roommates because they understand the typical problems of sharing a room.
5 Some students ask to live with school friends but we don't like doing that. It's good for students to ________ **new friends**.

6 **Write five sentences about yourself using the phrases with *do* and *make* from Exercise 5.**

I sometimes do questionnaires online.

7 **In groups, write five questions for a roommate questionnaire. Then compare your questions with another group and choose the best ten questions.**

ROOMMATE QUESTIONNAIRE

1 What time do you get up and go to bed?
2 When do you usually study?
3 What types of music do you like?

8 **SPEAKING Ask the questions in your questionnaire in your group. Compare answers and find the best roommate for you in the group.**

☐ **I can identify specific information in an interview and talk about roommates.**

2F SPEAKING

1 **In pairs, read the advert and answer the questions.**

1 Which adjectives describe the flat?
2 When can you rent the flat?

INFORMATION | REVIEWS (0) | LOCATION

Modern, tidy flat London, England
NEW ON THE WEBSITE TODAY
4 Guests 2 Bedrooms 2 Beds
Description: quiet flat, only 10 minutes' walk from Shoreditch underground station.
Available now! Minimum two nights.

2 6 1.33 **Look at the photo. Then watch or listen to the conversation and answer the questions.**

1 Which adjectives from Exercise 1 are not true about the flat?
2 When does Emma want to rent the flat?
3 Is the flat ready for rent? Say why.

3 **Study the Speaking box. In pairs, from memory, write down Ryan's answers to the questions in the box. Then read the conversation again and check.**

Ryan That's it, Amber. The flat's on the website.

____

Ryan Hello.
Emma Hi. My name's Emma. Can you give me some information about the flat for rent?
Ryan The flat? Yes, of course. How can I help?
Emma How many bathrooms are there?
Ryan Just one.
Emma Is there a shower?
Ryan Yes. There's a bath and a new shower.
Amber Ryan! The shower doesn't work yet!
Emma Has the flat got a garden? Can we cook outside?
Ryan There's a small garden and … a BBQ.
Emma What do you mean by 'small'?
Ryan Well, there's space for four people.
Amber Ryan! Four people here? It's impossible!
Emma What's that noise?
Ryan That's just the, um, the washing machine.
Emma Oh, OK. Have you got a dishwasher? I hate washing up!
Ryan Um, sorry, no. I hate washing up too.
Amber Ryan! Your flat is so untidy! It's terrible!
Emma OK … I've got a few more questions …

____

Ryan So when do you want to rent the flat?
Emma From Saturday to Saturday.
Ryan That's the 16th until …
Emma No, the 9th until the 16th.
Ryan The 9th?! But that's tomorrow.
Emma Yes. Is that OK?
Ryan Um, that's fine.
Emma OK. See you tomorrow. About 12 p.m.? Bye!
Ryan Bye.
Amber Ryan! Tomorrow? Seriously? It's impossible!

SPEAKING | Asking for information

Can you give me some information about the flat for rent?
How many bathrooms are there?
Is there a shower?
Has the flat got a garden?
Can we cook outside?
What do you mean by 'small'?
Have you got a dishwasher?

4 **Study the Speaking box again and complete the conversation.**

A [1] *Can you give me some* information about the house for rent in Bristol?
B Yes, of course. What do you want to know?
A [2] ______________ are there?
B There are three bedrooms. And an extra bed in the living room.
A [3] ______________ by 'extra bed'?
B The sofa in the living room is also a bed.
A Ah, OK. Is [4] ______________?
B Yes, there's a TV in the living room.
A And [5] ______________ bring a dog?
B Yes, you can. Pets are welcome.
A Great! Also, has the flat [6] ______________?
B Yes, there's a big fridge-freezer in the kitchen.

5 **In pairs, role play the situations. Student A, go to page 175. Student B, go to page 176.**

☐ **I can ask for information about a house or flat.**

2G WRITING | A description of a place

Holly

My room is always clean and tidy because I like to know where all my stuff is.
I love art so there are pictures by my favourite artists on the walls. I sometimes sit at my round table and draw, but I only put the good pieces of art up for people to see. There's a big red armchair in front of the window. I often go to sleep in it because it's so comfortable!
And there's a big bed with beautiful red covers on it next to the window.
Opposite the bed there is a big wardrobe for my clothes. There is a big mirror on it so I can check how I look before I go out!
At weekends my friends come over and we listen to music. My parents usually tell us to turn it down because it's too noisy.
I really like my room because it's comfortable and shows my personality and interests!

comment

1 Look at the picture and read Holly's online post. Does the post show Holly's personality and interests?

2 Read the post again and tick ✓ the true sentences.

1 ☑ Holly's room is clean and tidy.
2 ☐ Her armchair is uncomfortable.
3 ☐ There is a double bed next to the window.
4 ☐ She likes listening to music with her friends.
5 ☐ There isn't a mirror in her room.

3 Complete Alastair's post with the words from the box.

but in front of ~~messy~~ on so wall

Alastair

I love my bedroom, but it's very [1]*messy* because I'm not good at keeping it tidy.

I've always got lots of books and papers [2]________ the desk. There's a comfortable chair [3]________ it.
It's light blue because I'm a Manchester City football fan. And there are some signed posters of my favourite players on the [4]________. There's a big bed under the window, [5]________ it's light in the morning when I wake up. There is also a big wardrobe in my room, [6]________ there aren't any clothes in it, they're all on the floor!

I like my room because it's my space.

comment

WRITING | A description of a place

Opening
Start with a general description of your room:
I love my bedroom but it's very messy.
My room is always clean and tidy.

Description
Describe your room in more detail. Include these things:
- furniture: armchair, bed, chair, desk, wardrobe
- parts of a room: door, floor, window
- prepositions of place: in front of, on, next to, under
- your hobby/interest: I'm a Manchester City football fan./ I sometimes draw.
- adjectives: comfortable, big, light blue, tidy
- linkers: and, because, but, so

Conclusion
Say why you like your room:
I really like my room because it's comfortable and shows my personality!
I like my room because it's my space.

4 WRITING TASK Write a description of your bedroom. Use the Writing box to help you.

☐ I can write a description of a place.

2A GRAMMAR AND VOCABULARY 5.8

attic (n) /'ætɪk/
balcony (n) /'bælkəni/
bathroom (n) /'bɑ:θrʊm/
bedroom (n) /'bedrʊm/
ceiling (n) /'si:lɪŋ/
cellar (n) /'selə/
climb up/down /ˌklaɪm 'ʌp/'daʊn/
dining room (n) /'daɪnɪŋ ru:m/
door (n) /dɔ:/
drawing (n) /'drɔ:ɪŋ/
floor (n) /flɔ: /
front (n) /frʌnt/
garage (n) /'gærɪdʒ/
garden (n) /'gɑ:dn/
hall (n) /hɔ:l/
high (adj) /haɪ/
horse (n) /hɔ:(r)s/
kitchen (n) /'kɪtʃɪn/
living room (n) /'lɪvɪŋ ru:m/
music studio (n) /'mju:zɪk ˌstju:diəʊ/
paint (v) /peɪnt/
painting (n) /'peɪntɪŋ/
paradise (n) /'pærədaɪs/
roof (n) /ru:f/
speakers (n) /'spi:kəz/
stairs (n) /steəz/
straight (adj) /streɪt/
study (n) /'stʌdi/
swimming pool (n) /'swɪmɪŋ pu:l/
terrace (n) /'terɪs/
upstairs/downstairs (adv) /ˌʌp'steəz/ˌdaʊn'steəz/
wall (n) /wɔ:l/
window (n) /'wɪndəʊ/

2B VOCABULARY 5.9

armchair (n) /'ɑ:mtʃeə/
attractive (adj) /ə'træktɪv/
bath (n) /bɑ:θ/
behind (prep) /bɪ'haɪnd/
between (prep) /bɪ'twi:n/
breakfast bar (n) /'brekfəst bɑ:/
carpet (n) /'kɑ:pɪt/
cooker (n) /'kʊkə/
cupboard (n) /'kʌbəd/
dishwasher (n) /'dɪʃˌwɒʃə/
fireplace (n) /'faɪəpleɪs/
for rent /fə 'rent/
fridge (n) /frɪdʒ/
furniture (n) /'fɜ:nɪtʃə/
LED TV (n) /ˌel i: ˌdi: ˌti: 'vi:/
light (adj) /laɪt/
lovely (adj) /'lʌvli/
microwave (n) /'maɪkrəweɪv/
mirror (n) /'mɪrə/
next to (prep) /'nekst tə/
opposite (prep) /'ɒpəzət/
perfect (adj) /'pɜ:fɪkt/
rug (n) /rʌg/
shelf (pl. shelves) (n) /ʃelf/ʃelvz/
shower (n) /ʃaʊə/
sink (n) /sɪŋk/
sofa (n) /'səʊfə/
ten-minute walk from /ˌten ˌmɪnət 'wɔ:k frəm/
toilet (n) /'tɔɪlɪt/
view (n) /vju:/
wardrobe (n) /'wɔ:drəʊb/
washbasin (n) /'wɒʃˌbeɪsən/
washing machine (n) /'wɒʃɪŋ məʃi:n/

2C GRAMMAR AND VOCABULARY 5.10

cook a meal /ˌkʊk ə 'mi:l/
do chores /ˌdu: 'tʃɔ:z/
do the washing-up /ˌdu: ðə ˌwɒʃɪŋ 'ʌp/
keep your room tidy /ˌki:p jə ˌru:m 'taɪdi/
leave home /ˌli:v 'həʊm/
sweep the floor /ˌswi:p ðə 'flɔ:/
vacuum the carpet /ˌvækjuəm ðə 'kɑ:pɪt/
wash/dry/iron clothes /ˌwɒʃ/ˌdraɪ/ˌaɪən 'kləʊðz/

2D READING AND VOCABULARY 5.11

building (n) /'bɪldɪŋ/
clean (adj) /kli:n/
cold (adj) /kəʊld/
comfortable (adj) /'kʌmftəbəl/
community (n) /kə'mju:nəti/
dangerous (adj) /'deɪndʒərəs/
dark (adj) /dɑ:k/
dirty (adj) /'dɜ:ti/
empty (adj) /'empti/
familiar atmosphere /fəˌmɪliə 'ætməsfɪə/
fantastic (adj) /fæn'tæstɪk/
feel homesick /ˌfi:l 'həʊmˌsɪk/
flat/apartment (n) /flæt/ə'pɑ:tmənt/
full of people /ˌfʊl əv 'pi:pəl/
hot (adj) /hɒt/
light (adj) /laɪt/
messy (adj) /'mesi/
modern (adj) /'mɒdn/
neighbour (n) /'neɪbə/
noisy (adj) /'nɔɪzi/
normal (adj) /'nɔ:məl/
object (n) /'ɒbdʒɪkt/
quiet (adj) /'kwaɪət/
special (adj) /'speʃəl/
sunny (adj) /'sʌni/
terrible (adj) /'terəbəl/
tidy (adj) /'taɪdi/
top floor (n) /ˌtɒp 'flɔ:/
traditional (adj) /trə'dɪʃənəl/
traffic (n) /'træfɪk/
uncomfortable (adj) /ʌn'kʌmftəbəl/

2E LISTENING AND VOCABULARY 5.12

do a questionnaire /ˌdu: ə ˌkwestʃə'neə/
do your best /ˌdu: jə 'best/
generous (adj) /'dʒenərəs/
habit (n) /'hæbɪt/
interests (n) /'ɪntrəsts/
make a mess /ˌmeɪk ə 'mes/
make a suggestion /ˌmeɪk ə sə'dʒestʃən/
make new friends /ˌmeɪk ˌnju: 'frendz/
match (v) /mætʃ/
roommate (n) /'ru:mˌmeɪt/
share a room /ˌʃeər ə 'ru:m/

2F SPEAKING 5.13

available (adj) /ə'veɪləbəl/
location (n) /ləʊ'keɪʃən/
noise (n) /nɔɪz/
rent (v) /rent/
space (n) /speɪs/

2G WRITING 5.14

cover (n) /'kʌvə/
desk (n) /desk/
poster (n) /'pəʊstə/

Remember More > page 174

VOCABULARY AND GRAMMAR

1 Read the descriptions and write the rooms or parts of a house.

1 You sleep here. *bedroom*
2 You cook here.
3 You relax here.
4 You wash yourself here.
5 You work here.
6 You park your car here.

2 Label the photos.

1 *armchair*

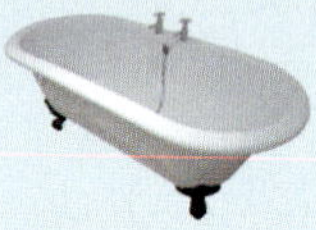
2 ________

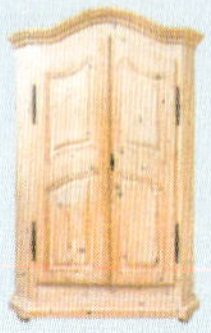
3 ________

4 ________

5 ________

6 ________

7 ________

8 ________

3 Look at the photo and complete the description of the room with the correct prepositions of place.

There's a big desk and a chair [1]*in front of* of the window. [2]________ the window, there's a comfortable bed. There is a big wardrobe full of clothes [3]________ it. On the floor, [4]________ the bed and the desk, there's a beautiful blue rug.
There's also a big map [5]________ the wall. On the desk there's a lamp and a computer [6]________ a little bookshelf.

4 Choose the correct words to complete the conversation.

Arron How's your house share? Do your housemates [1]*do / make* a mess all the time?
Molly Some people [2]*do / make* their best to keep the house [3]*clean / dirty* and tidy, but others don't.
Arron Well, that's [4]*normal / special* when you share a house with other people.
Molly I suppose. The rooms are really [5]*cold / warm* as well because there's no heating!
Arron Oh, no! What about your housemates?
Molly They seem cool. The house is always [6]*empty / full* of people so it's easy to [7]*make / do* new friends.
Arron Great! I guess there are lots of [8]*fantastic / terrible* parties too! Right?
Molly There are parties every weekend and I can't sleep because they are so [9]*noisy / quiet*!
Arron It sounds like my dream house!

5 Complete the post with the correct form of *there is*, *there are*, *some* or *any*.

Topic: Typical British houses

Question: What are British houses like?
How many rooms [1]*are there*?
Are there [2]________ special features in British houses?
Answer: My house

Cleo

[3]________ two floors in my house. Downstairs [4]________ a bathroom, a big living room and a kitchen. [5]________ a dining room, but in the kitchen [6]________ a big table and there are [7]________ chairs. Upstairs [8]________ another bathroom and three bedrooms. Like in all old British houses, the rooms have high ceilings and big windows, but there aren't [9]________ balconies! In front of the house there are [10]________ parking spaces for cars and a lovely garden behind.

6 Complete the conversation with *can/can't* and the verbs in brackets.

Sam What things around the house [1]*can you do* (you/do)?
Becky I [2]________ (keep) my room tidy.
Sam Everyone [3]________ (do) that!
Becky My sister [4]________! Her room is always messy!
Sam [5]________ (iron) your clothes?
Becky Yes, I [6]________!
Sam But I bet you [7]________ (not/cook)!
Becky No, I [8]________! [9]________ (you/cook)?
Sam Yes, my brother and I [10]________ (make) spaghetti bolognese. We make it every Saturday for our parents.

USE OF ENGLISH

7 **Choose the correct words a–d to complete the text.**

House | 2 bedrooms | 1 bathroom | sleeps 4

Seaview Cottage is a lovely place for a family holiday. It's a(n) [1]__ house for a perfect countryside experience, but with all the things you need for modern-day life.

• • •

When you open the front [2]__ and walk into the living room, there is a lovely fireplace and [3]__ comfortable sofas and armchairs. There's a big kitchen [4]__ to the living room with a cooker, a fridge and a microwave. There's also a bathroom with a toilet, washbasin and bath [5]__ it. Upstairs [6]__ two bedrooms with windows looking out on the garden. One of the windows is a door to the outside [7]__.

The house is in Brixham village, so you can walk everywhere and we are happy to make [8]__ about good places to eat or visit in the area.

Please [9]__ our visitor questionnaire before you leave to help us improve the service we provide.

Thank you!

Click here for more information and available dates.

1	**a** dark	**b** light	**c** modern	**d** traditional
2	**a** door	**b** floor	**c** wall	**d** window
3	**a** an	**b** any	**c** some	**d** the
4	**a** behind	**b** between	**c** in front	**d** next
5	**a** in	**b** on	**c** between	**d** under
6	**a** there is	**b** there isn't	**c** there are	**d** there aren't
7	**a** attic	**b** cellar	**c** roof	**d** terrace
8	**a** things	**b** suggestions	**c** questions	**d** ideas
9	**a** do	**b** have	**c** make	**d** write

Use of English > page 172

LISTENING

8 *1.34* **You will hear an answerphone message about a flat. Complete the notes below with one or two words in each gap.**

STRATEGY | Notes completion

Read the notes you need to complete carefully before you hear the recording for the first time. Try to predict if the word or information you need to listen for is a place, a name, a number etc.

41a HAMILTON ROAD

It's perfect for us – there are [1]*four* big bedrooms!

The kitchen's very new – it's only [2]________ old.

In the kitchen there's a sink, a [3]________, a cooker, a microwave and a washing machine.

When it's sunny, the best room in the flat is the [4]________.

The flat doesn't have a dining room but there's a [5]________ in the kitchen.

When it's warm and sunny, you can sit outside but the garden's a bit [6]________.

SPEAKING

9 **In pairs, role play the situation below. Then change roles and do the task again.**

Student A

Phone Student B to ask about a flat for rent. Ask for some information about the flat. Ask:

- how many bedrooms there are.
- some questions about the kitchen.
- how many bathrooms there are.
- some questions about the living room.
- if the flat has a garden or a balcony.

Student B

You have a flat for rent. Write some notes about the flat before you start, using the prompts below. Student A wants some information about the flat. Answer his/her questions.

- Number of bedrooms.
- What's in the kitchen?
- Number of bathrooms.
- What's in the living room?
- Garden or balcony?

WRITING

10 **Imagine you are renting a beautiful flat in London for two weeks in the summer holidays. Write a postcard to a friend in your country, telling him/her about the flat.**

In your postcard tell your friend:

- where the flat is.
- how many bedrooms there are.
- how many bathrooms there are.
- if there is a garden or balcony.
- some interesting information about the flat.

WATCH OUT FOR TIME WASTERS!

You send us your study problems. We give you advice.

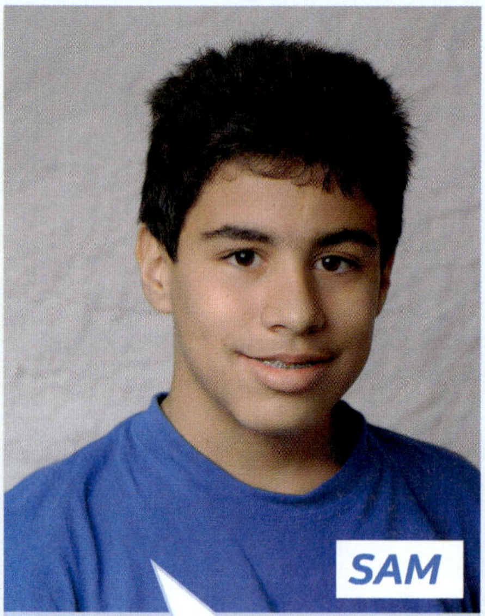

I'm really untidy. My school bag is a mess and I can never find anything on my desk. I waste a lot of time trying to find my homework, my books, a ruler or a rubber.

Our advice:

First, tidy your desk, your bag and your pencil case. Do it now and do it every day! Before you start your homework, put everything you need (textbook, exercise book, dictionary, pens, pencils, rubber, etc.) on your desk. That way you don't need to stop studying to look for things.

For me the biggest problem is social media. I've got lots of friends on social media sites. I get a notification from somebody every few minutes so it's really hard for me to study.

Our advice:

Why don't you reduce the number of your contacts on social media? Seriously, how many of your 'friends' are really friends? Keep your close friends and family and lose the others. It's also a good idea to mute group chats on your phone so they don't distract you from your homework.

Sometimes when I do my homework I can't concentrate. I start thinking about other things, like my favourite TV programmes, my football team's next match or other distractions.

Our advice:

You can concentrate on your work better if you give yourself a reward. So after forty-five minutes, stop studying and have a short break. Phone a friend, listen to some music or have a snack. Then start studying again.

GLOSSARY

distraction – something that stops you concentrating on what you are doing

notification – an automatically sent message to inform you about activity on your social media account

mute – stop someone's messages, pictures, etc. appearing on a social media website when you look at it

1 **In pairs, ask and answer these questions about your study habits.**

1 Where do you usually study/do your homework?
2 Do you check your phone for messages/go on social media when you study?
3 Is your desk always tidy?
4 What's your favourite time for studying?

2 **Read the website. Then in pairs, discuss the questions.**

1 Which person has similar problems to you?
2 What do you think of the advice?

3 **Read the website again and write Sam, Molly or Jake.**

1 Who has problems with his/her studies because of social media? *Molly*
2 Who finds it difficult to find things?
3 Who doesn't always focus very well on his/her homework?
4 Who needs to limit the number of his/her friends on social media?
5 Who needs to have a short break after studying for some time?
6 Who needs to organise his/her things better?

4 1.35 **Listen to an interview with an expert on how to avoid time wasters when studying. Then, in pairs, answer the questions.**

1 Which of the problems from the text does the expert mention?
2 What other problems does she talk about?

5 1.35 **Listen again and complete the advice with the words and phrases from the box.**

busy close desk off ~~quiet~~ remove room switch

LIFE SKILLS | How to avoid time wasters

- Find somewhere [1]*quiet* to study, for example, in your bedroom or in the library.
- [2]________ your email and social media and turn [3]________ your notifications.
- [4]________ off your phone or put it in another [5]________.
- [6]________ magazines, books, photos and computer games from your [7]________.
- Say 'no' to people when you're [8]________.

6 **Order the tips in the Life Skills box from 1–5 according to how useful they are (1= very important, 5 = not so important). Then discuss in pairs.**

7 **Complete the table and calculate the number of free hours you have for studying. Compare your answers in pairs.**

QUIZ

HOW MANY HOURS A WEEK DO YOU HAVE FREE FOR STUDYING?

ACTIVITY	NO. OF HOURS PER DAY	NO. OF DAYS	NO. OF HOURS PER WEEK
sleep		× 7 =	
meals (breakfast, lunch, dinner)		× 7 =	
school		× 5 =	
after-school clubs		× ____ =	
travel to/from school		× 5 =	
jobs at home		× 7 =	
extra activities (sport, languages, music, etc.)		× ____ =	
time with friends		× ____ =	
TV/computer games		× 7 =	
social media		× 7 =	
			Total: ____

There are 168 hours per week. After all of my activities, I have: 168 - ______ hours = ______ hours free for studying.

8 **Do the task below.**

LIFE SKILLS | Project

A Look again at your results in the table in Exercise 7. Decide what your time wasters are. Make a plan to avoid them and to find more time for studying. Use the ideas in this lesson and in the Life Skills box in Exercise 5 to help you design a good plan.
B Follow your plan for one week.
C After the week is over, tell your class which parts of your plan work for you and which don't. Say why.

03 Eat in – eat out

VOCABULARY	Food and drink, containers, prices, phrasal verbs
GRAMMAR	Countable and uncountable nouns with *some/any/no*, quantifiers **Use of English** > page 172
SPEAKING	Ordering food
WRITING	A café review
VIDEO	Grammar ▷ Communication ▷ Documentary ▷

THE RIGHT DIET FOR YOUR JOB

What do you need to eat every day? Well, sometimes it depends on the job you have.

INDIA BLACKWELL
18 | acrobat

India is a trapeze artist with Circomania, a modern circus with no animals, only acrobats. She does tricks above the circus ring, but she doesn't use lots of calories. She needs to keep her body weight down. It's important what and how much she eats so she cooks her meals herself.

For breakfast, India usually eats [1]some eggs with bread and butter, and drinks [2]some milk. She doesn't drink [3]any coffee. She loves Japanese and Mexican food, so lunch is sushi rice with tuna and spinach, and some water. And today's dinner is taco beef with some cheese, tomatoes and lettuce. She doesn't usually eat any desserts, but her favourites are ice cream and chocolate.

SAM CLARK
20 | cycle courier

Sam works for a company called Citysprint and takes packages around the city. His day usually starts with some coffee, [4]a sandwich and then some cake before the first courier call. Sam always carries special energy biscuits and some fruit with him. Does he carry [5]any crisps or energy drinks? No, he doesn't – just some juice. He doesn't stop for lunch because it slows him down! By dinner time he's really hungry so he eats some pasta or some meat with potatoes and other vegetables, and sometimes dessert.

So, how much food does Sam eat every day? That depends on how many kilometres he cycles. He does about eighty kilometres so he usually eats a lot.

3A GRAMMAR AND VOCABULARY

1 SPEAKING In pairs, look at the photos and tick the items you can see. Then read the texts. How is your diet different from India's and from Sam's?

☑ beef ☐ bread ☐ biscuits ☐ butter ☐ cake ☐ chocolate ☐ coffee ☐ crisps ☐ eggs ☐ ice cream ☐ juice ☐ lettuce ☐ milk ☐ pasta ☐ potatoes ☐ rice ☐ sandwich ☐ tomatoes ☐ water

India doesn't drink coffee, but I do.

2 1.36 Add the food and drinks from Exercise 1 to the table. Use one of the words in two groups. Listen and check.

Fruit and Vegetables	Dairy	Meat	Fish	Drinks	Others
apples *C* spinach *U*	yoghurt cheese	chicken	sardines tuna	tea	cereal

3 SPEAKING Tell your partner which foods you love, like, don't like or can't stand.

I love bread and chocolate, but I can't stand spinach!

Countable and uncountable nouns with *some/any/no*

4 Look at the names of the food and drinks in Exercise 2 again. Write C for the things you can count and U for the things you can't count.

5 Match phrases 1–5 in the texts with explanations a–d. Then check your answers in the Grammar box.

a ☐ We use *a(n)* / *some* with singular countable nouns.
b ☐ We use *a(n)* / *some* with plural countable nouns.
c ☐ We use *a(n)* / *some* with uncountable nouns.
d ☐ ☐ We use *any* / *some* in questions and in negative sentences with uncountable nouns and plural countable nouns.

Countable and uncountable nouns with *some/any/no*

	Countable	Uncountable
+	I often have **an** apple. I eat **some** sandwiches.	I eat **some** cereal.
–	There isn't **a** fridge. There aren't **any** eggs. There are **no** eggs.	There isn't **any** rice. There is **no** rice.
?	Have you got **a** snack? Do you eat **any** eggs?	Do you drink **any** milk?

How much?/How many?

	How many potatoes do you want?	**How much** coffee do you drink?

Grammar Reference and Practice > page 163

6 1.37 Study *Watch out!* then complete the dialogue with *a*, *an*, *some*, *any* or *no*.

Louis I'm hungry. What is there to eat?
India There's [1]*an* apple.
Louis Oh! Have you got [2]_________ chocolate?
India No, I haven't, but there's [3]_________ banana if you want it.
Louis You know I hate fruit! Have you got [4]_________ biscuits?
India No, I'm sorry there are [5]_________ biscuits or chocolate in the house!
Louis You're so healthy! Come on, let's go and buy [6]_________ ice cream!

WATCH OUT!

We can use *no* to mean the same as *not any*:
*There **isn't any** milk. = There **is no** milk.*

7 Complete the questions with *How much* or *How many*. Then answer the questions in pairs.

1 *How much* chocolate do you eat every day?
2 _________ sandwiches do you have a week?
3 _________ biscuits do you eat every day?
4 _________ water do you drink every day?
5 _________ fruit do you eat every week?
6 _________ snacks do you have in the evening?

A *How much chocolate do you eat every day?*
B *I drink a cup of hot chocolate every morning.*

8 SPEAKING Work in pairs. What do you usually have for breakfast, lunch and dinner?

I usually have some cereal with milk. I drink some orange juice, but I never have any tea or coffee.

7 Read the questions and watch the video. Say what the speakers answer. Then in pairs, ask and answer the questions.

1 How many meals do you have every day?
2 What do you usually have for breakfast?

☐ I can use countable and uncountable nouns to talk about diets.

3B VOCABULARY | Containers, prices

1 🔊 *1.38* **Look at the pictures and complete labels a–h with the words from the box. Then listen and check.**

bag bottle ~~box~~ can carton jar packet tin

a a *box* of chocolates

b a ______ of sweets

c a ______ of cola

d a ______ of juice

e a ______ of water

f a ______ of tuna

g a ______ of mayonnaise

h a ______ of biscuits

2 🔊 *1.38* **PRONUNCIATION Listen and repeat the phrases in Exercise 1. Notice how you pronounce *of* /əv/.**

3 **Make a shopping list with the eight containers in Exercise 1. Then, in pairs, find out which things are on your partner's shopping list.**

A *Have you got a packet of crisps?*
B *Yes, I have. Have you got a jar of coffee?*
A *No, I haven't*

4 🔊 *1.39* **Read and match the prices with how you say them. Then listen and check.**

1 ☐ £2.50	**a** one pound ninety-nine
2 ☐ £3.00	**b** two pounds fifty
3 ☐ £4.60	**c** three pounds
4 ☐ £1.99	**d** four pounds sixty
5 ☐ 70p	**e** seventy pence

5 🔊 *1.40* **Listen and write the prices.**

SHOPEROO'S SPECIAL OFFERS

ONE JAR OF COFFEE ¹£*3.46*

THREE TINS OF SARDINES IN TOMATO SAUCE ²£______

SIX PACKETS OF CRISPS ³£______

BUY ONE, GET ONE FREE!

TWO BOTTLES OF LEMONADE ⁴£______

TWO BAGS OF SALAD ⁵£______

6 **SPEAKING In pairs, role play the situations. Student A go to page 175. Student B go to page 176.**

☐ **I can talk about food products, containers and prices.**

3C SPEAKING

1 **Look at the photo on page 41. In pairs, discuss the questions.**

1. Are there any cafés near your home or your school?
2. How often do you go there?
3. Who do you go with?

2 ▷ *8* 🔊 *1.41* **Watch or listen to Part 1 of the conversation. Decide if statements 1–4 are true or false.**

1. ☐ Robin is at the café.
2. ☐ Leila orders two tuna salads.
3. ☐ There isn't any carrot cake.
4. ☐ Leila's order is £12.50.

3 ▷ *8* 🔊 *1.41* **Look at the menu and answer the questions. Watch or listen again to check your answers.**

1. What does Leila order for herself?
2. What does Leila order for Robin?

CARIBOU CAFÉ

SANDWICHES

tuna mayonnaise	£3
chicken and cheese	£4
chicken and salad	£4.50

SALADS

spinach and rice salad	£4.50
tuna salad	£5
chicken salad	£6

DESSERTS

yoghurt and fruit	£2.50
carrot cake	£3
chocolate cake	£3

HOT DRINKS

tea	£1.50
coffee	£2.50
hot chocolate	£2

COLD DRINKS

water – sparkling/still	£1.50
orange juice	£2.50
apple juice	£2.50

4 ▷ *9* 🔊 *1.42* **Watch or listen to Part 2. What's the problem with Robin's food?**

5 **Study the Speaking box and complete the conversation with one or two words in each gap.**

Server Hi. How can I [1]*help* you?
Leila Hi. I'd like … Sorry … Hi, Robin. Where are you?
Robin Sorry, Leila. I'm on my way. Where are you?
Leila I'm in the café. What would you like?
Robin A tuna salad – and a sandwich.
Server Are you [2]_________ to order?
Robin Maybe cheese? And a white coffee and …
Leila OK. Bye. Sorry about that. Em… Can I [3]_________ a tuna salad please? And …
Server Two salads. Which? We've got tuna, chicken …
Leila No. One tuna salad, please. And I'd [4]_________ a spinach and rice salad.
Server OK. So two salads. Anything else?
Leila Yes, my friend would like a cheese sandwich.
Server We haven't got any cheese sandwiches. Is chicken and cheese OK?
Leila Um, maybe I can check … No, chicken and cheese. That's fine.
Server [5]_________ you like any cake or desserts?
Leila Yes, I'd like a piece of carrot cake, please.
Server Sorry. There isn't any carrot cake. There's chocolate …
Leila Yes, OK.
Server [6]_________ to drink?
Leila Yes, a cup of coffee and a glass of apple juice please.
Server White or black?
Leila Sorry? Oh, the coffee. White, please.
Server One white coffee.
Leila [7]_________ much is that?
Server [8]_________ £21.50, please.
Leila Here you are.
Server Thank you. Oh, eh! Sorry! Excuse me! Sorry, but it's £21.50 and this is £12.50.
Leila Oh, I'm so sorry. Here you are.
Server Thank you.

SPEAKING | Ordering food

Taking orders	Giving orders
How can I help you?	Can I have (a tuna salad), please?
Are you ready to order?	I'd like a/some …, please.
What would you like to eat/ drink?	Yes, I want …, please.
Would you like any cake or desserts?	How much is that?
Anything else?	Here you are.
Anything to drink?	Thank you.
Is that all?	
That's £21.50, please.	
You're welcome.	

6 ▶ ***1.43*** **Put the conversation in the correct order. Then listen and check.**

☐ **Server** OK. That's £8.50, please.
☐ **Server** You're welcome.
[*1*] **Server** Are you ready to order?
☐ **Server** OK. A chicken and salad sandwich. Is that all? Would you like any cake or dessert?
☐ **Server** What would you like?
☐ **Server** Sure. Would you like anything to drink?
☐ **Customer** Here you are. Thank you.
☐ **Customer** I'd like a bottle of sparkling water, please.
☐ **Customer** Yes.
☐ **Customer** Yes, I'd like some yoghurt and fruit, please.
☐ **Customer** Can I have a chicken and salad sandwich, please?

7 **In pairs, practise the dialogue in Exercise 6.**

8 **In pairs, role play the situations. Student A, go to page 175. Student B, go to page 176.**

☐ **I can order food and drinks in a café.**

1 SPEAKING **Work in pairs. What do you think are the top three types of food people waste?**

bananas bread cheese eggs fish meat milk potatoes salad tomatoes

I think people waste a lot of bread.

2 1.44 **Listen to an expert and check your answers to Exercise 1.**

Quantifiers: *a lot of, too many, too much, a few, a little, not many, not much*

3 Decide if the underlined nouns are countable (C) or uncountable (U).

1. We all waste **too much** food. *U*
2. **Not many** people try to change this.
3. That's **a lot of** money.
4. We don't just waste **a little** bread.
5. We each throw away **a few** potatoes.
6. That's **a lot of** chips!
7. Stop buying **too many** things.
8. How much milk have we got? **Not much.**

4 Study the Grammar box and check your answers to Exercise 3.

Quantifiers: *a lot of, too many, too much, a few, a little, not many, not much*

	Countable	Uncountable
+	They have **a lot of** cakes! There are **too many** olives in this salad. There are **a few** chips in the bag.	There's **a lot of** cheese on this pizza. You put **too much** sugar in your tea! There's **a little** water in the bottle.
–	Oh, there are**n't many** biscuits in the packet!	There is**n't much** coffee in the jar.
?	Are there **many** chocolates in the box?	Do people eat **much** rice in South America?

Grammar Reference and Practice > page 164

5 Look again at the sentences in Exercise 3 and decide which refer to a small amount, a big amount or more than you need.

1. small amount: ________, ________, ________, ________
2. big amount: ________, ________
3. more than you need: *1*, ________

6 Choose the correct words to complete the poster.

Stop food waste

SHOP SMART!

- Don't buy too [1]*much / many* food when you shop – make a shopping list.

  Shop more often and only buy [2]*a few / a little* milk and bread and a [3]a *few / little* fresh vegetables.

STORE SMART!

- Don't keep too [4]*much / many* tins in the cupboard and check use-by dates.
- Make sure there isn't [5]*much / many* meat or fish in your fridge.

EAT SMART!

- Don't put [6]*a lot of / much* things on your plate at one time, you can always have some more.
- Just have a [7]*few / little* pasta or rice and a [8]*few / little* chips or potatoes. Don't waste food!

7 Think of your fridge and cupboards at home and write sentences about what food and drink there is in them. Then, in pairs, compare your answers.

1. There's a lot of …
2. There isn't much …
3. There are too many …
4. There are only a few …
5. There's a little …
6. There aren't many …

1 There's a lot of orange juice in my fridge.

8 REFLECT | Society **In pairs, ask and answer the questions.**

1. Do you waste a lot of food? What do you waste and why?
2. What do you do with the leftovers? (E.g. throw them away, eat them the next day, freeze them.)

☐ **I can use quantifiers to talk about amounts.**

3E LISTENING AND VOCABULARY

1 **Match definitions 1–7 with the jobs in the box.**

baker butcher chef ~~dietician~~ food photographer restaurant reviewer waiter

1. gives advice about healthy food and eating *dietician*
2. makes and sells bread
3. serves customers in a restaurant or café
4. visits restaurants, tries the food and writes about it
5. sells meat in a shop
6. takes photos of food for websites, magazines, etc.
7. cooks food in a restaurant

2 ***1.45*** **Listen to the first part of an interview with Rachel. What's her job?**

3 ***1.45*** **Read the questions. Listen again. Which question does Rachel answer?**

1. Is food important to you personally?
2. Can you describe your typical day?
3. Where do you usually work?

4 **Read the first part of the interview. How do you know the answers to Exercise 2 and 3? Find the key phrases.**

I love food. I love eating it and I also love looking at it. I visit a lot of good restaurants and some amazing chefs come to my studio. So I see and try some fantastic food. I enjoy cooking too but I'm not a professional. There is actually another food photographer – he's quite famous – called Francesco Tonelli. He's a chef too. When he photographs food, he also cooks a meal for everyone!

5 ***1.46*** **Study Active Listening and read questions 1–4. Then listen to the rest of the interview and match the questions to answers A–D in the interview.**

1. What tips do you have?
2. What equipment do you need?
3. What happens to the food after you finish your work?
4. What food is difficult to work with?

ACTIVE LISTENING | Understanding the main idea

- Think what you know about the topic and listen for key words and phrases.
- Listen to the whole recording without stopping.
- Don't try to understand every word.

6 ***1.47*** **Listen to the whole interview and complete the sentences with one word in each gap.**

1. Francesco Tonelli is a professional chef and ________ ________.
2. Rachel thinks you can use ________ on ________ for a blog.
3. ________ and ________ ________ are two examples of difficult food to photograph.
4. Rachel uses water to make ________ and ________ look fresh.
5. Unfortunately, Rachel ________ a lot of the food she uses during a photo shoot.

7 ***1.48*** **Look at the photos and match items a–g with the words in the box. Then, listen to the descriptions of the photos and check.**

☐ bowl ☐ cup ☐ fork ☐ glass ☐ knife ☐ plate ☐ spoon

8 **SPEAKING | Complete the sentences with the correct form of the words from Exercise 7. Then, in pairs, ask and answer the questions.**

1. How many *cups* of tea or coffee do you drink every day?
2. Do you have a ________ of cereal for breakfast in the morning?
3. Do you keep a ________ of water next to your bed at night?
4. You need a ________ and a ________ to eat steak. How do you eat a pizza?
5. Some people eat spaghetti with a ________ and a fork and some with just a fork. How do you eat spaghetti?

☐ **I can understand the main idea of a radio interview and talk about people and food.**

3F READING AND VOCABULARY

1 **SPEAKING | In pairs, look at photos A and B and discuss the questions.**

1 Do you ever go out for a meal? What do you usually eat?
2 Where do you go to: fast food chains, restaurants, pizzerias?
3 Which of the two restaurants in the photos do you like more? Say why.

A

B

2 **What do you think an ethical restaurant is? In pairs, discuss the ideas below.**

it helps homeless people
it uses natural or local ingredients
it's cheap or you pay very little it's expensive but the money goes to charity the food comes from other countries it only serves vegetarian food

I think an ethical restaurant is cheap and uses natural or local ingredients.

3 **Read the text and check your answers to Exercise 2.**

4 **Read the text again and choose the correct answers.**

1 Why do people often eat at home these days?
a Because home-cooked meals taste great.
b Because they want to use special ingredients.
c Because they like cooking.
d Because they don't want to spend a lot of money.

2 What is true about JBJ?
a You can work with a chef.
b You can only eat at the weekends.
c You never pay for a meal.
d You can become famous.

3 Which of the following is not true about *Rosa's*?
a It's in Philadelphia.
b Homeless people can't eat there.
c It's a pizza restaurant.
d There are messages on all the walls.

4 What can you do at *Indian Veg*?
a Work for free in the kitchen.
b Meet famous vegetarians.
c Learn about vegetarianism.
d Eat delicious meat dishes.

5 What do we learn about ethical restaurants from the article?
a They are all vegetarian.
b They all have the same rules.
c They are not very popular.
d They all try to help people in some way.

5 **Read the text again and answer the questions.**

1 How much do you pay at the *JBJ* restaurant?
2 How many courses can you have at the *JBJ* restaurant?
3 How much does an extra piece of pizza cost at *Rosa's*?
4 How many pieces of pizza do homeless people eat at *Rosa's* in nine months?
5 How many dishes do they offer at *Indian Veg*?
6 How much do you pay at *Indian Veg* to eat all you can?

6 **Look at the phrasal verbs highlighted in the text and choose the correct option.**

1 I want to *find / give* out what happens when you cook an egg in the microwave!
2 Sit *down / out*, the food is almost ready!
3 Sometimes we eat *in / out* at a restaurant.
4 My brother and I *find / help* out at our aunt's restaurant once a week.
5 It's difficult but don't give *out / up*!
6 They often *give / help* out leaflets about new restaurants in town.

7 **Write questions with four phrasal verbs from the box. Then ask and answer the questions in pairs.**

eat in eat out find out give out give up help out sit down

A *Do you sometimes help out at home?*
B *Yes, I often do the washing-up and help make dinner.*

☐ **I can identify specific information in an article and talk about restaurants.**

Ethical restaurants

2.1

These days people often cook and eat in – this saves some money and people can also choose what ingredients they use for their meals. But here are some interesting places around the world to eat out and taste great food. They aren't expensive and you can help a few people at the same time.

The JBJ Soul Foundation community restaurant in New Jersey, USA, is a 'pay what you can' restaurant. People who have got money pay $10 or more. But people without money work in the restaurant and get free meals. You can also pay and help out with one of the famous guest chefs in the kitchen – you can wash up or make food. Every day there are delicious meals of starters, main courses and desserts, with ingredients from their organic garden or the local area.

Rosa's Fresh Pizza Restaurant in Philadelphia, USA, is the first 'pay it forward' restaurant. You pay just $1 for an extra piece of pizza and a homeless person can eat it later. At Rosa's, staff give out post-it notes and customers write personal messages on them. In fact, there are post-it notes all over the restaurant walls, with messages like: 'Have a great day!' 'Don't give up!' and 'Enjoy your pizza!' There are also a lot of 'Thank you' messages from homeless people. Around thirty to forty homeless people eat at Rosa's every day, that's 8,500 pieces of pizza in nine months!

Indian Veg is an 'all you can eat' restaurant in London. You pay £4.50 for thirty different vegetarian dishes – almost too many to choose from! Office workers, students, tourists and homeless people sit down to eat together. On the walls there are facts and figures about how vegetarians help animals, people and the environment. You can even find out which famous people are vegetarian from the photos and posters on the walls. You can also see how healthy and tasty vegetarian food is. Every year they offer free meals to homeless people on Christmas Day.

8 2.2 **Listen to someone talking about an app for restaurants and cafés and choose the correct words to complete the sentences.**

NAME OF APP:
Too Good To Go (TGTG)

What the app does: helps to stop [1]*food / paper* waste in restaurants and cafés.

Information in the app: number of [2]*dishes / meals* and their price.

How to search: by [3]*area / town* or by the name of a café or restaurant.

How to order: [4]*click / call*, pay and collect.

9 REFLECT | Values **In pairs, discuss the questions.**

1. Do you like the idea of the app?
2. Is it useful? Say why.
3. Is there a similar app in your country?

10 WATCH AND REFLECT **Go to page 152. Watch the documentary *The Real Junk Food Project* and do the exercises.**

3G WRITING | A café review

1 SPEAKING In pairs, ask and answer the questions.

1. What's your favourite café?
2. Why do you like it?

2 Read the café review 1 and answer the questions.

1. What's the name of the café?
2. What is the writer's favourite dish?
3. What does the writer like about the café?
4. How many LMNH! cafés are there and where are they?
5. When is the café open?

3 Read review 1 again and tick the things that have capital letters in English. Is it the same in your language?

☑ countries/nationalities ☐ days/months
☐ the pronoun 'I' ☐ names of cities and streets
☐ new sentences ☐ parts of the day
☐ people's names/surnames

4 Read the second review and put capital letters where they are missing.

5 Study the Writing box. Read the examples from Jennie's review and find more examples in Miklós's review.

WRITING | A café review

- Write the name and the type of the café:
  look mum no hands! isn't just a café, it's also a bike repair shop.
- Describe it and say why people like it:
  It's very popular because it serves very good food.
- Give information about the menu and your favourite dish:
  It serves tasty hot and cold food and drink. My favourite dish is the speciality 'English breakfast'.
- Say what you particularly like about the café:
  I really like the cycle theme, the comfortable chairs and free wi-fi.
- Give the location and the opening hours:
  There are two LMNKs in London, in Old Street and in Back Church Lane, open all day Monday to Sunday.

Don't forget to check your spelling and capital letters!

6 WRITING TASK Write a café review. Use the Writing box to help you.

***Jennie Cooke,** September 2018*

1 look mum no hands! isn't just a café with a strange name, it's also a bike repair shop. It's very popular because it serves very good hot and cold food and drink. My favourite dish is the speciality 'English breakfast' – but it's only available in the morning.

I really like the cycle theme, the comfortable chairs and the free wi-fi. The staff are cool too because they don't ask you to leave when you finish your coffee!
There are two LMNHs in London, in Old Street and in Back Church Lane, open all day Monday to Sunday. But there are also pop-up LMNHs around the UK.

***miklós arany,** April 2018*

2 Cat café, Budapest is a cat café in the hungarian capital. it's a cool new place to enjoy a drink and a snack with cats all around you.
on the cat theme menu, there are speciality drinks, like my favourite cat-puccino! and there are just too many fantastic cakes to choose from, all with cute cat art on them. The staff are really friendly and helpful, but the cats are awesome – i love them! you can visit the café from monday to sunday, between 10 a.m. and 9 p.m. at 3 révay street, Budapest.

3A GRAMMAR AND VOCABULARY 5.15

apple (n) /'æpəl/
banana (n) /bə'nɑːnə/
beef (n) /biːf/
biscuit (n) /'bɪskɪt/
body weight (n) /'bɒdi weɪt/
bread (n) /bred/
butter (n) /'bʌtə/
cake (n) /keɪk/
calorie (n) /'kæləri/
cereal (n) /'sɪəriəl/
cheese (n) /tʃiːz/
chicken (n) /'tʃɪkɪn/
chocolate (n) /'tʃɒklət/
coffee (n) /'kɒfi/
crisps (n) /krɪsps/
dairy (n) /'deəri/
dessert (n) /dɪ'zɜːt/
diet (n) /'daɪət/
drink (n, v) /drɪŋk/
eggs (n) /egz/
energy drink (n) /'enədʒi drɪŋk/
fish (n) /fɪʃ/
fruit (n) /fruːt/
ham (n) /hæm/
hungry (adj) /'hʌŋgri/
ice cream (n) /ˌaɪs 'kriːm/
juice (n) /dʒuːs/
lettuce (n) /'letɪs/
meat (n) /miːt/
milk (n) /mɪlk/
orange (n) /'ɒrɪndʒ/
pasta (n) /'pæstə/
pizza (n) /'piːtsə/
potato (n) /pə'teɪtəʊ/
rice (n) /raɪs/
sardines (n) /ˌsɑː'diːnz/
snack (n) /snæk/
spinach (n) /'spɪnɪdʒ/
tea (n) /tiː/
sandwich (n) /sænwɪdʒ/
tomato (n) /tə'mɑːtəʊ/
tuna (n) /'tjuːnə/
vegetables (n) /'vedʒtəbəlz/
water (n) /'wɔːtə/
yoghurt (n) /'jɒgət/

3B VOCABULARY 5.16

bag (n) /bæg/
bottle (n) /'bɒtl/
box (n) /bɒks/
can (n) /kæn/
carton (n) /'kɑːtn/
free (adv) /friː/
jar (n) /dʒɑː/
lemonade (n) /ˌlemə'neɪd/
mayonnaise (n) /ˌmeɪə'neɪz/
packet (n) /'pækɪt/
pence (n) /pens/
pound (n) /paʊnd/
price (n) /praɪs/
salad (n) /'sæləd/
special offer (n) /ˌspeʃəl 'ɒfə/
sweets (n) /swiːts/
tin (n) /tɪn/
tomato sauce (n) /tə'mɑːtəʊ sɔːs/

3C SPEAKING 5.17

carrot cake (n) /'kærət keɪk/
change (n) /tʃeɪndʒ/
customer (n) /'kʌstəmə/
order (n, v) /'ɔːdə/
server (n) /'sɜːvə/
sparkling/still water (n) /ˌspɑːklɪŋ/ˌstɪl 'wɔːtə/

3D GRAMMAR 5.18

chips (n) /tʃɪps/
food waste (n) /'fuːd weɪst/
freeze (v) /friːz/
keep (v) /kiːp/
leftovers (n) /'leftəʊvəz/
shopping list (n) /'ʃɒpɪŋ lɪst/
smart (adj, adv) /smɑːt/
store (v) /stɔː/
sugar (n) /'ʃʊgə/
throw away /ˌθrəʊ ə'weɪ/
use-by date (n) /'juːz baɪ deɪt/

3E LISTENING AND VOCABULARY 5.19

baker (n) /'beɪkə/
bowl (n) /bəʊl/
butcher (n) /'bʊtʃə/
chef (n) /ʃef/
cup (n) /kʌp/
dietician (n) /ˌdaɪə'tɪʃən/
equipment (n) /ɪ'kwɪpmənt/
food photographer (n) /'fuːd fəˌtɒgrəfə/
fork (n) /fɔːk/
fresh (adj) /freʃ/
glass (n) /glɑːs/
job (n) /dʒɒb/
knife (n) /naɪf/
plate (n) /pleɪt/
restaurant reviewer (n) /'restərɒnt rɪˌvjuːə/
sell (v) /sel/
spoon (n) /spuːn/
steak (n) /steɪk/
waiter (n) /'weɪtə/

3F READING AND VOCABULARY 5.20

cheap (adj) /tʃiːp/
collect (v) /kə'lekt/
cost (v) /kɒst/
delicious (adj) /dɪ'lɪʃəs/
dish (n) /dɪʃ/
eat in /ˌiːt 'ɪn/
eat out /ˌiːt 'aʊt/
environment (n) /ɪn'vaɪrənmənt/
ethical (adj) /'eθɪkəl/
find out /ˌfaɪnd 'aʊt/
give out /ˌgɪv 'aʊt/
give up /ˌgɪv 'ʌp/
help out /ˌhelp 'aʊt/
homeless people (n) /'həʊmləs ˌpiːpəl/
main course (n) /ˌmeɪn 'kɔːs/
natural/local ingredients /ˌnætʃərəl/ˌləʊkəl ɪn'griːdiənts/
organic (adj) /ɔː'gænɪk/
pizzeria/pizza restaurant (n) /ˌpiːtsə'riːə/'piːtsə ˌrestərɒnt/
search (by sth) (v) /'sɜːtʃ (baɪ ˌsʌmθɪŋ)/
serve (v) /sɜːv /
sit down /ˌsɪt 'daʊn/
spend/save money /ˌspend/ˌseɪv 'mʌni/
starter (n) /'stɑːtə/
taste (v) /teɪst/
vegetarian (n, adj) /ˌvedʒə'teəriən/

3G WRITING 5.21

opening hours (n) /'əʊpənɪŋ ˌaʊəz/
speciality (n) /ˌspeʃi'æləti/

Remember More > page 174

VOCABULARY AND GRAMMAR

1 Compete the shopping list with the words from the box.

~~beef~~ butter cheese chicken drinks ice cream juice lettuce meat potatoes sardines spinach tea tomatoes tuna yoghurt

Shopping list
Fruit and vegetables: *apples* ______, ______, ______, ______
______: *beef* ______
Fish: ______, ______
Dairy: ______, ______, milk, ______, ______
______: coffee, milk, ______, ______

2 Match the foods with the containers.

1 [b] a box of — a mayonnaise
2 [ ] a can of — b chocolates
3 [ ] a carton of — c tuna
4 [ ] a jar of — d juice
5 [ ] a tin of — e cola

3 Write two food-related jobs for each category.

Restaurant jobs: ______, ______
Shop jobs: ______, ______
Newspaper/magazine jobs: ______, ______

4 Match the items in pictures a-g with the words from the box.

[a] bowl [ ] cup [ ] fork [ ] glass [ ] knife [ ] plate [ ] spoon

5 Complete the table with the words from Exercise 1.

Countable	Uncountable
apples	

6 Choose the correct words to complete the sentences.

1 I usually eat *a* / *(an)* apple at break time every day.
2 John has *any* / *no* breakfast before he goes to school, so he's hungry by ten o'clock.
3 There isn't *a* / *any* meat in this dish – it's vegetarian.
4 I'd like *any* / *some* coffee please, black with *any* / *no* milk.
5 There's *a* / *an* packet of biscuits in the cupboard if you want *no* / *some*.
6 Are there *any* / *no* nuts in this cake? I'm allergic to them.

7 Complete the conversation with the phrases from the box. There is one extra phrase.

a few a little how many ~~how much~~ not many not much too many too much

Gwen [1]*How much* milk have we got in the fridge?
Adam [2]______! We need some more.
Gwen What about eggs? [3]______ are there in the carton?
Adam Let me look. There are only [4]______ eggs left – just four.
Gwen That's [5]______. We need to go shopping. I want to make some cakes later.
Adam Do you need butter? We have only got [6]______, just half a packet.
Gwen It's OK. I don't want to make a cake with [7]______ butter. It's not good for you.
Adam True. And [8]______ cakes are not good for you, so I think I should eat them all!

USE OF ENGLISH

8 Choose the correct words a–d to complete the text.

THE RED CHILLI

A new Indian restaurant is now open in your area.
Come and eat [1]____ or take out with our free local delivery service.
We offer a range of meat: [2]____, beef or lamb, fish and vegetable meals.
Take a look at our online menu to [3]____ out what today's special dishes are.
And we plan to give [4]____ free homemade desserts to our first 100 customers! Don't miss out because our specialist [5]____ makes excellent cakes!

So hurry up and come to our restaurant. You can book a table Monday to Sunday for [6]____ (12–3 p.m.), or dinner (6–10 p.m.). Alternatively, [7]____ your meals online at **redchilly.co.uk**!

	a	b	c	d
1	at	down	in	under
2	chicken	kitchen	spinach	eggs
3	eat	find	give	help
4	on	off	out	up
5	baker	butcher	customer	waiter
6	breakfast	eat	food	lunch
7	do	like	make	order

Use of English > page 172

The Health KITCHEN

A There's a great new restaurant opposite the station. It's called the *Health Kitchen* and the food's amazing. It isn't very expensive, so it's always very busy. You can't book a table so it's best to go there early.

At lunchtime they serve sandwiches, soup and salads. The prices are quite low. For example, chicken soup with bread and butter costs £4.95 and a tuna salad with chips is just £6.50. They also have a few very tasty cakes and ice creams. Again, these aren't very expensive: a piece of carrot cake is only £2.45 and ice cream is just £1.95.

In the evenings you can have a three-course meal and there are lots of dishes to choose from. Their chef cooks all kinds of dishes from all over the world. For example, you can choose a Thai chicken curry, a Spanish paella, an Italian pasta dish or a French fish soup. They also have some very tasty vegetarian dishes and some amazing salads.

B So why is the restaurant called the Health Kitchen? Well, there are two reasons. The first is because all the food is 100 percent organic and is 'zero kilometre'. This means that all ingredients come from the local area. The second reason is because they tell you the number of calories in each dish. This means that you can make sure you're eating a healthy meal.

The staff are really friendly and helpful – they know a lot about the chef's food so they can recommend the best dishes for you to try. The service is fast: there are a lot of waiters so you never have to wait a long time for your food to arrive.

In my opinion, it's a fantastic restaurant and I love going there. It's my birthday next month so maybe I can celebrate it with a few of my friends at the *Health Kitchen*!

By Helen Compton

READING

9 Read Part A of the text and answer the questions.

1 Where is the *Health Kitchen*?
2 Why is the restaurant always busy?
3 What kind of food can you have there at lunchtime?
4 What kind of food do they serve in the evenings?

10 Read Part B of the text and complete the notes. Write no more than three words in each gap.

STRATEGY | Notes completion

Use key words to look for information and grammatical clues to decide what kind of word is needed in each gap. Read through all your answers to check that the completed sentences make sense and are grammatically correct.

1 *The Health Kitchen* uses food products from ________.
2 When you choose a dish, you know ________ calories it has.
3 ________ can give you advice about the dishes.
4 Your food arrives quickly because there are ________ waiters.
5 Helen wants to go to the *Health Kitchen* next month because it's ________.

SPEAKING

11 Look at the photo of the shopping basket. In pairs, ask and answer the questions below.

1 Which vegetables can you see in the basket?
2 What kind of dairy food is there in the basket?
3 What's your favourite dish and how often do you eat it?

WRITING

12 Look at Helen Compton's review of the *Health Kitchen* restaurant again. Write an email to a friend. Write the following information:

- tell him/her about the *Health Kitchen*
- say what kind of food you can eat there
- ask him/her to go there with you on your birthday

04 School life

VOCABULARY School, education collocations
GRAMMAR Present Continuous, Present Simple and Present Continuous
Use of English> page 172
SPEAKING Asking for, giving or refusing permission
WRITING An Internet forum post
VIDEO Grammar ▷ Documentary ▷ Communication ▷

Josh Is she coming?

Carrie No, she isn't. Oh, wait ... No, it's Mr Blake. Hold on. Hi, Mr Blake!

Mr Blake Oh, hello Carrie. What are you doing in the hallway? Lessons are starting now. And are you making phone calls in school? You know the rules, Carrie – only before lessons and at lunch time, please.

Carrie I'm not talking to anyone, Mr Blake. I'm, um, doing some new subjects this term so I'm checking my timetable. It's on my phone. Ah, yes. My next lesson is in the art room.

Mr Blake Ah, with Miss Stobart? Well, she's sitting in the staffroom with Mr Taylor at the moment. She's a bit sad today ... Anyway, I've got a class in the library and I'm late. And you are too!

Carrie Yes, Mr Blake. I'm going now ... Josh? I'm back. She isn't coming. She's still in the staffroom.

Josh OK. Wait there. We need a few minutes.

Carrie OK. I can see her! She's walking along the corridor. I'm coming back right now. And listen, you're all making too much noise .... Be quiet! ... Shhh!

Miss Stobart Sorry, everyone. Oh!

4A GRAMMAR AND VOCABULARY

1 SPEAKING **Look at the words in the box. Say which rooms or places you go to each day of the week.**

art room canteen computer room gym hallway library music room playing fields science lab staffroom

On Mondays I have classes in the music room and the science lab. I go to the canteen every day.

2 🔊 ***2.3*** **Read and listen to the conversation and look at the photos on page 50. Which places from Exercise 1 are the people in?**

3 🔊 ***2.3*** **Read and listen to the conversation again. Where is Carrie? Where are her friends? Where is Miss Stobart?**

Present Continuous

4 **Read the sentences. Then choose the correct option in the rule below.**

I'm not talking to anyone.

I'm checking my timetable.

We use the Present Continuous to talk about activities that *happen regularly / are happening now*.

5 **Read the Grammar box and check your answers to Exercise 4.**

Present Continuous

We use the **Present Continuous** to talk about actions that are happening now, at the moment of speaking.

+	I'**m having** lunch at the moment. She'**s getting** up now. They'**re playing** games.
–	I'**m not talking** to anyone. He **isn't coming**. You **aren't listening**.
?	**Are** you **doing** your homework? Yes, I **am**./No, **I'm not**.
Wh-?	Where **is** she **going**?

Spelling rules:
do → doing, write → writing, swim → swimming

Grammar Reference and Practice > page 164

6 **Complete the sentences. Use the Present Continuous affirmative or negative. Then check with the conversation on page 50.**

1 Carrie and Mr Blake *aren't talking* (talk) in the staffroom.
2 Miss Stobart _________ (feel) happy.
3 Josh _________ (wait) in the art room.
4 Carrie _________ (sit) in a classroom.
5 The students in the art room _________ (make) a lot of noise.

7 **Look again at the photos on page 50. Use the prompts to describe what is happening.**

1 Carrie/talk/teacher
2 Carrie/stand/hallway.
3 Students/prepare/decorations/classroom
4 Josh/talk to Carrie/on the phone

8 🔊 ***2.4*** **Listen and answer the questions.**

1 Why are the students feeling sad?
2 What is happening in the classroom now?

9 **Write sentences about people in your classroom. Use the words and phrases from the box to make affirmative and negative sentences in the Present Continuous.**

ask the teacher a question do an exercise eat
play a game read sit on chairs write in a notebook

1 I'm …
2 One person …
3 A few students …
4 Our teacher …
5 A lot of students …

1 I'm doing an exercise now.

10 **SPEAKING In pairs, think of one person in your classroom. Take turns to ask and answer questions and guess the people.**

A *Is the person writing at the moment?*
B *No, he isn't.*
A *Is he doing an exercise?*
B *Yes, he is.*

11 **Study *Watch out!* and read the sentences. Is the speaker describing an event happening now or a temporary situation?**

1 We're leaving right now. Do you want to come? *now*
2 I'm learning Spanish at school this year.
3 I can't talk now. I'm having breakfast.
4 We're reading Shakespeare this term.
5 Look! Deb isn't wearing her school uniform.

WATCH OUT!

We also use the Present Continuous to talk about temporary situations that aren't happening exactly at the time of speaking:

*I'**m doing** some new subjects this term.*

12 **SPEAKING In pairs, ask and answer the questions.**

1 What TV shows are you watching at the moment?
2 Are you reading any interesting books at the moment?
3 Are you doing any after-school clubs this term?
4 What subjects are you really enjoying this term?

▶ ***11*** **Read the question and watch the video. Say what the speakers answer. Then, in pairs, ask and answer the question.**

Are you learning anything new at the moment?

☐ **I can use the Present Continuous to talk about things happening now or temporary situations.**

4B VOCABULARY | School subjects and classroom objects

1 Match the school subjects with definitions 1–12.

Art ~~Biology~~ Chemistry Computer Science Drama Foreign Languages Geography History Maths Music Physical Education (PE) Physics

1 In *Biology* we learn about animals and plants.
2 In _________ we study important events from the past.
3 In _________ we learn how to sing and play an instrument.
4 In _________ we learn about electricity and atoms.
5 In _________ we study elements and substances.
6 In _________ we exercise and play sport.
7 In _________ we learn how to draw and paint.
8 In _________ we study numbers.
9 In _________ we learn how to act.
10 In _________ we learn how to use computers and write computer programs.
11 In _________ we study things like continents or climate.
12 In _________ we learn how to speak, read and write in a different language.

2 2.5 Listen and match the school subjects in Exercise 1 with lessons 1–6 in the recording.

1 *Art* 3 _________ 5 _________
2 _________ 4 _________ 6 _________

3 SPEAKING In pairs, take turns to describe a school subject for your partner to guess.

A *We have it on Mondays and Thursdays. We learn about animals, humans and plants.*
B *It's Biology.*

4 Match objects 1–11 in the pictures with the words from the box.

[2] calculator [ ] dictionary [ ] folders [ ] headphones [ ] highlighters [ ] keys [ ] notebooks [ ] ruler [ ] school backpack [ ] textbook [ ] tissues

5 2.6 Listen to the descriptions of six objects. Put objects a–f with recordings 1–6.

a [ ] highlighters
b [ ] tissues
c [ ] textbook
d [ ] dictionary
e [1] headphones
f [ ] calculator

6 2.7 PRONUNCIATION Listen and notice the number of syllables and the stress. Then listen again and repeat the words.

●•	●••	●•••	•●••	••●•
Music	Chemistry	calculator	Biology	education
_________	_________	_________	_________	_________

7 2.8 Listen to five more words and write them in the correct column in the table in Exercise 6.

8 SPEAKING In groups, discuss the questions.

1 What subjects are easy or difficult for you?
2 What foreign languages are you learning at school this year?
3 Which teachers give you a lot of homework?
4 How many objects in the picture in Exercise 4 are you carrying in your school bag/backpack right now?
5 What other things do you always carry? Make a list. Is there anything surprising about other students' answers?

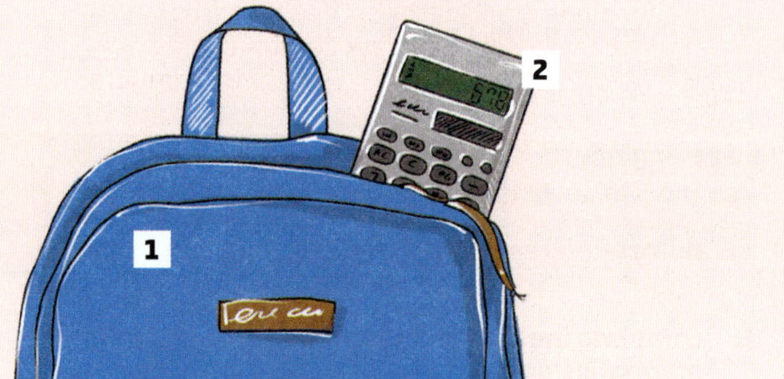

[ ] **I can talk about school, school subjects and classroom objects.**

4C GRAMMAR

NO PENS DAY WEDNESDAY

This looks like a normal classroom in the UK. The students are wearing uniforms and right now they're having a debate. There are some books and folders on the desks, but there aren't any pens.

'No Pens Day Wednesday' happens once a year, every year in the UK. The aim of the day is to improve students' listening and speaking skills. Thousands of schools join the event. For one day, students put down their pens. They don't write anything all day. In every lesson, from languages to Maths and even Art, students only do speaking activities.

'It's a great idea,' says Emma Davis, a student in Brighton. 'On Wednesdays we usually practise writing essays but today we're talking about our favourite characters in the book that we're reading this term.'

1 SPEAKING **Look at the photo and answer the questions.**

1 What are the students doing?
2 Is it a typical lesson? Say why.

2 **Read the article and check your answers in Exercise 1. Then, in pairs, discuss the questions.**

1 Do you think 'No Pens Day Wednesday' is a good idea?
2 Would you like a day like this in your school? Say why.

Present Simple and Present Continuous

3 **Are the underlined verbs in the sentences in the Present Simple (PS), Present Continuous for now (PC for now), or Present Continuous for temporary situation (PC temporary)?**

1 Right now they're having a debate. *PC for now*
2 *No Pens Wednesday* happens once a year, every year in the UK. _____
3 On Wednesdays we usually practise writing essays but today we're talking about our favourite characters in the book we're reading this term. _____ _____ _____

4 **Read the Grammar box and check your answers to Exercise 3.**

Present Simple and Present Continuous

We use the **Present Simple** to talk about regular actions/activities and facts.

We **have** music lessons twice a week.

Time expressions: always, usually, every day, once a week, etc.

We use the **Present Continuous**:
- to talk about actions/activities happening now
- to talk about temporary situations.

Today we**'re practising** for a concert.

This term I**'m learning** to play the guitar.

Time expressions: now, at the moment, this week/month/term, etc.

Grammar Reference and Practice > page 164

5 **Choose the correct form of the verb to complete the sentences.**

1 We *have / are having* Maths classes twice a week.
2 *Do you eat / Are you eating*? Please don't eat in the classroom.
3 Sports Day *happens / is happening* once a year at our school.
4 I *learn / 'm learning* to write computer code this term.
5 Jamie's angry about something. He *doesn't talk / isn't talking* to me at the moment.
6 There's chicken on this pizza. *Do you eat / Are you eating* meat or are you a vegetarian?

6 **Complete the email with the correct Present Simple and Present Continuous forms of the verbs in brackets.**

Hi Jin,
Today is Takeover Day in my school. It [1]*happens* (happen) once a year. Students take over adult roles at school for just one day. For example, some students [2]_________ (become) teachers for the day, others [3]_________ (be) cooks or school secretaries. I'm the assistant head teacher of my school today. At the moment, I [4]_________ (sit) in a meeting about school meals. Head teachers [5]_________ (have) a lot of boring meetings but I [6]_________ (enjoy) this one. All the other teachers [7]_________ (listen) to my opinions!

7 SPEAKING **In pairs, ask and answer the questions.**

1 What do you usually do after school on Wednesdays?
2 Are you learning to play a sport or an instrument at the moment? What is it?
3 What do you usually do on your way to school (listen to music, talk to friends, etc.)?
4 What is your teacher doing now?

☐ **I can use the Present Simple and the Present Continuous to talk about regular actions and activities happening now.**

4D READING AND VOCABULARY

1 SPEAKING **Imagine you can study at any school. What's important to you? Put the phrases in order 1–6 (1 = very important). Then compare your ideas in groups.**

- ☐ subjects you can study
- ☐ the school building
- ☐ opinions about the school
- ☐ the sports
- ☐ the distance from your house
- ☐ friends at the same school

2 **Read the article quickly. Choose the best answer. The author of the article is**

a thinking about studying at the Studio.
b a new student at the Studio.
c an adult.

3 **Study Active Reading and read the text again. Complete the school profile.**

Name	[1]*The Studio*	
Where	[2]__________, UK	
The school day	Starts: [3]__________	Finishes: [4]__________
Number of students	About: [5]__________	
Subjects	Typical subjects and designing [6]__________	

ACTIVE READING | Finding specific information

- Read the questions or task. Think about what information you need, e.g. a number, a name, or a date.
- Read the text quickly and find the parts of the text with the information you need. Don't worry about the rest of the text.

4 **Read the article again. Answer the questions.**

1 How old are the students at the school?
2 How much is breakfast at the school?
3 What do students often do for the computer game companies near the school?
4 When does the canteen serve food?
5 What adjectives does the author use to describe the students at the end of the article?

5 **Look at the highlighted phrases in the article. Complete the collocations with the words from the box.**

break exam (x2) grades project qualification ~~subject~~

1 do a *subject*
a __________
2 take an __________
a __________
3 get a __________
good/bad __________
4 pass/fail an __________

6 **Choose the correct words to complete the article.**

At the ESBC school in Berlin, Germany, students can't pass or [1]__________ exams because they don't get any grades until they are fifteen. After that, students only [2]__________ exams when they want to.

Students do normal [3]__________, such as German, Maths and English. But in a subject called 'Challenge' they also do [4]__________ based on real life. For example, the school gives them €150 each to plan an 'adventure' by themselves, from kayaking to working on farms.

1	**a** do	**b** fail	**c** get
2	**a** make	**b** pass	**c** take
3	**a** subjects	**b** activities	**c** languages
4	**a** practice	**b** projects	**c** qualifications

7 SPEAKING **Tick the sentences that are true for you. Then, in pairs, compare your answers.**

1 ☐ I take a break from studying every half an hour.
2 ☐ I'm doing an art project at the moment.
3 ☐ I like taking exams.
4 ☐ I don't usually get good grades in Maths.
5 ☐ When I pass an exam, my mum usually cooks me my favourite dinner!

8 REFLECT | Society **In pairs, discuss the questions.**

1 Do you think practical subjects like designing computer games or planning an adventure are useful or a waste of time? Say why.
2 Do you do any unusual subjects at your school?
3 What new subjects would you like to do at school? Say why.
4 Look at the list of features of *The Studio and ESBC in Berlin*. Which would you like to have at your school?

'real life' projects a school cinema an all-day canteen
free breakfast lessons until 5 p.m. optional exams

▶ *12* WATCH AND REFLECT **Go to page 153. Watch the documentary *A different kind of school* and do the exercises.**

☐ **I can identify specific information in an article and talk about school life.**

The UK's first gaming school

04

by Thomas Rogers

2.9

Today I'm visiting *The Studio* in Liverpool. It's the UK's first gaming school for students between the ages of fourteen and nineteen. The school is different from normal schools: students mix lessons with real work and each day starts at 9 a.m. and finishes at 5 p.m., like a typical working day.

The time is 8.45 a.m. and some students are arriving at school. Some are already enjoying a free breakfast inside. They're all wearing uniforms and they look smart. The school looks cool, like the office of an Internet tech company.

It's now 9 a.m. and school is starting. First there's an assembly, in the school cinema. I'm sitting in a really comfortable chair. This isn't like my old school ...

Lessons usually start at 9.20 a.m. But today is Games Day at the school and the students are doing projects in teams all day. Each team is designing, writing and making a computer game. They have adults to help them. But the adults aren't teachers - they're real games designers. In fact, there are a lot of computer game companies near the school. Students often test games for the companies and sometimes they get money for it.

Suddenly it's 1 p.m. and I'm getting hungry. When is lunch?

'There isn't a special time,' a student tells me. 'The school serves food all day so students can take a break when they need to - like in the working world.'

In the canteen, students and teachers are eating together and talking about their games. In total, there are about 250 students at The Studio.

Students don't only study games, of course. They do typical subjects like Maths, Foreign Languages and History. They take exams too. But at the end of their time at the school, they also get a qualification in designing computer games.

The students at the school look happy and motivated. They want to learn, they want to pass their exams and get good grades.

This really isn't like my old school. I want to be a student again. But in this school.

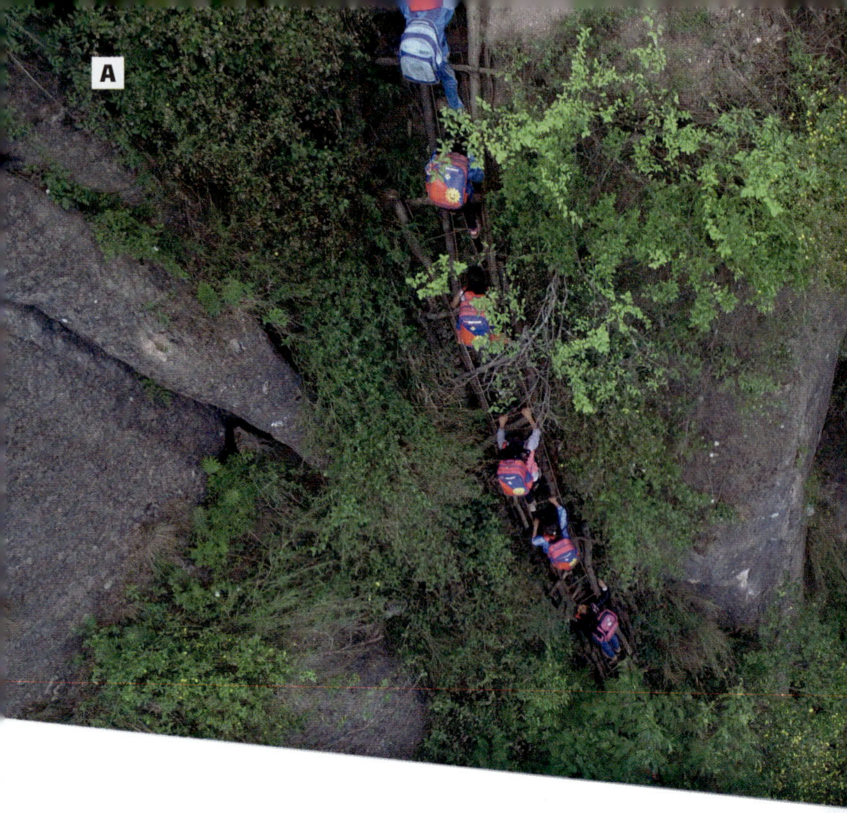

4E LISTENING AND VOCABULARY

1 SPEAKING **In pairs, discuss the questions.**

1. How do you usually get to school? By car, by public transport or on foot?
2. How long does the journey take?
3. What do you usually do on the journey?

2 **Look at the photos. Find these things in the photos.**

canal ladders plane skaters

3 🔊 *2.10* **Listen to the podcast. Number the photos A–C in the order the speaker mentions them.**

1 ☐ 2 ☐ 3 ☐

4 🔊 *2.10* **Read the questions. Then listen again and choose the correct answer.**

1. Josie gets to school
   a by car.
   b by bus.
   c on foot.
2. The students in China
   a use the ladders to go to school every day.
   b don't see their parents at weekends.
   c live about a kilometre from their school.
3. The Rideau Canal
   a is eight kilometres long.
   b is open for skating for about two months.
   c is closed in the afternoons.
4. Jonathan Davey
   a studies at a university in Poland.
   b takes a flight on Wednesdays and Fridays.
   c spends £10,000 on flights every year.

5 🔊 *2.11* **Complete the sentences from the podcast with the adjectives from the box. Then listen and check.**

crowded dangerous expensive freezing fun ~~simple~~ tiny

1. I have a *simple* journey in the morning.
2. The bus is always really _________, so I can never sit down.
3. These Chinese students are from a _________ village in the mountains.
4. That looks like a _________ journey for children.
5. It looks cold – in fact, it's _________!
6. Ice-skating! That's a _________ way to get to school.
7. But London is really _________ so Jonathan lives in Gdańsk, Poland.

6 🔊 *2.12* **Dictation. Listen to a short part of a podcast. Then listen again and write exactly what you hear.**

7 REFLECT | Society **Read the advert and in pairs, discuss the questions.**

1. What does the advert ask students to do?
2. What are the good things about walking to school in the advert? Can you think of any others?
3. Are there similar challenges at your school?

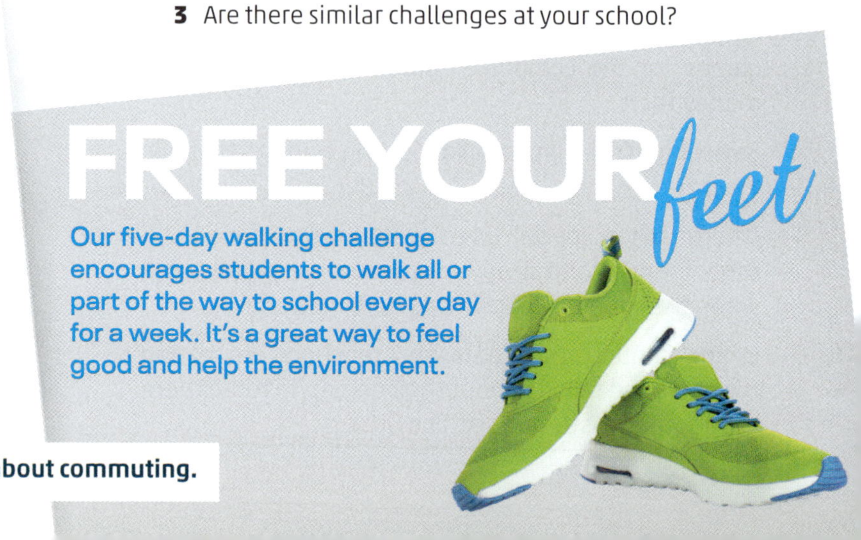

☐ **I can identify key details in a podcast and talk about commuting.**

4F SPEAKING

1 **Look at the photo and answer the questions.**

1 Who are the people in the photo?
2 Where are they?
3 What do you think they are talking about?

2 ▷ *13* 🔊 *2.13* **Watch or listen to Lucas and Zoe's conversation. Why does Zoe feel annoyed with Lucas?**

3 ▷ *13* 🔊 *2.13* **Which things does Lucas ask to borrow from Zoe? Which of them does she not give him? Read the dialogue and complete the gaps from memory. Watch or listen again to check.**

Lucas Hi, Zoe. Is anyone sitting here?
Zoe Hi, Lucas. No ... That's all my stuff. Sorry. Your music's quite loud!
Lucas Sorry!
Zoe Shhhh!
Lucas Sorry. Can I borrow your [1] __________, please?
Zoe Yes, of course. Here you are.
Lucas Zoe. Could I borrow your [2] __________? Mine is at home.
Zoe Yes, sure. But I have physics homework today so I need it soon. There are apps, you know ... for your phone.
Lucas I know, but I don't have one. Thanks. Just ask when you need it.
Everyone Shhhh!
Lucas Just one more thing ... Is it OK if I use your [3] __________?
Zoe No, sorry but you can't. I'm using it at the moment. OK?
Librarian Zoe! Please be quiet. This is a library!
Zoe Thanks a lot, Lucas!

4 **Study the Speaking box and complete the conversations with one or two words in each gap.**

1 **A** __________ ask you a question?
B Yes, __________
2 **A** Is it __________ I use your dictionary?
B __________ but you can't. It's at home.
3 **A** Could __________ your highlighter?
B Yes, that's fine. __________ are.

SPEAKING | Asking for, giving and refusing permission

Asking for permission
Can I borrow your headphones, please?
Could I borrow your calculator?
Is it OK if I use your ruler?

Saying 'yes'
Yes, of course.
Yes, sure. Here you are.
Yes, that's fine.
That's no problem.

Saying 'no' (and giving a reason)
No, sorry. (I don't have one.)
I'm sorry but you can't. (I'm using it at the moment.)

5 **Study *Watch out!* and complete the sentences with *one* or *ones*.**

1 That train is really crowded. Let's take the next *one*.
2 I need some new glasses. My old __________ are really old.
3 Buy two bottles of water and get a third __________ free!
4 Can you see the two girls? The tall __________ is Cassie and the other __________ is Marta.
5 These tissues are really expensive. Have you got any cheaper __________?
6 We do a lot of different subjects at school, but my favourite __________ are Art and Music.

WATCH OUT!

We use *one* and *ones* to avoid repeating countable nouns.
Can I borrow a pen? Yes, of course. Which ***one*** *do you want?*
Which headphones are yours? The red ***ones****.*

6 **In pairs, take turns to ask for permission and respond.**

1 borrow your phone?
2 look at your answers?
3 go to the toilet?
4 go out with my friends?
5 take a break?
6 use your highlighter?
7 move your backpack?

A *Can I borrow your phone, please?*
B *No, sorry. I don't have it with me*

7 **In pairs, role play the situation. Student A turn to page 175. Student B, go to page 176. Then change roles.**

☐ **I can ask for and give, or refuse permission.**

What is a typical school day like in England?

Elijah Watson, Secondary School student in York, England. Chelsea FC fan

I'm at Bridge School, in York, England. I'm sixteen and I'm in Year 11.

Our school day starts at 8.45 a.m. We have an assembly in the gym. The head teacher talks about news at the school. Then we have two hours of lessons.

At 11 o'clock there is a 15-minute break. We usually have a snack and chat with friends. Then there are two more lessons before lunchtime.

We have lunch at 12.45 p.m. The school canteen gets really crowded! Some students bring sandwiches from home but you can buy food, like pasta, salads, and burgers. A lot of it is quite healthy so I eat at school. After lunch I play football outside on the playing fields.

Afternoon lessons finish at 3.30 p.m. but there are lots of after-school clubs. This term I'm doing Spanish.

4G WRITING | An Internet forum post

1 SPEAKING **Look at the photo. What are the students doing?**

2 **Read the question on the website and Elijah's answer. Choose three topics Elijah mentions.**

extra classes after school   the computers at school
the food at lunchtime   his favourite subjects   sport

3 **Study the Writing box. Find the phrases in Elijah's post.**

WRITING | An Internet forum post

- Introduce yourself (your name, your school, your age, your year):
  I'm at Bridge School.
  I'm in Year …
- Say what happens in the morning:
  Our school day starts at …
  Then we have …
  At 11 o'clock …
- Say what happens at lunchtime:
  We have lunch at …
  You can buy food, like …
- Talk about the afternoon and after-school activities:
  Afternoon lessons finish at …
  This term I'm doing …

4 **Study *Watch out!* Then replace the underlined words and phrases in 1–4 with a pronoun.**

1. I really enjoy English. English is my best subject.
2. I never bring sandwiches to school. I can't stand sandwiches!
3. We like our Maths teacher, Mr Thomas. But Mr Thomas gives us a lot of homework.
4. We're lucky because we have great playing fields at our school. The playing fields are really big!

I really enjoy English. It is my best subject.

WATCH OUT!

We use pronouns to avoid repeating nouns:
*You can also buy **food**, like pasta, salads, and burgers. A lot of **it** is quite healthy.*

5 SPEAKING **Work in pairs. Compare your school and Elijah's school. Use the prompts in Exercise 2 to help you.**

6 WRITING TASK **Write about your school. Use the text in Exercise 2 to help you. Use the Writing box as a guide.**

- Use pronouns to avoid repeating nouns.
- Use linking words: *and*, *but*, and *then*.

☐ **I can describe a typical day at my school.**

4A GRAMMAR AND VOCABULARY 5.22

afterschool club (n) /ˌɑːftəˈskuːl klʌb/
art room (n) /ˈɑːt ruːm/
be late /ˌbi ˈleɪt/
canteen (n) /kænˈtiːn/
check your timetable /ˌtʃek jə ˈtaɪmˌteɪbəl/
classroom (n) /ˈklɑːsrʊm/
computer room (n) /kəmˈpjuːtə ruːm/
documentary (n) /ˌdɒkjəˈmentəri/
gym (n) /dʒɪm/
hallway (n) /ˈhɔːlweɪ/
hold on /ˌhəʊld ˈɒn/
library (n) /ˈlaɪbrəri/
make a phone call /ˌmeɪk ə ˈfəʊn kɔːl/
music room (n) /ˈmjuːzɪk ruːm/
playing fields (n) /ˈpleɪɪŋ fiːəldz/
prepare (v) /prɪˈpeə/
school uniform (n) /ˌskuːl ˈjuːnəfɔːm/
science lab (n) /ˈsaɪəns læb/
staffroom (n) /ˈstɑːfruːm/
term (n) /tɜːm/

4B VOCABULARY 5.23

act (v) /ækt/
Art (n) /ɑːt/
atom (n) /ˈætəm/
backpack (n) /ˈbækˌpæk/
Biology (n) /baɪˈɒlədʒi/
calculator (n) /ˈkælkjəleɪtə/
Chemistry (n) /ˈkeməstri/
climate (n) /ˈklaɪmət/
Computer Science (n) /kəmˌpjuːtə ˈsaɪəns/
continent (n) /ˈkɒntɪnənt/
dictionary (n) /ˈdɪkʃənəri/
Drama (n) /ˈdrɑːmə/
education (n) /ˌedjʊˈkeɪʃən/
electricity (n) /ɪˌlekˈtrɪsəti/
element (n) /ˈeləmənt/
folder (n) /ˈfəʊldə/
foreign languages (n) /ˌfɒrɪn ˈlæŋgwɪdʒɪz/
Geography (n) /dʒiˈɒgrəfi/
headphones (n) /ˈhedfəʊnz/
highlighter (n) /ˈhaɪlaɪtə/
History (n) /ˈhɪstəri/
keys (n) /kiːz/
Maths (n) /mæθs/
Music (n) /ˈmjuːzɪk/
notebook (n) /ˈnəʊtbʊk/
object (n) /ˈɒbdʒɪkt/
Physical Education (n) /ˌfɪzɪkəl ˌedjʊˈkeɪʃən/
Physics (n) /ˈfɪzɪks/
plant (n) /plɑːnt/
play an instrument /ˌpleɪ ən ˈɪnstrəmənt/
ruler (n) /ˈruːlə/
school bag (n) /ˈskuːl bæg/
substance (n) /ˈsʌbstəns/
textbook (n) /ˈtekstbʊk/
the past (n) /ðə ˈpɑːst/
tissue (n) /ˈtɪʃuː/

4C GRAMMAR 5.24

assistant head teacher (n) /əˌsɪstənt hed ˈtiːtʃə/
character (n) /ˈkærəktə/
computer code (n) /kəmˈpjuːtə kəʊd/
essay (n) /ˈeseɪ/
have a debate /ˌhæv ə dɪˈbeɪt/
improve (v) /ɪmˈpruːv/
join (v) /dʒɔɪn/
listening/speaking skills (n) /ˈlɪsənɪŋ/ˈspiːkɪŋ skɪlz/
meeting (n) /ˈmiːtɪŋ/
pen (n) /pen/
practise doing sth /ˌpræktɪs ˈduːɪŋ ˌsʌmθɪŋ/
role (n) /rəʊl/
take over /ˌteɪk ˈəʊvə/
takeover (n) /ˈteɪkˌəʊvə/

4D READING AND VOCABULARY 5.25

adventure (n) /ədˈventʃə/
arrive at (school) (v) /əˌraɪv ət (ˈskuːl)/
assembly (n) /əˈsembli/
design a computer game /dɪˌzaɪn ə kəmˈpjuːtə geɪm/
do a project /ˌduː ə ˈprɒdʒekt/
do a subject /ˌduː ə ˈsʌbdʒɪkt/
games designer (n) /ˈgeɪmz dɪˌzaɪnə/
gaming (n) /ˈgeɪmɪŋ/
get a qualification in sth /ˌget ə ˌkwɒlɪfɪˈkeɪʃən ɪn ˌsʌmθɪŋ/
get good grades /ˌget gʊd ˈgreɪdz/
mix (v) /mɪks/
motivated (adj) /ˈməʊtəveɪtəd/
office (n) /ˈɒfɪs/
optional (adj) /ˈɒpʃənəl/
pass/fail an exam /ˌpɑːs/ˌfeɪl ən ɪgˈzæm/
practical (adj) /ˈpræktɪkəl/
smart (adj) /smɑːt/
take a break (from sth) /ˌteɪk ə ˈbreɪk (frəm ˌsʌmθɪŋ)/
take an exam /ˌteɪk ən ɪgˈzæm/
test (v) /test/
working day (n) /ˌwɜːkɪŋ ˈdeɪ/

4E LISTENING AND VOCABULARY 5.26

advert (n) /ˈædvɜːt/
by car/bus/public transport /ˌbaɪ ˈkɑː/ˈbʌs/ˌpʌblɪk ˈtrænspɔːt/
canal (n) /kəˈnæl/
challenge (n) /ˈtʃæləndʒ/
closed (adj) /kləʊzd/
crowded (adj) /ˈkraʊdɪd/
dangerous (adj) /ˈdeɪndʒərəs/
expensive (adj) /ɪkˈspensɪv/
free (v) /friː/
freezing (adj) /ˈfriːzɪŋ/
fun (adj) /fʌn/
get to school /ˌget tə ˈskuːl/
journey (n) /ˈdʒɜːni/
kilometre (n) /ˈkɪləˌmiːtə/
ladder (n) /ˈlædə/
on foot /ɒn ˈfʊt/
plane (n) /pleɪn/
simple (adj) /ˈsɪmpəl/
skater (n) /ˈskeɪtə/
skating/ice-skating (n) /ˈskeɪtɪŋ/ˈaɪs ˌskeɪtɪŋ/
take (v) /teɪk/
take a flight /ˌteɪk ə ˈflaɪt/
tiny (adj) /ˈtaɪni/
travel (v) /ˈtrævəl/
village (n) /ˈvɪlɪdʒ/
walk (v) /wɔːk/

4F SPEAKING 5.27

borrow (v) /ˈbɒrəʊ/
go to the toilet /ˌgəʊ tə ðə ˈtɔɪlɪt/
loud (adj) /laʊd/

4G WRITING 5.28

chat with friends /ˌtʃæt wɪð ˈfrendz/
give a talk /ˌgɪv ə ˈtɔːk/
Internet forum post (n) /ˌɪntənet ˈfɔːrəm pəʊst/
secondary school (n) /ˈsekəndəri skuːl /

Remember More > page 174

VOCABULARY AND GRAMMAR

1 Match definitions 1–10 with the words in the box. There are two extra words.

☐ Art ☐ Biology ☐ canteen ☐ Chemistry ☐ Drama ☐ Geography ☐ gym ☐ hallway ☐ History ☑1 library ☐ Music ☐ staffroom

1 You read books here.
2 You learn about the past in this subject.
3 You eat your school lunch here.
4 Teachers meet and prepare lessons here.
5 You act in plays in this lesson.
6 You do Physical Education (PE) here.
7 You draw pictures in this lesson.
8 You study plant and animal life in this lesson.
9 You play instruments or sing in this lesson.
10 You learn about the world in this lesson.

2 Choose the correct words to complete the sentences.

1 Turn to page 21 in your *notebooks* / *textbooks*, please!
2 You need to use a *calculator* / *dictionary* to solve this Maths problem.
3 I haven't got any *headphones* / *highlighters* to mark the important parts in the book.
4 Class! Put your things away in your *folders* / *backpacks*. It's break time.

3 Complete the sentences with the words from the box.

break cool exams expensive grade pass simple ~~subjects~~

Josh Which [1]*subjects* are you studying at the moment, Lana?
Lana Maths. I want a really good [2]_________ this year.
Josh That's [3]_________ for you! You never fail any [4]_________, not like me!
Lana Hey! Why don't we take a [5]_________ tonight, stop studying and have some fun?
Josh That sounds [6]_________! There's a new pizza place in town. It's not very [7]_________. And who knows, a night out with a genius could help me [8]_________ my exams too!

4 Complete the sentences with the Present Continuous forms of the verbs (in brackets). Tick the sentences that talk about temporary situations.

1 ☐ The students _________ (not listen) to the teacher, they _________ (play) a game of cards.
2 ☐ John _________ (not do) his homework, he _______ (use) his mobile phone.
3 ☐ I _________ (not run) this week because I feel ill.
4 ☐ 'What _________ (you read)?' 'It's a book about art.'
5 ☐ '_________ (the girls have) lunch?' 'No, they _______ (not be). They _________ (eat) chocolate!'
6 ☐ '_________ (you study) the Romans this term?' 'Yes, I _________ (be).'

5 Complete the text with the Present Simple or Present Continuous forms of the verbs in brackets.

OUTDOOR CLASSROOM DAY

Across the world today students [1]*are not studying* (not study) in their classrooms, they [2]_________ (take part) in Outdoor Classroom Day.
For example, at this time on Thursdays, Pablo in Rio usually [3]_________ (study) Physics in the Science room, but today he [4]_________ (learn) about nature in the fields around his school. In fact, the whole school [5]_________ (do) a project on nature this term.
Maria in Athens usually [6]_________ (have) double Maths now, but today she and her classmates [7]_________ (measure) an area outside the school for a new vegetable garden. This is because Greek schools [8]_________ (try) to become green this year.
Sven and Anna [9]_________ (not leave) their school in Stockholm very often, but today they [10]_________ (clean) a local beach.
What about you? Tell us what [11]_________ (usually/you/do) at school and what [12]_________ (happen) today!

USE OF ENGLISH

6 Choose the correct words a–c to complete the texts.

1

School is closed this week because it's __ and the central heating isn't working.

a tiny **b** cool **c** cold

2

SPORTS DAY starts at 9 a.m. on the school __ fields. Don't be late!

a drama **b** playing **c** game

3

This year all students studying __ languages can take part in our school exchange project.

a foreign **b** funny **c** strange

4

PLEASE WEAR __ AND NOT SHOES IN THE SCHOOL GYM AT ALL TIMES!

a headphones **b** tissues **c** trainers

5

If you are interested in __ a programming project this term please come to the computer room at 3 p.m.

a doing **b** getting **c** taking

6

Please don't climb over the school walls. It's against the rules and it's __.

a crowded **b** dangerous **c** expensive

Use of English > page 172

LISTENING

7 2.14 Read questions 1–5 and study the pictures. Then listen and choose the correct answer for each recording.

STRATEGY | Multiple choice task with picture options

Look at the pictures and questions carefully to check that you understand what the pictures show. This will give you an idea of what sort of information to look for.

1 How does Jodie usually travel to school?

2 What does Jamie borrow from Amy?

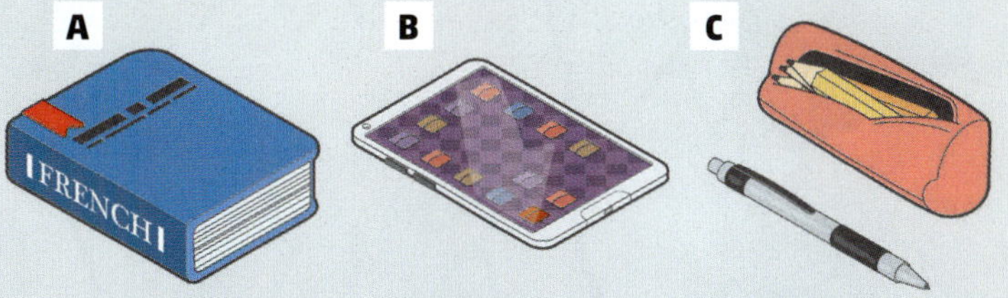

3 Which homework is Becky doing?

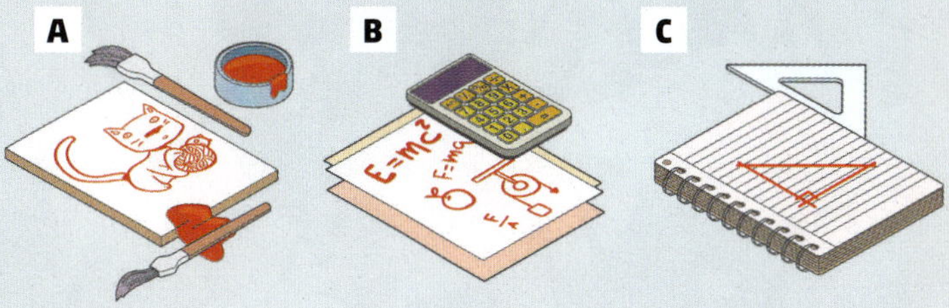

SPEAKING

8 In pairs, take turns to ask and answer the questions.

1. What time do you usually finish school?
2. What is your favourite subject?
3. Which subjects don't you enjoy studying?
4. What are you learning in English at the moment?
5. Which sports are you doing at the moment?
6. What kind of music are you listening to these days?

WRITING

9 Write an email to an English-speaking friend about your typical school day in which you:

- introduce yourself (your name, your school, your age, your year)
- say what happens in the morning
- say what happens at lunchtime
- talk about the afternoon and after-school activities.

From: danrob@qmail.com
To: steven04@qmail.com
Subject:

Hi Steven

LIFE SKILLS

How to manage exam stress

STUDY FORUM

Sal06	I find revising for exams really stressful. Any ideas on how to reduce the stress?
Kirsten	Don't study all the time. Get up and do something! I go for a run and that really helps me to relax.
Edi39	I find it helps to revise late at night. I often stay up till 2 a.m. It's quieter and there's nobody around to annoy me.
LauraX	I get very nervous when I'm revising on my own. I start thinking I don't know anything. So I do past exam papers with my best friend and I feel less stressed.
Mark2	It's easy to feel worried when there's so much to do. I read all my notes quickly and highlight the things I'm not sure about. Then the exams seem less scary.

1 **Order these situations from the least (1) to the most (6) stressful. Then compare in pairs. Can you think of anything more stressful?**

- ☐ you lose your phone
- ☐ you get up late and miss the bus to school
- ☐ you have an argument with your best friend
- ☐ your parents ask you to do some housework while you're studying
- ☐ your end of year exams start tomorrow
- ☐ you are sitting an important exam

2 **Discuss in pairs. What can you do to avoid stress in situations like those in Exercise 1?**

3 **Read the comments on the study forum. In pairs, say who has the best idea for reducing exam stress. What do you do to feel less stressed before exams?**

4 **Read the article and match headings A–F with the advice for revising 1–6.**

A Don't be afraid to ask
B Be organised and start early
C Make it interesting
D Eat and sleep well
E Don't keep your stress to yourself
F Healthy body, healthy brain

Taking stress out of exams

This month, Jonathan Pearson, director of the Student Support Centre discusses how to cope with the stress of exams.

Pre-exam stress is one of the biggest problems in students' lives. It makes you feel bad and stops you from thinking clearly. So here are my tips to help you revise, relax and reduce the stress of exams.

1 ☐ The best way to cope with exam stress is to have a good study plan. Decide which subjects to study every day and how much time to spend on each one. And don't wait until just before the exam to begin your revision.

2 ☐ When you get bored, you don't learn so well. So take a short break every 45-60 minutes. Change the subject you're studying when you start feeling bored. And try studying with a friend. It's more fun when there are two of you.

3 ☐ When we don't understand something, we feel stressed. It's normal. But don't worry about it, do something about it! Ask your teacher for help. You may find it hard to believe but all teachers want their students to do well in exams.

4 ☐ Your body needs exercise for your brain to work better. So don't study all the time. It can just make you more stressed. Do some sport, go to the gym or just go for a walk but get up and move!

5 ☐ It's important for your brain to rest so try to get eight hours' sleep every night. Eat a healthy diet and avoid drinks with caffeine that can stop you from sleeping well.

6 ☐ Finally, if after following all this advice, you still feel stressed, then don't keep it a secret. Talk to someone, your mum or your dad, a friend or a teacher and tell them how you feel. We all need help sometimes.

5 2.15 **Listen to Laura asking her brother Mark for tips for the day of her exam. Complete Mark's advice with 2–3 words in each gap.**

- Go [1]*to bed early* the night before the exam.
- Have a [2]________ so you don't feel hungry.
- Take a [3]________ to the exam, it's good for your brain.
- Leave [4]________ so you aren't late for the exam.
- When you get the exam paper, [5]________ very carefully.
- Answer the [6]________ first. It makes you feel good.
- Plan [7]________ to spend on each question.
- If you panic in the exam, try to relax. [8]________ and take deep breaths.

6 In pairs, answer the questions.

1. Which of Mark's tips do you usually follow?
2. Which ones would you like to try?

7 Complete the Life Skills box with the words below.

answer breaks carefully early eight exercise late ~~revising~~ talk teacher

LIFE SKILLS | How to manage exam stress

Start [1]*revising* a long time before the exam but don't study all the time – take short [2]________ often. Take care of yourself: try to get [3]________ hours' sleep every night, have a healthy diet and get lots of physical [4]________. Ask your [5]________ to explain complicated things and [6]________ to someone if you feel stressed. The night before the exam, go to bed [7]________. In the morning have a good breakfast but don't be [8]________ for your exam. Read the exam paper [9]________, make a plan and [10]________ the easy questions first.

8 Do the task below.

LIFE SKILLS | Project

A Imagine you have an important test in two weeks' time.

Plan your revision timetable. Decide:

- which subjects to study
- what to do when you aren't studying
- when and where to study
- when to have breaks/relax/see friends
- what kind of exercise to do and when to do it
- when to sleep

B Present your timetable to the class. What do you think of your classmates' timetables?

05 Appearances

VOCABULARY Personality adjectives, appearance, clothes
GRAMMAR *Past Simple* **Use of English** > page 172
SPEAKING Shopping for clothes
WRITING An informal email
VIDEO Grammar ▷ Communication ▷ Documentary ▷

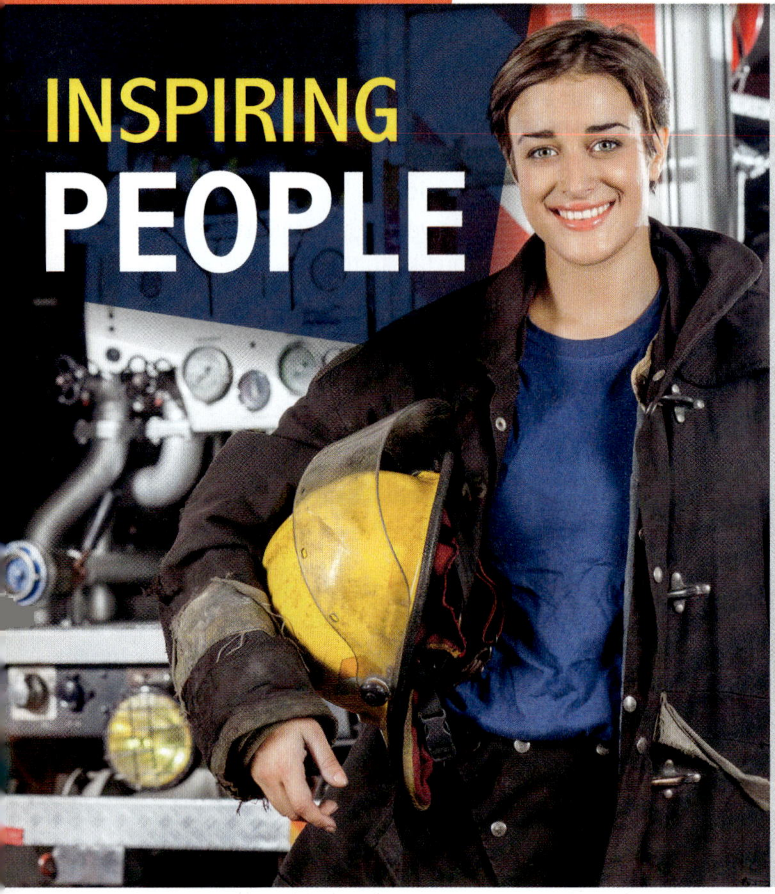

INSPIRING PEOPLE

Last week we asked readers to write about their heroes when they were kids. Who were they? What could they do?

1 When I was four, there was a fire in my house. I was in bed upstairs and my parents couldn't reach me. Fortunately, our neighbour Rosie was a firefighter. She climbed a ladder and saved me. She was so brave! After that Rosie was my hero and my friend. My parents weren't often around so I was with Rosie a lot. She wasn't very patient but she was creative and full of good ideas. She could climb trees, ride a horse, ski and lots more. Unfortunately, she doesn't live here now. I miss her.
JESSE, INVERNESS

2 When I was eight, I started at a new school. On my first day, I felt nervous and lonely. I pushed open a door and went into the wrong classroom. Some of the pupils laughed at me. But then a teacher came into the room and the children stopped laughing. The teacher's name was Mrs McKay. She did so much for me. She was always very helpful. I wasn't confident. I had learning difficulties. But Mrs McKay taught me to believe in myself. Thanks to her, I became a serious student. I studied hard and got good results. She was easy-going and funny but she also inspired her students. I cried when she moved away.
ALEX, BRIGHTON

5A GRAMMAR AND VOCABULARY

1 **Describe the photo. Then read the texts quickly. Does the photo show text 1, 2 or both?**

2 **Read the texts again. What are the heroes' names and why were they heroes?**

Past Simple: *to be* and *can*

3 **Look at the examples underlined in the introduction and text 1. Complete the sentences with *could or was/were*. Then find questions and negative forms of *can* and *to be* in the past.**

1 We use ________ to talk about ability in the past.
2 We use ________ and ________ for the verb *to be* in the past.

Past Simple: *to be* and *can*

	to be	
	I • He • She • It	We • You • They
+	I **was** happy.	We **were** brave.
-	It **wasn't** funny.	You **weren't** helpful.
?	**Was** he patient? Yes, he **was**./No, he **wasn't**.	**Were** they confident? Yes, they **were**./No, they **weren't**.

	can
	I • You • He • She • It • We • They
+	We **could** draw very well.
-	I **couldn't** dance.
?	**Could** they sing? Yes, they **could**./ No, they **couldn't**.

Grammar Reference and Practice > page 165

4 **In pairs, complete the conversation with the correct forms of *could*, *was* or *were*. Then have a similar conversation beginning with the first question.**

Matt Who [1]*was* your hero when you [2]__________ little?
Emma My sister Jodie.
Matt [3]__________ you the same age?
Emma No, we [4]__________. She [5]__________ two years older.
Matt [6]__________ you do the same things as her?
Emma No, obviously I [7]__________ do all the things that she [8]__________ do because I [9]__________ big and strong like her but she [10]__________ always very patient with me.

Past Simple: affirmative

5 **Look at the examples and answer the questions.**

Some of the pupils laughed at me.

A teacher came into the room. She did so much for me.

1. What do you add to a regular verb to make it past?
2. Which two verbs have irregular forms?

Past Simple: affirmative

We use the **Past Simple** to talk about things that started and finished in the past.

I • You • He • She • It • We • They

Regular verbs	Irregular verbs
We **watched** TV last night.	We **went** to Greece in 2014.

Time expressions

last week/night/year/month, yesterday, thirty years/two minutes/five days ago, in 1950/April/the 1990s

Grammar Reference and Practice > page 165

6 **Find the Past Simple forms of the verbs in the box in the texts and decide if they are regular or irregular.**

~~ask~~ ~~become~~ come cry do feel get go have inspire laugh move push start stop study teach

Regular verbs	Irregular verbs
asked	*became*

7 *2.16* **Complete the text with some of the verbs from Exercise 6. Then listen and check.**

My grandad George [1]*came* from a small town in Wales. When he was seven, his family [2]__________ house to London. When he [3]__________ school there he couldn't read or write but his teachers [4]__________ him well and he [5]__________ hard. He [6]__________ the first person in our family to go to university. After university he [7]__________ a job at the BBC. During his life he [8]__________ many hobbies, especially skiing and he [9]__________ some amazing things. In 2004 he [10]__________ to the South Pole to make a documentary. He was my hero.

8 *2.17* **PRONUNCIATION Listen and put the verbs from the box in the correct column. Then listen again and check.**

~~asked~~ ~~cried~~ ~~decided~~ described died ended pushed saved shouted started stopped watched

/t/	/d/	/ɪd/
asked	*cried*	*decided*

9 **Put these past time expressions in order from the most recent. Then use them to write sentences about your life. Read them to your partner.**

in 2003 last weekend last night two months ago yesterday morning

I watched a great film on TV last night.

10 **Match the highlighted adjectives in the text in Exercise 1 with the definitions.**

1. My brother makes me laugh. He's really *funny*.
2. My mum's afraid of nothing. She is very __________.
3. My best friend has a lot of imagination. She is very __________.
4. I'm generally relaxed and calm. I'm __________.
5. My sister is always ready to do things for other people. She is so __________!
6. Our neighbour never laughs or smiles. He's always __________.
7. My dad can wait without becoming angry or upset. He is so __________.
8. I don't believe in myself. I'm not __________

11 **Write six sentences about people you know. Use the adjectives from Exercise 10.**

Tanya is really funny. She always makes me laugh.

12 **SPEAKING In pairs, talk about your heros. Say what they were like and what they could do.**

My older brother was my hero. He could play football really well and taught me how to play.

14 **Read the question and watch the video. Say what the speakers answer. Then in pairs, talk about yourselves.**

What were you like as a child?

☐ **I can use the Past Simple to talk about the past.**

5B VOCABULARY | Appearance, clothes

1 Match the words in the box with the clothes 1–20 in the pictures.

☐ boots ☐ cardigan ☐ coat ☐ dress ☐ gloves
☐ hat ☐ hoody ☐ *1* jacket ☐ jeans ☐ jumper
☐ scarf ☐ shirt ☐ shoes ☐ skirt ☐ socks ☐ T-shirt
☐ top ☐ tracksuit bottoms ☐ trainers ☐ trousers

2 *2.18* Listen and match the names with the people in the photos.

Bill Jake Josh Julia Ling Leon Mandy Susie

Photo A: (left to right): ________, ________, ________, ________

Photo B: ________ Photo D: ________
Photo C: ________ Photo E: ________

3 Read the descriptions and look at photos A–E. Complete the vocabulary map using the words from the descriptions.

Susie is quite short, slim and pretty. She has got long, red, wavy hair and green eyes. She's wearing a really cool hat!

Ling has got medium-length, brown, straight hair and brown eyes. She's got a nice smile.

Leon is tall, well-built and good-looking. He has got short, black hair, brown eyes and a beard.

General
Opinion: *pretty*, ______,
Age: young, middle-aged, old

Face
eyes: blue, grey, ______, ______
other: *beard*, ______

APPEARANCE

Body
Height: ______, ______
Build: thin, ______, ______

Hair
Colour: dark, fair, grey, white, blond(e), ______, ______, ______
Type: curly, ______, ______
Length: bald, ______, ______, ______

4 Study Watch Out! and complete the sentences with the words in the correct order.

1 Jane has got (blonde / hair / long / straight).
2 My mum has got (big / blue / eyes / lovely).
3 My dad is bald and has got a (beard / grey / short).
4 Ben has got (hair / curly / black / beautiful).
5 Mr Jones is a (good-looking / man / young).

WATCH OUT!

For appearance we use this order of adjectives:

opinion	length/size	age	colour	type	noun
beautiful	*short*		*brown*	*curly*	*hair*
attractive	*tall*	*young*			*woman*

5 Write descriptions of three of the other people in the photos.

Bill is slim and quite tall. He's got short dark hair and brown eyes. He's wearing a grey hoody and tracksuit bottoms.

6 SPEAKING In pairs, take turns to describe a person in your class. Your partner guesses who it is.

A *This person is quite tall and slim and she has got long, brown, straight hair and blue eyes. She is wearing jeans, a red T-shirt and black trainers.*

B *It's Maria!*

7 REFLECT | Society In pairs, discuss the questions.

1 Which adjectives are better to describe somebody: *ugly or not very attractive, short or not very tall, old or not very young*? Say why.
2 Do you think it's important to be positive when talking about other people's appearance or personality? Say why.

shopit Rose@retro_rose

A

B

C

D

E

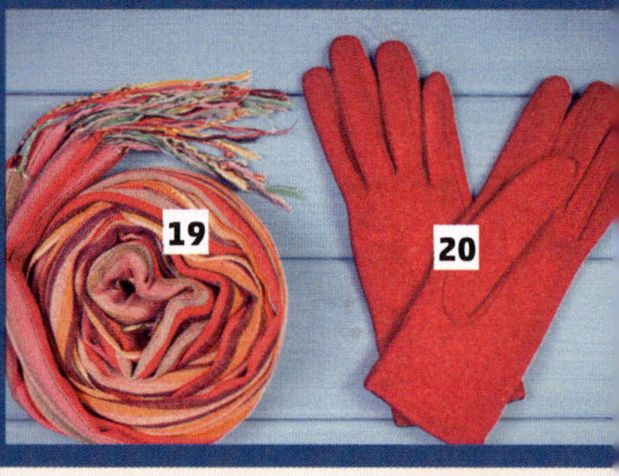

☐ **I can talk about people's appearance and clothes.**

5C SPEAKING

1 **In pairs, discuss the questions.**

1 How often do you go shopping for clothes?
2 Which shops do you go to?
3 Do you prefer shopping for clothes alone or with friends? Say why.
4 Do you enjoy going shopping for clothes? Say why.

2 **Look at the photo. Who wants to buy some clothes, Theo or Katie? Who is not interested? How do you know?**

3 *15* *2.19* **Watch or listen to the conversation. What items of clothing do Katie and Theo decide to buy?**

4 *15* *2.19* **Study the Speaking box and complete the dialogue with one word in each gap. Watch or listen to check.**

Katie	Oh, please, Theo. I just want to look at a few things.
Theo	OK. But don't be a long time. I don't need any clothes.
Assistant	Can I [1] *help* you?
Theo	No, thanks. I'm just [2] ________.
Katie	Um. Yes, please. I'm looking [3] ________ a green T-shirt.
Assistant	OK. There are some here. What [4] ________ are you?
Katie	Medium.
Assistant	Here you are.
Katie	Thanks.
Ten minutes later …	
Katie	Can I try these [5] ________?
Assistant	Of course. The changing [6] ________ are over there.
Katie	Thanks.
Katie	Hey, Theo, what do you think of this T-shirt and these jeans? I really like them!
Theo	Um, yeah, cool. Look, I've got a few things too.
Katie	Wow! Trousers, T-shirts, jeans, a jumper … You don't need any clothes, eh?
Theo	Yeah, well.
Assistant	[7] ________ they fit?
Katie	The jeans are great. But have you got this T-shirt in a small?
Assistant	Sorry. No.
Katie	Theo? Are you ready to go?
Theo	Just a minute!
Katie	Theo! Hurry up. I'm bored!
Theo	I'm ready. I only like this T-shirt. Does it [8] ________ me?
Katie	Yes, it's [9] ________. Can we go?
Theo	No, it doesn't [10] ________ right. I don't like it anymore.
Katie	OK. I need to pay for these jeans.
Theo	What? Katie! Hurry up! I'm bored!

SPEAKING | Shopping for clothes

What sales assistants say	What customers say
Can I help you?	Yes, please. I'm looking for …
Do you need any help?	No, thanks. I'm just looking.
What size are you?	Small/Medium/Large
The changing rooms are (over there).	Can I try this/these on?
Does it/Do they fit?	Yes, it's/they're perfect.
	Have you got this (T-shirt) in a small/medium/large?
	Does it/Do they suit me?
	No, it doesn't look right.

5 *2.20* **Put the conversation in the correct order. Listen and check.**

a ☐ **Assistant** Here you are.
b ☐ **Assistant** Of course. The changing rooms are over there.
c ☐ **Assistant** What do you think? Does it fit?
d *1* **Assistant** Hi. Can I help you?
e ☐ **Assistant** OK. We have three different ones at the moment. What size are you?
f ☐ **Customer** Medium, please.
g ☐ **Customer** Where? Oh, there. OK. Thanks.
h ☐ **Customer** Thanks. Can I try it on?
i ☐ **Customer** Yes, it does. I really like it.
j ☐ **Customer** Yes, please. I'm looking for a blue jacket.

6 **Think of an item of clothing you want to buy. In pairs, practise the conversation in Exercise 5.**

7 **In pairs, role play the situation. Student A, go to page 175. Student B go to page 176.**

☐ **I can shop for clothes.**

5D GRAMMAR

1 **SPEAKING In pairs, describe the people in the photo and compare their appearance with the way people look today.**

2 **2.21 Listen and read the conversation between Elsa and Didi. Who are the people in the photo?**

Didi Did you find the photo album, Elsa?
Elsa Oh! No, I didn't. Where did you put it?
Didi I put it on the coffee table last night. Here it is. Oh, look! That's me when I was eighteen.
Elsa You look so pretty! Did Grandpa take that photo?
Didi No, he didn't. That's Grandpa next to me.
Elsa What did you say?
Didi That's Grandpa. He had wavy hair and a beard when he was young. He didn't go bald until he was forty.
Elsa Did you always dress like that in those days?
Didi No, we didn't dress like that at work.
Elsa I love your dress! Did you keep it?
Didi Yes, I did. It's in my wardrobe.
Elsa Oh! Can I try it on? Please!

Past Simple: negative and question forms

3 **Look at the examples. Then complete rules 1–2.**

Did you find the photo album?
We didn't dress like that at work.

1 To make negative sentences in the Past Simple we use ________ + infinitive.
2 To make questions in the Past Simple we use ________ + *I/you/he/she/it/we/they* + infinitive.

4 **Study the Grammar box. Then find more examples of the Past Simple in Elsa and Didi's conversation.**

Past Simple: negative and question forms	
	I • You • He • She • It • We • They
+	He **liked** her. They **had** a conversation.
-	He **didn't tell** her. They **didn't talk** about his T-shirt collection.
?	**Did** he **like** her? Yes, he **did**./No, he **didn't**.
Wh-?	What **did** you **eat**?

Grammar Reference and Practice > page 166

5 **2.22 Complete the conversation with the correct forms of the words in brackets. Then listen and check your answers.**

Elsa You look so different in these photos. When [1]*did you take* (you/take) them?
Didi In 1973 when [2]________ (we/see) David Bowie in concert.
Elsa [3]________ (Grandpa/wear) make-up all the time in 1973?
Didi No, [4]________ (he/not do), only when [5]________ (we/go) to glam rock concerts. And [6]________ (he/not wear) platform shoes very often either, thank goodness!
Elsa You look great! [7]________ (you/like) your hair long?
Didi Yes, [8]________ (I/do).
Elsa So, why [9]________ (you/change) it?
Didi Because [10]________ (I/not want) to be unfashionable.

6 **Make the sentences negative.**

1 I went shopping last weekend.
I didn't go shopping last weekend.
2 I bought a new phone yesterday.
3 I went to a great party on Saturday.
4 I met my best friend when I was four.
5 My parents gave me a guitar for my birthday.
6 My sister and I played video games last night.
7 I really enjoyed the last film I saw at the cinema.
8 Our Maths teacher gave us some homework this morning.

7 **SPEAKING Use the sentences in Exercise 6 to make questions. Then, ask and answer the questions in pairs.**

A *Did you go shopping last weekend?*
B *Yes, I did.*
A *What did you buy?*
B *I didn't buy much but I bought a case for my phone.*

☐ **I can use the Past Simple to ask questions and give affirmative or negative answers.**

5E LISTENING AND VOCABULARY

1 **Look at the photo. Is it a boy or a girl? How do you know?**

2 **2.23 Listen to the first part of the interview to check your answers in Exercise1. Were you surprised? Say why.**

3 **2.24 Listen to the rest of the interview. What is the main topic?**

a Young children's clothes in the 19th century.
b Why pink is a traditional colour for girls.
c Changes in fashion for boys and girls.

4 **Study Active Listening. Then read sentences 1–6 and decide what information you need.**

1. At the end of the 19th century, boys under six in the western world often had ________.
2. At that time boys also wore ________ until they were six.
3. When good quality coloured clothes became available, they were ________ colours.
4. Until the early ________ century, boys and girls both wore pink and blue clothes.
5. The article from 1918 says blue is the best colour for ________.
6. In the 1980s, in ________, pink became the only colour for girls' clothes.

ACTIVE LISTENING | Finding specific information

- Think about the topic before you listen.
- Read sentences or questions before you listen and decide what information you need. For example, what kind of word do you need – an adjective, a noun or a verb. Do you need a number, a place, a date or something else?
- Listen for the information you need. Don't try to understand every word.

5 **2.25 Listen to the interview again and complete the sentences in Exercise 4 with one or two words.**

6 **Study Watch out! Then complete the sentences with the verbs from the box.**

fit go with ~~match~~ suit

1. Your socks don't *match*! One is black and the other is blue!
2. Jeans ________ well ________ everything. I wear them all the time.
3. This top doesn't ________ me anymore. It's really small.
4. I never wear light-coloured clothing. Dark colours ___ me.

WATCH OUT!

fit, suit, go with, match

These trousers ***fit*** *me.* They are the correct size.

Red ***suits*** *you.* You look great in red.

Those shoes don't ***go with*** *that dress.* They don't look good together.

Your T-shirt ***matches*** *your trainers.* They look good together.

7 **REFLECT | Society In pairs, read the text and answer the questions. Then compare your answers with other pairs.**

1. What type of toys did you play with when you were young?
2. Do you think it is important for girls and boys to play with the same toys? Why?
3. How strong is the tradition of blue for boys and pink for girls in your country?
4. What do you think about this tradition?

Many shops offer different toys for boys and girls. Boys' toys often involve building or technology while girls' toys involve role-playing and arty things – and too many of them are pink! The people behind the campaign, *Let Toys be Toys*, want to stop this gender stereotyping. They say kids should be free to choose which toys to play with and that all children need to play with different toys to develop different skills.

☐ **I can identify specific information in an interview and talk about clothes.**

DIGITAL DOPPELGÄNGERS

A

B

2.26

Is it possible to find someone who looks like you but is not part of your family?

Most people look very different from each other. [1]________ However, these genes can combine by chance to produce faces that look very similar to ours. They are not exactly the same – there's usually a small difference: a different smile, different shaped eyes, etc.

Many people today are interested in finding their doubles and thanks to a new website, it is now possible to find your lookalike online. The process is simple: you register, upload current photos, then answer questions about your appearance (the shape and size of your face, eyes, mouth, nose, etc.). A computer matches people who look similar and then you can contact your doppelgängers through the website.

I wanted to find out more about digital doppelgängers, so I spoke to some people who found their doubles online. Douglas, aged 23 from Scotland, met Vincent, also 23, from France, via webcam. 'I couldn't believe my eyes! We were identical. [2]________'. We both had a beard and the same colour hair, although Vincent's was longer. But our accents were so different we started to laugh when we spoke!'

Sophie, 19, and Gracie, 18, were born just ten miles apart in London, but they didn't know each other before their online match. 'In the online photos I thought we actually looked quite different from each other, because I've got brown hair and green eyes and Gracie's got blonde hair and blue eyes,' Sophie told me. [3]________ We both play with our hair when we're nervous, and we even talk the same way!' said Gracie.

The doppelgänger website is very popular. Why? 'Because when you meet someone who looks like you, you feel an instant connection, you do not feel alone,' says Anna, another person I interviewed.

I think she has a point. Right! It's time for me to find my twin!

C

D

5F READING AND VOCABULARY

1 **SPEAKING** **Work in pairs. Describe the pairs of people in photos A–D. What's similar and what's different about them? Talk about the things below.**

age build clothes eye colour height
hair (style, colour, length) other features

I think the two men in picture B are similar, but they have got different hair styles and they are wearing different clothes.

2 **Read the text on page 70. What's a doppelgänger?**

3 **Read the text again. Match sentences A–E with gaps 1–3. There are two extra sentences.**

A The differences in our appearance depend on a small number of genes.
B But you can't always find a match.
C 'But when we met face to face, we discovered a lot of similarities.'
D It was like looking in the mirror!
E It would be great to meet my twin!

4 **Read the text and answer the questions.**

1. What decides the way we look?
   Our genes.
2. Who/What matches digital doppelgängers on the website?
3. How did Douglas and Vincent meet for the first time?
4. What was similar about them?
5. Why did Sophie and Gracie seem different in the photo?
6. According to one person in the text, what do we feel when we meet a person who looks like us?

5 **Complete the sentences with the correct form of the words from the box.**

different from lookalikes look different ~~look like~~
similar to identical the same

1. I *look like* my grandmother, tall and slim.
2. My little sister is _________ the rest of my family – she's very serious but we tell jokes all the time.
3. Is that your mother in the photo? You don't look very _________ her!
4. I'm exactly _________ as my dad – we're both very easy-going!
5. My brother _________ from the rest of the family because he's the only one with red hair.
6. My twin brother and I are _________ – we're the same height and our faces are similar – but we're not _________ – he's got blue eyes and mine are brown – and our personalities are really different.

6 **Use the phrases from Exercise 5 to write four sentences about your family.**

I'm different from my two sisters – they're both confident but I'm quite shy.
We look different too because …

7 **2.27** **Listen to a podcast interview about working as lookalikes and complete the notes.**

Do you want to work as a lookalike?

What you need

Anyone can work as a lookalike if they look similar to a [1]*famous* person.
You need to sound like them or walk like them or even [2]_________ or dance like them.
You can be successful if you've got a lot in [3]_________ with your lookalike.

What you do

You go to public events and private VIP [4]_________.
You do photo shoots for a [5]_________ or open a new building.
Some lookalikes work as actors' doubles in [6]_________.

8 **SPEAKING** **In pairs, ask and answer the questions.**

1. Do you look like a famous person or do you know anybody who does?
2. How are you or they similar to and different from the famous person?
   My brother looks a bit like tennis player Novak Djokovic. He's got the same colour hair and eyes and he's very tall, but he can't play tennis like him!

9 **REFLECT | Society** **In pairs, discuss the questions.**

1. What are the advantages or disadvantages of being famous?
2. Would you like to be famous? Say why. What would you like to be famous for?

16 WATCH AND REFLECT **Go to page 154. Watch the documentary *Lifestyles now and then* and do the exercises.**

☐ **I can understand the structure of a text and talk about family and lookalikes.**

5G WRITING | An informal email

1 Read the email and put the things below in the order they are mentioned in the text.

☐ Interests
☐ Appearance
☐ Personality

New message from Chris

Hi John,
How are you? What's new? Guess what! I met a guy called Seb last Saturday and he knows you! He says he was in your class at primary school. Do you remember him?
He's quite tall and he's got short dark hair and green eyes. He looks a bit like the French footballer Olivier Giroud, but without the beard!
He seemed quite shy at first because he didn't say much. Then we started talking about football and friends – and he's actually really funny and easy-going. We have a lot in common.
He really likes sport – he plays in a local basketball team. He also loves skateboarding and hip hop like me.
Do you fancy meeting Seb and me in town next weekend? Text me!
Bye for now,
Chris

2 Match questions 1–3 with the categories from the box. Then find the answers to the questions about Seb in the email.

☐ appearance ☐ personality ☐ interests

1 What does he like?
2 What does he look like?
3 What is he like?

3 Study the Writing box. Then put Saskia's email to Brigette in the correct order.

WRITING | An informal email

- Open the email:
  Hi John,
  How are you?
- Say who it is about:
  I met a guy called Seb last Saturday.
- Describe the person's appearance:
  He looks a bit like the French footballer Olivier Giroud, but without the beard!
- Describe the person's character:
  He seemed quite shy at first because he didn't say much.
- Talk about their interests/what you have in common:
  He really likes sport – he plays in a local basketball team. He also loves skateboarding and hip hop music like me.
- Suggest something to do together:
  Do you fancy meeting Seb and me in town next weekend? Text me!
- End the email:
  Bye for now,
  Chris

a ☐ A new girl from Singapore called Leila moved to my school last month. She sits next to me in class and we're great friends!

b [1] Hello Brigette, How are you? How's school?

c ☐ Leila's confident and very creative and she's really helpful, especially in Maths because she's really good at it.

d ☐ See you in the summer. Bye for now,
Saskia

e ☐ She's short and slim and she's got long black straight hair and brown eyes. In fact, she's very pretty and looks like a model, but she's still really nice!

f ☐ We've got the same interests – photography and cinema, but we don't like PE or Computer Science!

g ☐ Why don't you come for a visit so you can meet her yourself?

4 WRITING TASK Write an email about a new friend. Use the Writing box to help you. In your email:

- describe how you met.
- describe your friend's appearance.
- describe your friend's personality.
- talk about his/her interests and what you have in common.
- suggest something to do together.

☐ **I can write an informal email.**

5A GRAMMAR AND VOCABULARY 5.29

accident (n) /'æksɪdənt/

brave (adj) /breɪv/

confident (adj) /'kɒnfɪdənt/

creative (adj) /kri'eɪtɪv/

cry (v) /kraɪ/

die (v) /daɪ/

easy-going (adj) /ˌi:zi 'gəʊɪŋ/

feel afraid/scared /ˌfi:l ə'freɪd/'skeəd/

fire (n) /faɪə/

firefighter (n) /'faɪəˌfaɪtə/

funny (adj) /'fʌni/

helpful (adj) /'helpfəl/

hero (n) /'hɪərəʊ/

inspire (v) /ɪn'spaɪə(r)/

move house /ˌmu:v 'haʊs/

patient (adj) /'peɪʃənt/

push (v) /pʊʃ/

reach (v) /ri:tʃ/

ride a horse /ˌraɪd ə 'hɔ:s/

save (v) /seɪv/

serious (adj) /'sɪəriəs/

shout at sb (v) /'ʃaʊt ət ˌsʌmbɒdi/

5B VOCABULARY 5.30

appearance (n) /ə'pɪərəns/

attractive (adj) /ə'træktɪv/

bald (adj) /bɔ:ld/

beard (n) /bɪəd/

blue/grey/brown/green eyes /ˌblu:/ˌgreɪ/ˌbraʊn/ˌgri:n 'aɪz/

boots (n) /bu:ts/

build (n) /bɪld/

cardigan (n) /'kɑ:dɪgən/

coat (n) /kəʊt/

curly/straight/wavy hair /ˌkɜ:li/ˌstreɪt/ˌweɪvi 'heə/

dark/fair/grey/white/blond(e)/red/brown/black hair /ˌdɑ:k/ˌfeə/ˌgreɪ/ˌwaɪt/ˌblɒnd/ˌred/ˌbraʊn/ˌblæk 'heə/

dress (n) /dres/

gloves (n) /glʌvz/

good-looking (adj) /ˌgʊd 'lʊkɪŋ /

hair colour/type/length (n) /'heə ˌkʌlə/ˌtaɪp/ˌleŋθ/

hat (n) /hæt/

height (n) /haɪt/

hoody (n) /'hʊdi/

jacket (n) /'dʒækɪt/

jeans (n) /dʒi:nz/

jumper (n) /'dʒʌmpə/

middle-aged (adj) /ˌmɪdəl 'eɪdʒd/

nice (adj) /naɪs/

old (adj) /əʊld/

pretty (adj) /'prɪti/

scarf (n) /skɑ:f/

shirt (n) /ʃɜ:t/

shoes (n) /ʃu:z/

short/medium-length/long hair /ˌʃɔ:t/ˌmi:diəm ˌleŋθ/ˌlɒŋ 'heə/

skirt (n) /skɜ:t/

slim (adj) /slɪm/

smile (n) /smaɪl/

socks (n) /sɒks/

tall (adj) /tɔ:l/

thin (adj) /θɪn/

top (n) /tɒp/

tracksuit bottoms (n) /'træksu:t ˌbɒtəmz/

trainers (n) /'treɪnəz/

trousers (n) /'traʊzəz/

T-shirt (n) /'ti: ʃɜ:t/

well-built (adj) /ˌwel 'bɪlt/

young (adj) /jʌŋ/

5C SPEAKING 5.31

changing room (n) /'tʃeɪndʒɪŋ ru:m/

fit (v) /fɪt/

go shopping for clothes /ˌgəʊ ʃɒpɪŋ fə 'kləʊðz/

sales assistant (n) /'seɪlz əˌsɪstənt/

size (n) /saɪz/

small/medium/large (adj) /smɔ:l/'mi:diəm/lɑ:dʒ/

suit (v) /su:t/

try on (v) /ˌtraɪ 'ɒn/

5D GRAMMAR 5.32

dress (v) /dres/

go bald /ˌgəʊ 'bɔ:ld/

platform shoes (n) /ˌplætfɔ:m 'ʃu:z/

unfashionable (adj) /ʌn'fæʃənəbəl/

wear make-up /ˌweə 'meɪkʌp/

5E LISTENING AND VOCABULARY 5.33

campaign (n) /kæm'peɪn/

century (n) /'sentʃəri/

construction (n) /kən'strʌkʃən/

fit (v) /fɪt/

gender (n) /'dʒendə/

go with sth /'gəʊ wɪð ˌsʌmθɪŋ/

good quality (adj) /ˌgʊd 'kwɒləti/

match (v) /mætʃ/

stereotyping (n) /'steriətaɪpɪŋ/

suit (v) /su:t/

toy (n) /tɔɪ/

western world /ˌwestən 'wɜ:ld/

5F READING AND VOCABULARY 5.34

combine (v) /kəm'baɪn/

contact (v) /'kɒntækt/

current photo (adj) /ˌkʌrənt 'fəʊtəʊ/

difference (n) /'dɪfərəns/

different from (adj) /'dɪfrənt frɒm/

doppelganger (n) /'dɒpəlgæŋə/

digital (adj) /'dɪdʒətl/

double (n) /'dʌbəl/

facial features (n) /ˌfeɪʃəl 'fi:tʃəz/

feel an instant connection /ˌfi:l ən ˌɪnstənt kə'nekʃən/

find a match /ˌfaɪnd ə 'mætʃ/

genes (n) /dʒi:nz/

have a lot in common /ˌhæv ə lɒt ɪn 'kɒmən/

have a point /ˌhæv ə 'pɔɪnt/

identical (adj) /aɪ'dentɪkəl/

look like sb /'lʊk laɪk ˌsʌmbɒdi/

look/seem different /ˌlʊk/ˌsi:m 'dɪfərənt/

lookalike (n) /'lʊkəlaɪk/

looks (n) /lʊks/

meet face to face /ˌmi:t ˌfeɪs tə 'feɪs/

qualities (n) /'kwɒlətiz/

shape (n) /ʃeɪp/

shy (adj) /ʃaɪ/

similar to sb (n) /'sɪmələ tə ˌsʌmbɒdi/

sound (v) /saʊnd/

specific (adj) /spə'sɪfɪk/

tell jokes /ˌtel 'dʒəʊks/

the same (as sb/sth) /ðə 'seɪm (əz ˌsʌmbɒdi/ˌsʌmθɪŋ)/

twin (n) /twɪn/

virtual (adj) /'vɜ:tʃuəl/

5G WRITING 5.35

fancy doing sth /ˌfænsi 'du:ɪŋ ˌsʌmθɪŋ/

primary school (n) /'praɪməri sku:l/

Remember More > page 174

VOCABULARY AND GRAMMAR

1 Complete the sentences with the words from the box. There is one extra word.

brave easy-going funny ~~patient~~ serious

1 My mum is very *patient*. She always sits with me and helps me do my homework.
2 Not many TV comedians are ________ these days. They just don't make you laugh!
3 George was very ________ in school and studied hard, so he decided to become a politician.
4 ________ people are generally more relaxed and calm.
5 As a child, Susan was very ________. She loved to meet new people and talked to everyone!

2 Complete the table with the words from the box.

~~boots~~ ~~cardigan~~ ~~coat~~ dress ~~gloves~~ hat hoody jacket jeans jumper scarf shirt shoes skirt socks T-shirt tracksuit bottoms trainers trousers

Shop by department
Footware: *boots*, ________, ________, ________
Tops and bottoms: *cardigan*, ________, ________, ________, ________, ________, ________, ________, ________, ________
Outdoor clothes: *coat*, ________
Others: *gloves*, ________, ________

3 Look at the pictures and complete the descriptions with the words from the box.

bald beard dark good-looking middle-aged short slim straight ~~young~~

Sid's a tall, [1]*young* man with short [2]________ hair and a [3]________.

Judy's a [4]________ woman with [5]________ blonde wavy hair and blue eyes.

Kim's a beautiful, [6]________, young woman with long brown [7]________ hair.

Chris is a [8]________, well-built, [9]________ man with brown eyes.

4 Match 1–6 with a–f to make sentences.

1 These shoes don't fit me,
2 I don't think this shirt
3 I look very similar
4 My brother is different from
5 The sisters are identical twins
6 Green really suits you

a because of the colour of your eyes.
b so they look the same.
c they're not my size.
d goes with this skirt.
e the rest of the family.
f to my mum.

5 Complete the conversation with the correct form of *was/were* or *could*. Add *not* if necessary.

Julie Dad, what [1]*were* you good at as a child?
Dad Well, I [2]________ a great footballer.
Julie Really? Mum said you [3]________ play sport!
Dad No, your mother [4]________ good at sport, but I was!
Julie So you [5]________ in the school team like me?
Dad Well, no. But me and my friends [6]________ in a band.
Julie Cool! [7]________ you play an instrument?
Dad Yes, we all [8]________, but there [9]________ really instruments in our band, we just sang.
Julie Dad!

6 Complete the sentences with the correct form of the verbs in brackets and complete the short answers. Which verbs are regular and which are irregular?

1 My parents *studied* (study) music in the 1990s.
2 John's team ________ (not win) last Saturday.
3 '________ (you/see) Alice this afternoon?' 'No, I ________. She ________ (leave) school at lunchtime!'
4 I ________ (go) shopping in town yesterday afternoon.
5 '________ (we/have) any English homework last week?' 'Yes, we ________.'
6 The Romans ________ (arrive) in Britain in 43 AD.

USE OF ENGLISH

7 Complete the text with the missing words.

Inspiring figures

William Shakespeare [1]*was* an important English writer. He [2]________ at least thirty-seven plays and many poems. He was probably [3]________ in Stratford-upon-Avon [4]________ April, 1564, and died there just over 400 years [5]________ . His parents [6]________ a successful merchant and a farmer's daughter, so the family wasn't poor. William probably [7]________ at King's New Grammar School. He got married at the age of eighteen and [8]________ three children. We don't know if he [9]________ write well at school, but around 1592 he started work as a professional playwright and poet in London. His plays are just as popular today as they [10]________ in the past.

Use of English > page 172

READING

8 Read the article and choose the correct answers a–d.

STRATEGY | Multiple choice task

First, read the text and the main parts of the questions without reading the answers. Try to answer the questions yourself. Then read the options a-d, if your answer is one of them, it's probably correct.

1 Why did Diana leave school when she was sixteen?
  - **a** She wasn't very confident.
  - **b** She didn't pass her exams.
  - **c** Her parents' marriage ended.
  - **d** She wanted to learn to play the piano.

2 When Diana married Charles
  - **a** there were guests from 750 countries.
  - **b** the ceremony was in Sandringham.
  - **c** it was two years after they met.
  - **d** millions of people watched the wedding on TV.

3 Which sentence is true about Diana?
  - **a** She liked to photograph women.
  - **b** She worked for newspapers around the world.
  - **c** She didn't belong to the Royal Family.
  - **d** She wanted to help people without homes.

4 After her divorce, Diana
  - **a** was no longer popular.
  - **b** created a new charity.
  - **c** started a new magazine 'People's Princess'.
  - **d** continued helping the charities.

SPEAKING

9 In pairs, discuss the questions.

1. What's your best friend like? Describe his/her personality.
2. What does your mother look like? Describe her appearance.
3. What did you buy when you last went shopping for clothes?
4. Would you like to wear a school uniform? Why/Why not?

WRITING

10 You made a new friend last weekend. Write an email to your friend and tell him/her about the person. Include the following information:

- describe how you met
- describe the person's appearance
- describe the person's personality
- talk about his/her interests and what they have in common
- suggest that they do something together

Lady Di

Diana Spencer was born in Sandringham, a village in the east of England, on 1st July, 1961. Her parents divorced when she was seven years old, so she didn't have a very happy childhood. As a teenager she was very shy. She didn't get very good grades at school but she could play the piano very well and was good at swimming and diving. When she was sixteen she failed her exams and left school.

In 1980 she started dating Prince Charles, the oldest son of Queen Elizabeth II, and he asked her to marry him a year later. When Charles and Diana got married, in July 1981, at St Paul's Cathedral in London, 750 million people around the world watched the ceremony on TV.

Diana soon became one of the most photographed women in the world. She was slim with short, blonde hair and she was very pretty. Her photos appeared in newspapers and magazines all over the world and she soon became a global fashion icon.

Diana used her position as a member of the British Royal Family to help people. She worked closely with charities that helped people who were ill. She also worked for a charity in London that helped the homeless – people who don't have anywhere to live and often sleep in the streets.

Diana and Charles had two children, William and Harry, but their marriage was not a happy one and they divorced in 1996. After her divorce, Diana continued to do a lot of work to help these charities. She was very popular and the newspapers called her the 'People's Princess'. The British people loved her because she was very kind and generous and they were very shocked and sad when she died in a car accident in Paris in 1997.

06 The arts around us

VOCABULARY The arts, jobs in the arts
GRAMMAR Comparative and superlative adjectives, (*not*) *as … as*, *too*, (*not*) *enough*
Use of English > page 172
SPEAKING Suggestions
WRITING A film review
VIDEO Grammar ▷ Documentary ▷ Communication ▷

EXTREME ARTS!

6A GRAMMAR AND VOCABULARY

1 **Look at the photos. What different types of arts can you see?**

dance film literature music painting photography sculpture theatre

2 **2.28 Complete the gaps with the people in the box. Then listen and check.**

~~choreographer~~ composer director poet scriptwriter

The arts	People
dance	[1]*choreographer*, dancer
film	actor/actress, [2]________, director
literature	writer, [3]________
music	[4]________, musician
painting	painter
photography	photographer
sculpture	sculptor
theatre	actor, [5]________

Find out about the longest films, the strangest songs, the smallest sculptures, and their creators.

In 2014 a Swedish director, Anders Weberg made a trailer for his film, *Ambiancé*. It was seventy-two minutes long. In 2016 he made a second trailer. It was longer than the first one – seven hours and nineteen minutes! So how long is the film? It's thirty days long! But *Ambiancé* isn't as long as the world record. Another Swedish film, called *Logistics*, is thirty-five days long.

Austrian artist Raoul Haspel's first record became the most popular piece of music in Austria in 2015. The record was one minute of silence.
Haspel's record wasn't an original idea. There are many 'silent' records, some by famous artists, such as John Lennon. However, Haspel's record was more successful and made €15,000.

South African, Jonty Hurwitz used 3D printing technology to create seven of the tiniest sculptures of people in the world. The biggest of Hurwitz's sculptures is as wide as a human hair.
The smallest one is a sculpture of a dancer. It's smaller than an ant's eye.
The first version of Jonty's dancer took him several months to make. But a photographer destroyed it by accident during a photo shoot – in a second!

3 SPEAKING **In pairs, discuss examples of the different types of arts and people in Exercise 2.**

I really like Pride and Prejudice by the writer Jane Austen. My favourite film director is Wes Anderson.

4 **Read the article quickly. Who are the people below and what did they create?**

Anders Weberg Raoul Haspel Jonty Hurwitz

Comparative and superlative adjectives

5 **Read the sentences. Then match fragments 1–3 with a–c to complete the rules.**

Comparative adjectives

The second trailer was longer than the first one.

Haspel's record was more successful.

Superlative adjectives

The smallest one is a sculpture of a dancer.

Haspel's record became the most popular piece of music in Austria in 2015.

1 We add *-er* or *-est*
2 We add *more* or *the most*
3 We often use *than*

a ☐ after comparatives.
b ☐ to one-syllable adjectives
c ☐ before adjectives with two or more syllables

6 **Study the Grammar box and check your answers to Exercise 5. Which two adjectives are irregular? Find more examples of comparatives and superlatives in the text.**

Comparative and superlative adjectives

	Adjective	Comparative	Superlative
one syllable	cold	**colder** (than)	**the coldest**
one syllable, ends in *-e*	wide	**wider** (than)	**the widest**
one syllable, ends in vowel + consonant	hot	**hotter** (than)	**the hottest**
two syllables, ends in *-y*	tidy	**tidier** (than)	**the tidiest**
two or more syllables	interesting	**more** interesting (than)	**the most** interesting
irregular	good	**better** (than)	**the best**
	bad	**worse** (than)	**the worst**

Grammar Reference and Practice > page 167

7 **Complete the sentences with the comparative forms of the adjectives in brackets. Add *than* if necessary.**

1 You're <u>*better than*</u> (good) me at photography.
2 The last *Harry Potter* film was __________ (scary) the first one.
3 These theatre tickets are __________ (expensive) because the seats are __________ (close) to the stage.
4 The film *Ambiancé* is __________ (short) *Logistics*.
5 Hurwitz's sculpture of a dancer is __________ (thin) a human hair.

8 *2.29* **Complete the sentences with the superlative form of the adjectives. Which records are the most surprising? Listen and check.**

busy expensive fast high ~~successful~~

RECORD-BREAKING ARTS

1 <u>*The most successful*</u> piece of literature of all time, with sales of over 500 million copies, is *Don Quixote* by Cervantes.
2 ______________ (and probably the coldest!) art gallery in the world is on a mountain in Argentina. It's over 4,000 metres above sea level.
3 The Louvre in Paris gets over seven million visitors a year. It's ______________ museum in Europe.
4 ______________ movie in the world was The Pirates of the Caribbean: At World's End. It cost over $370 million but it earned almost a billion dollars.
5 ______________ rapping is in a song by Eminem. The singer says 1,560 words in six minutes and four seconds. That's 4.28 words every second.

9 **Study *Watch out!* and rewrite the sentences with (*not*) *as … as*.**

1 Rock music is more popular than hip-hop.
Hip-hop isn't as popular as rock music.
2 TV series are more interesting than films.
Films ______________.
3 The earlier *Star Wars* films are better than the latest ones.
The latest *Star Wars* films ______________.
4 In my opinion films are more exciting than theatre.
I don't think theatre ______________.

WATCH OUT!

We can also compare two things with (*not*) *as … as*:

But Ambiancé still ***isn't as long as*** *the world record.*

The biggest sculpture is about ***as wide as*** *a human hair.*

10 SPEAKING **Discuss in pairs. Do you agree with the sentences in Exercise 9?**

1 I don't agree. I don't think rock music is as popular as hip-hop.

17 **Read the question and watch the video. Say what the speakers answer. Then in pairs, ask and answer the question.**

Which is better - watching a film at home or going to the cinema? Why?

☐ **I can use comparative and superlative adjectives to talk about people and objects.**

A brief guide to … Glastonbury

Everything you need to know about the UK's number 1 music and arts festival

🔊 *2.30*

It started on a farm in 1970, the day after American rock star Jimi Hendrix died. Tickets cost £1 and 1,500 people showed up for two days of rock and folk music. There was also free milk for everyone! The next year, the festival got its famous 'Pyramid Stage'. Singer David Bowie was the headliner and there were around 8,000 people. This time the festival was free.

Now, Glastonbury is the biggest annual music and arts festival in the UK and it's still on the same farm. Every June, the tiny village of Pilton (population: 996) welcomes 180,000 guests, including 2,000 of the most talented and popular performers in the world.

It's now also a longer festival than in the past – with five days of live shows from music of every kind, to dance, theatre, comedy, film and literature. It isn't as cheap as it was, of course. Ticket prices now start at £250. Even at this price, they usually sell out in a few hours but the festival is still free for people from Pilton! You can bring a tent or rent one – the most luxurious, with four bedrooms and two bathrooms, costs £9,000.

When so many people spend five days in a field, it's not surprising that they make a lot of mess. And it's worse when it rains during the festival because, at the end, many people leave their wet and dirty things on the farm. In 2016, the wettest year in the festival's history, people left 11,000 kg of clothes and camping equipment including 2,200 chairs and 5,500 tents. It took two weeks to clean up the farm!

What are your experiences of Glastonbury? Have you got any tips?

Comments (64)

Marla: I volunteered at Glastonbury last year. You don't earn any money but when you aren't working, you can enjoy the festival. It was an awesome experience. I hung out a lot with the other volunteers and I made a lot of interesting new friends.

Simon: Don't believe the weather forecast. It almost always rains at Glastonbury. But it's still a brilliant festival. I buy a ticket every year. Just wear your wellies!

Michael: I never go! Stay at home and watch it on TV. Glastonbury's really crowded. The weather is usually awful and the food at all festivals is disgusting!

Reply

Cass: I'm sorry, but what a boring comment! And the food at festivals is often delicious. It isn't cheap, of course …

6B READING AND VOCABULARY

1 SPEAKING In pairs, discuss the questions.

1 What music or arts festivals do you know in your country or abroad?
2 Which one would you like to go to? Say why.

2 Read the article quickly and complete the notes.

Glastonbury – the facts

When it started:	1 *1970*
When it happens:	2 in ________, every year
Where it happens:	3 in ________, in the UK
How many people go now:	4 ________
The number of performers now:	5 ________
The price of the cheapest ticket:	6 ________

3 Read the article again and choose the correct answers.

1 How did Glastonbury change between 1970 and 1971?
 a It got a new name 'The Pyramid stage'.
 b The tickets became more expensive.
 c It became more popular.
2 What does Glastonbury now have in common with Glastonbury in 1970?
 a It is still in the same village.
 b It is still two days long.
 c It is still only rock and folk music.
3 What is different about the Glastonbury Festival today?
 a It is now free to people from Pilton.
 b You can now pay to borrow a tent on the farm.
 c It attracts talented and famous musicians.
4 How many tents did people leave at Glastonbury in 2016?
 a 2,200 **b** 5,500 **c** 11,000

4 Read the comments. Complete the sentences with the correct name.

1 *Marla* and ________ didn't buy a ticket last year.
2 ________ thinks the food is expensive.
3 ________ gives advice about clothes.

5 Study Active Reading. Then look at the underlined words and choose their correct meanings below.

1 *Showed up* means
 a arrived. **b** left.
2 *Headliner* means
 a main organiser. **b** biggest star.
3 When something *sells out* it means
 a it becomes cheaper for a short period of time.
 b you can't buy it because there aren't any left.
4 *Luxurious* means
 a expensive and beautiful **b** cheap but beautiful
5 *Earn* means
 a receive money. **b** pay money.
6 *Wellies* are shoes you wear in
 a good weather. **b** bad weather.

ACTIVE READING | Understanding new words

- Read the whole sentence with the new word.
- Decide if the word is a verb, noun or adjective.
- Read the sentences around the new word and use the context to understand its meaning.

6 Study the highlighted adjectives in the comments. Then find:

1 two opinion adjectives with opposite meanings to describe food.
 delicious, disgusting
2 an opinion adjective with the opposite meaning to 'interesting'.
3 two opinion adjectives that mean 'very good'.
4 an opinion adjective that means 'very bad'.

7 Complete the sentences with adjectives from Exercise 6. Sometimes more than one answer is possible.

1 This pasta is *delicious*. Can I have some more, please?
2 Bob can't come? Oh, no! That's ________ news.
3 I tried to read that book but I fell asleep. It was really ________.
4 There's too much salt in this. It's ________!
5 You won the competition! That's ________ news!

8 2.31 Listen to the report about volunteers at festivals. Are the sentences true or false?

1 ☐ Over 1,500 people volunteer to work at Glastonbury.
2 ☐ Volunteers usually start work on the first day of the festival.
3 ☐ Volunteers don't need experience of this kind of work.
4 ☐ Volunteers finish working when the festival ends.

9 REFLECT | Culture In pairs, discuss the questions.

1 Do you think volunteering at a festival is a good idea?
2 What kind of festival jobs can you think of? Which of them would you like to do?
3 What good things and bad things about volunteering at a festival can you think of?

18 WATCH AND REFLECT Go to page 155. **Watch the documentary *High school musical awards* and do the exercises.**

☐ **I can understand new words in a text and talk about music festivals.**

The Grinch

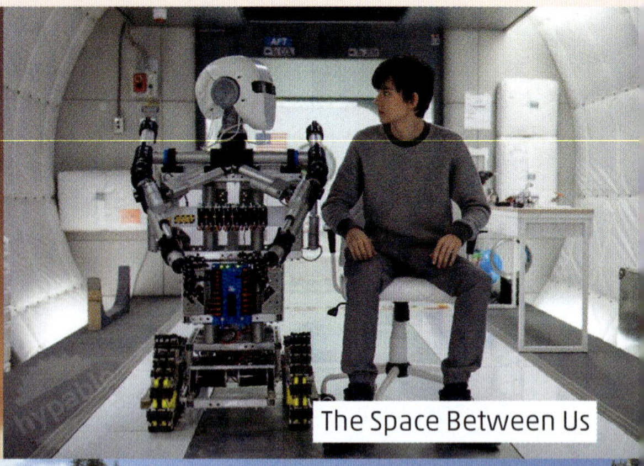
The Space Between Us

Titanic

How to Train Your Dragon

Classic MOVIE CHOICE!

Choose the types of film you are interested in.

1 SPEAKING What types of film can you see in the posters? What films do you like watching?

action animated film comedy documentary drama fantasy horror musical romance science fiction superhero western

I really like science fiction. Star Wars is my favourite film.

2 2.32 Listen to four people talking about films. What type of film did each person see?

3 2.33 Match definitions 1–8 with the words in the box. Then listen and check.

☐1 audience ☐ cast ☐ character ☐ ending ☐ plot ☐ scene ☐ soundtrack ☐ special effects

1 the people who watch a film
2 all the actors in a film
3 the story of a film
4 a person in a film
5 the music from a film
6 computer-generated images in a film
7 a short part of a film
8 the way that a story finishes

4 2.34 Check you understand the highlighted words. Read the review and choose the correct adjectives. Then listen and check.

This film cost $200 million so I expected another **1** big-budget / low-budget superhero film, with some good special effects but **2** an exciting / a predictable plot – superhero fights bad person, superhero wins! But actually there were lots of new ideas and the plot was really **3** disappointing / original and unusual. The main character is really **4** funny / scary – I laughed a lot. And the action scenes were, at times, quite **5** funny / scary. I couldn't watch the scene in the restaurant. I covered my face with my hands! The only **6** disappointing / original thing was the soundtrack. I hate heavy metal!

5 SPEAKING Complete the sentences with the names of films you know. Then, in pairs, discuss your answers.

The film with the ...
1 funniest character is ...
2 scariest character is ...
3 most disappointing ending is ...
4 most predictable plot is ...
5 most original plot is ...

6 SPEAKING Take turns to describe a film but don't say its title. Can your partner guess what it is?

☐ **I can talk about films.**

6D GRAMMAR

1 **SPEAKING In pairs, look at the photo and answer the questions.**

1. Who are your favourite film directors?
2. What films did they make?

2 **What are the most important qualities for a film director? Say why. Discuss in pairs.**

brave confident creative easy-going funny patient talented

3 **2.35 Listen to an interview with film director Frances Campbell. Which adjectives from Exercise 2 does she use to describe a good film director?**

4 **2.35 Complete the sentences with adjectives from Exercise 2. Listen again to check.**

1. That was a very *funny* comedy.
2. I'm sometimes not ________ enough. I want things to go right first time.
3. You also need to believe in yourself, to be ________ to ask actors to do a scene again and again.
4. Actors aren't always the most ________ people in the world – they can be very tense!
5. You have to be ________ enough to find a clever solution that isn't too complicated.
6. If you think you're ________ enough, then just start!
7. Do it right now! Be ________! Don't wait!

Too, (not) enough

5 **Read sentences 1–3 and match them with a–c to make rules. Study the Grammar box to check.**

In the past the equipment was too expensive.

I'm sometimes not patient enough.

Your mobile phone is good enough to make your first film.

1. We use *too* + adjective when
2. We use adjective + *enough* when
3. We use *not* + adjective + *enough* when

a. something is less than you need or want.
b. something is more than you need or want.
c. something is suitable for what you need or want.

Too, (not) enough	
too + adjective	The story was **too** complicated.
adjective + *enough*	He's creative **enough** to be an artist.
not + adjective + *enough*	The plot was **not** interesting **enough**.

We use:
- *enough* when there is the right amount of something
- *not enough* when there is less than we need or want
- *too* when there is more than we need or want.

Grammar Reference and Practice > page 167

6 **2.36 Complete the conversations. Use *too* and *enough* with pairs of adjectives from the box. Listen and check.**

interesting / long short / loud talented / worried

A Did you enjoy the concert?
B It was OK but they only played for forty minutes. It was [1]________. And the lead singer wasn't [2]________ – I couldn't hear her!

A Why aren't you in the school play?
B I'm not [3]________ and I'm [4]________ about performing in front of the whole school.

A What's that book like?
B The story's [5]________ but it's [6]________. It took me a month to read.

7 **Rewrite the sentences with *too* + adjective or (not) adjective + *enough*.**

1. We're too young to go to the concert.
2. The cinema screen isn't big enough.
3. These paintings are too traditional for me.
4. The plot wasn't original enough.
5. The film was too short.

8 **2.37 PRONUNCIATION Listen and then put the words from the box in the correct column.**

~~actor~~ art cast drama fantasy fastest largest made patient small

/a:/	/eɪ/	/ae/	/ɔ:/
dance	play	romance *actor*	awful

9 **2.38 PRONUNCIATION Listen and check your answers to Exercise 8. Then practise saying the words.**

10 **SPEAKING In pairs, talk about these things. Use *too*+adjective, (*not*) adjective + *enough* to give reasons.**

1. a film you don't like
2. a type of music you don't listen to
3. a book you didn't finish
4. a type of film you never watch

☐ **I can use '*too*' and '(*not*) *enough*' to talk about the quantity of something.**

6E LISTENING AND VOCABULARY

1 **Do the quiz in pairs. Check the answers on page 176.**

2 *3.1* **Listen to a conversation and decide who is speaking.**

- **a** a radio interviewer and a graffiti artist
- **b** two graffiti artists
- **c** a radio interviewer and an expert on street art

3 *3.1* **Read the questions. Then listen again and choose the correct answers.**

1. What does Thomas say about his first experience with graffiti?
   - **a** His dad was really pleased.
   - **b** He painted his name on his bedroom door.
   - **c** His dad's reaction surprised him.
2. How did Thomas feel about art classes at school?
   - **a** He only liked modern art.
   - **b** He enjoyed doing the homework.
   - **c** He liked the teacher.
3. Where did Thomas get his first tagging name from?
   - **a** It was his favourite type of music at that time.
   - **b** It's the place where he lives.
   - **c** It's a shorter version of his first name.
4. Why did Thomas start painting larger paintings?
   - **a** He got bored with small paintings.
   - **b** He wanted grey, empty walls to look nicer.
   - **c** People who lived or worked there asked him to do so.
5. How did Thomas's first customer find him?
   - **a** He contacted Thomas's parents.
   - **b** He saw Thomas's name in a local newspaper.
   - **c** He met Thomas in a bar.
6. Thomas thinks that many graffiti artists
   - **a** are lucky.
   - **b** were unsuccessful at school.
   - **c** were very different from him.

4 **Look at the examples of *get* from the audio script. Match each use of *get* to one of the meanings a–d.**

1. ☐ As soon as my dad **got home** I showed it to him.
2. ☐ I wore a hoody and I even **got a mask**.
3. ☐ I **got too confident**.
4. ☐ I **got a £1000 fine**.
5. ☐ Then I **got a call** from a local bar owner.
6. ☐ They **got bored** as teenagers.

a arrive **b** become **c** buy **d** receive

5 **Complete the sentences with the correct forms of *get* and the words and phrases from the box.**

~~a good grade~~ angry a ticket warm something to eat to school

1. I *got a good grade* in the exam.
2. I'm hungry. Where can I ________ near here?
3. Thomas's father ________ when he saw the graffiti on the door.
4. What time do usually you ________?
5. She waited until it ________ before she went for a walk.
6. Did you ________ me ________ for the concert? How much was it?

6 **REFLECT | Society** **Read the article. Then in groups discuss the questions.**

1. What types of graffiti are there in your town?
2. Do you like any of it?
3. When does graffiti become street art?

In big cities in the UK, there are special graffiti walls for artists to use. People who paint graffiti in other places can get fines or even go to prison But it's still a big problem. The cost of cleaning graffiti from British walls is now over £1 billion every year.

☐ **I can identify specific information in an interview and talk about graffiti.**

SPEAKING | Suggestions

Making suggestions
What/How about (playing) ...
Why don't we (go) ...
Let's (go) ...

Accepting suggestions
That's a good idea.
Yes, why not?
OK, let's do that.
Sounds good/great/amazing.

Refusing suggestions
No way! (informal)
I don't think that's a great idea.
I don't think so.
I'm not sure.

Suggesting an alternative
Why don't we ... instead?
Let's ... instead.

1 **In pairs, ask and answer the questions.**

1 Which of these things do you do when you're bored?
2 What other things do you do?

check my phone   do sport   go for a walk   go to an exhibition
listen to podcasts   phone a friend   play games   watch a film

When I'm bored I go for a walk or I phone a friend.

2 ▶ *19* 🔊 *3.2* **Watch or listen to the conversation. Which activities does Tanya suggest?**

3 **Study the Speaking box. Then read the dialogue and find the phrases Tanya and Steven use to make, accept and refuse suggestions.**

Tanya What's up?
Steven My phone's dead and I was in your street.
Tanya Come on, then.
Steven Let's do something.
Tanya Sure. I know. Why don't we go to that graffiti exhibition?
Steven That's a good idea. Where is it?
Tanya In the centre of town.
Steven No way! That's too far!
Tanya OK. What about going to the cinema? I want to see that fantasy ...
Steven I don't think so. I haven't got any money.
Tanya OK. Let's play football in the park instead.
Steven I don't think that's a great idea. I'm wearing my best trainers.
Tanya I haven't got any more ideas. How about watching that new series online?
Steven OK, let's do that. Is it OK if I charge my phone?
Tanya Sure.
Steven That's strange. Five messages from my parents. Oh, no. I forgot! It's my cousin's birthday today. There's a party at his house this afternoon. I need to go. Now!
Tanya What?
Steven Um ... do you want to do something tomorrow?
Tanya Sure. Call me later ... But check your diary first!

4 **Choose the correct phrase to compete the suggestions.**

1 *How about / Let's* calling Jack?
2 *Why don't we / How about* eat out tonight?
3 *What about / Let's* buy some tickets to a music festival.
4 *What about / Why don't we* going shopping today?
5 *Let's / Why don't* watch that new *X-men* film at the cinema.

5 **Complete the replies with the missing words.**

a Yes, *why* not? I need some new clothes.
b _________ way! I made a curry. It's delicious!
c _________ amazing! But we need permission first ...
d I don't think that's a great _________. He and I are not talking at the moment.
e I'm not _________. It looks the same as the last one.

6 🔊 *3.3* **Match questions 1–5 in Exercise 4 with replies a–e in Exercise 5. Listen and check.**

1 ___ **2** ___ **3** ___ **4** ___ **5** ___

7 **In pairs, practise the short conversations in Exercises 4 and 5.**

8 **In pairs, role play the situations. Student A go to page 175. Student B go to page 176.**

☐ **I can make and accept or refuse suggestions.**

6G WRITING | A film review

1 SPEAKING In pairs, discuss the questions.

1 Do you read film reviews? Do you read them before or after you watch films? Say why.
2 In your opinion, what's the best place to find good reviews?
3 What information do you expect to find in a film review?

2 Read Maria's review. Which pieces of information from question 3 in Exercise 1 does she mention?

3 Read the review again. Complete the table.

Title	[1]*La La Land*
Type of film	[2]_________
Location	[3]_________
Main actors	[4]_________
Director	[5]_________
Plot	A(n) [6]_________ meets a [7]_________ and they fall in love.
Maria's opinion	[8]_________ acting, singing and dancing

4 Study the Writing box. Find similar phrases in Maria's review.

WRITING | A film review

- Give general information about the film (title, type, year, actors, director, prizes)
  ... is a (science fiction film)
  It came out in ...
  The cast includes ...
  The director is ...
  The film won ...
- Describe characters and story
  The main characters are ...
  The plot is ...
  The film is set in ...
- Give your opinion
  The special effects were incredible.
  My favourite scene was in the traffic jam.
  The ending was surprising.
  It made me feel happy.
- Summarise
  Overall, I (don't) think ...
  I would/wouldn't recommend this film to ...

WATCH OUT!

We use present tenses to describe the plot of a film:
Mia and Sebastian both ***live*** *in Los Angeles. Mia* ***is trying*** *to find work as an actress.*

Maria's film reviews

La La Land is a musical, a romance and a drama. It came out in 2017 and the cast includes Emma Stone and Ryan Gosling. The film won seven Oscars, including Best Actress for Stone and Best Director for Damien Chazelle.
The film is set in Los Angeles and the plot is simple: Mia (Stone) is trying to find work as an actress. Sebastian (Gosling) wants to be a professional musician with his own jazz club. They meet and fall in love but is their friendship strong enough? Or are their ambitions stronger?
I usually prefer more exciting movies but this film surprised me. Stone and Gosling's acting, singing and dancing are awesome. Gosling even learned to play the piano for this role!
From the beginning of the film, when Mia and Sebastian meet in a traffic jam, to the surprising ending (my favourite scene), *La La Land* made me feel both happy, and sometimes, sad. I would recommend it to anyone.

5 3.4 Read part of a film review and choose the correct answers. Listen and check.

Brothers is a comedy film. It came [1]_________ over five years ago. The film is set [2]_________ an American high school and the main [3]_________ are two brothers with very different personalities. My favourite [4]_________ was in the Science lesson but I didn't laugh a lot in this film. And the [5]_________ is very predictable. [6]_________, I don't think it was very good and I wouldn't [7]_________ this film to anyone.

1 **a** in **b** out **c** up
2 **a** about **b** on **c** in
3 **a** characters **b** cast **c** plots
4 **a** ending **b** soundtrack **c** scene
5 **a** final **b** ending **c** finish
6 **a** Overall **b** Above **c** Around
7 **a** recommend **b** tell **c** talk

6 WRITING TASK Write a review of a film.

- Use the table in Exercise 3 to plan your review.
- Use the phrases in the Writing box.
- Use present tenses to describe the plot.
- Use opinion adjectives.

☐ I can write a film review.

6A GRAMMAR AND VOCABULARY 5.36

3D printing (n) /ˌθriː ˌdiː ˈprɪntɪŋ/

actor/actress (n) /ˈæktə/ˈæktrɪs/

art gallery (n) /ˈɑːt ˌɡæləri/

choreographer (n) /ˌkɒriˈɒɡrəfə/

composer (n) /kəmˈpəʊzə/

copy (n) /ˈkɒpi/

create (v) /kriˈeɪt/

creator (n) /kriˈeɪtə/

dance (n) /dɑːns/

dancer (n) /ˈdɑːnsə/

director (n) /dəˈrektə/

fast (adj) /fɑːst/

film (n) /fɪlm/

literature (n) /ˈlɪtərətʃə/

movie (n) /ˈmuːvi/

museum (n) /mjuːˈziəm/

music (n) /ˈmjuːzɪk/

musician (n) /mjuːˈzɪʃən/

painter (n) /ˈpeɪntə/

painting (n) /ˈpeɪntɪŋ/

photographer (n) /fəˈtɒɡrəfə/

photography (n) /fəˈtɒɡrəfi/

piece of music/literature /ˌpiːs əv ˈmjuːzɪk/ ˈlɪtərətʃə/

poet (n) /ˈpəʊɪt/

rap (v) /ræp/

record (n) /ˈrekɔːd/

record-breaking (adj) /ˈrekɔːd ˌbreɪkɪŋ/

sales (n) /seɪəlz/

scriptwriter (n) /ˈskrɪptˌraɪtə/

sculptor (n) /ˈskʌlptə/

sculpture (n) /ˈskʌlptʃə/

seat (n) /siːt/

stage (n) /steɪdʒ/

talented (adj) /ˈtæləntɪd/

theatre (n) /ˈθɪətə/

trailer (n) /ˈtreɪlə/

version (n) /ˈvɜːʃən/

visitor (n) /ˈvɪzɪtə/

world record (n) /ˌwɜːld ˈrekɔːd/

writer (n) /ˈraɪtə/

6B READING AND VOCABULARY 5.37

annual (adj) /ˈænjuəl/

attract (v) /əˈtrækt/

awesome (adj) /ˈɔːsəm/

awful (adj) /ˈɔːfəl/

boring (adj) /ˈbɔːrɪŋ/

brief (adj) /briːf/

brilliant (adj) /ˈbrɪljənt/

clean up /ˌkliːn ˈʌp/

delicious (adj) /dɪˈlɪʃəs/

disgusting (adj) /dɪsˈɡʌstɪŋ/

earn (v) /ɜːn/

guide to sth (n) /ˈɡaɪd tə ˌsʌmθɪŋ/

headliner (n) /ˈhedlaɪnə/

live show /ˌlaɪv ˈʃəʊ/

luxurious (adj) /lʌɡˈzjʊəriəs/

music/arts festival (n) /ˈmjuːzɪk/ˈɑːts ˌfestəvəl/

performer (n) /pəˈfɔːmə/

population (n) /ˌpɒpjəˈleɪʃən/

sell out /ˌsel ˈaʊt/

show up /ˌʃəʊ ˈʌp/

star (n) /stɑː/

talented (adj) /ˈtæləntɪd/

tent (n) /tent/

volunteer (n, v) /ˌvɒlənˈtɪə/

weather forecast (n) /ˈweðə ˌfɔːkɑːst/

wellies (n) /ˈweliz/

wet (adj) /wet/

6C VOCABULARY 5.38

action film (n) /ˈækʃən fɪlm/

animated film (n) /ˈænəmətɪd fɪlm/

audience (n) /ˈɔːdiəns/

big-/low-budget (adj) /ˌbɪɡ/ˌləʊ ˈbʌdʒɪt/

cast (n) /kɑːst /

character (n) /ˈkærɪktə(r)/

comedy (n) /ˈkɒmədi/

computer-generated images (adj) /kəmˌpjuːtə ˌdʒenəreɪtɪd ˈɪmɪdʒɪz/

disappointing (adj) /ˌdɪsəˈpɔɪntɪŋ/

documentary (n) /ˌdɒkjəˈmentəri/

drama (n) /ˈdrɑːmə/

ending (n) /ˈendɪŋ/

exciting (adj) /ɪkˈsaɪtɪŋ/

fantasy film (n) /ˈfæntəsi fɪlm/

funny (adj) /ˈfʌni/

horror film (n) /ˈhɒrə fɪlm/

main character (n) /ˌmeɪn ˈkærəktə/

musical (n) /ˈmjuːzɪkəl/

original (adj) /əˈrɪdʒɪnəl/

plot (n) /plɒt/

predictable (adj) /prɪˈdɪktəbəl/

romance (n) /ˈrəʊmæns/

scary (adj) /ˈskeəri/

scene (n) /siːn/

science fiction film (n) /ˌsaɪəns ˈfɪkʃən fɪlm/

soundtrack (n) /ˈsaʊndtræk/

special effects (n) /ˌspeʃəl ɪˈfekts/

superhero film (n) /ˈsuːpəˌhɪərəʊ fɪlm/

unusual (adj) /ʌnˈjuːʒuəl/

western (n) /ˈwestən/

6D GRAMMAR 5.39

camera (n) /ˈkæmərə/

direct (v) /dəˈrekt/

perform (v) /pəˈfɔːm/

school play (n) /ˌskuːl ˈpleɪ/

screen (n) /skriːn/

6E LISTENING AND VOCABULARY 5.40

be unsuccessful /bi ˌʌnsəkˈsesfəl/

get a call /ˌget ə ˈkɔːl/

get a fine /ˌget ə ˈfaɪn/

get a good grade /ˌget ə ˌɡʊd ˈɡreɪd/

get bored/angry /ˌget ˈbɔːd/ˈæŋɡri/

get dark /ˌget ˈdɑːk/

get home/to school /ˌget ˈhəʊm/tə ˈskuːl/

get worse /ˌget ˈwɜːs/

graffiti artist (n) /ɡræˈfiːti ˌɑːtɪst/

mask (n) /mɑːsk/

modern art (n) /ˌmɒdn ˈɑːt/

spray paint (n) /ˈspreɪ peɪnt/

street art (n) /ˈstriːt ɑːt/

tagging (n) /ˈtæɡɪŋ/

6F SPEAKING 5.41

check your diary /ˌtʃek jə ˈdaɪəri/

go to an exhibition /ˌɡəʊ tə ən ˌeksəˈbɪʃən/

watch a series /ˌwɒtʃ ə ˈsɪəriːz/

6G WRITING 5.42

acting (n) /ˈæktɪŋ/

be set in … /bi ˈset ɪn/

beginning (n) /bɪˈɡɪnɪŋ/

incredible (adj) /ɪnˈkredəbəl/

recommend (v) /ˌrekəˈmend/

win an Oscar /ˌwɪn ən ˈɒskə/

Remember More > page 174

VOCABULARY AND GRAMMAR

1 Read the definitions and write the words.

1 a film with singing and dancing in it *musical*
2 a person who writes the story of a film
3 a scary film
4 a person who writes classical music
5 a film based on drawings
6 the music in a film
7 a film about real people and events
8 moving to music, often with a partner

2 Complete the film review with the words from the box.

audience big-budget cast characters ~~director~~ drama plot scenes special effects

DUNKIRK

Critics love [1]*director* Christopher Nolan's latest film *Dunkirk* because it tells the story of real events in a new and interesting way. The [2]________ tells the story of how civilian ships came to Dunkirk to rescue British soldiers from France in World War II. But Dunkirk isn't just a war film, it's a [3]________. It tells the story of real people and the cost of war on their lives.
Despite the big names in the [4]________: Kenneth Branagh, Mark Rylance and even singer Harry Styles, this is not really a [5]________ film compared to $378.5 million for *Pirates of the Caribbean* (2011). What is even more surprising for a film of this genre, it doesn't rely on amazing [6]________ to tell the story.
The exciting opening [7]________ include perfect camera work and close-up. This makes the [8]________ feel that they are at the centre of the action. As a result, they believe in the events and really care about what happens to the [9]________ in the story.

3 Choose the correct words to complete the sentences.

1 George Orwell is the *literature* / *writer* of the book *Animal Farm*.
2 I want to see a *photographer* / *photography* exhibition at the National Portrait Gallery.
3 Which *actor* / *director* did you like the most in the play?
4 *The Kiss* by Rodin is one of the most famous *sculptors* / *sculptures* in the world.
5 My favourite *painter* / *musician* is Leonardo da Vinci. I love the 'Mona Lisa' at the Louvre Gallery.
6 The tickets for the concert *sold out* / *showed up* in 24 hours.
7 'What do you think of this burger?' 'It's *delicious* / *disgusting*! I'm going to order another one!'

4 Match sentences 1–4 with the uses of *get*.

☐ arrive ☐ become ☐ buy ☐ receive

1 Tom's got me a ticket to Glastonbury Festival.
2 Dad never gets angry with us – he's great!
3 I always get to school late in the morning.
4 I got good grades in all my subjects at school this year.

5 Complete the sentences with the comparative or superlative forms of the adjectives in brackets.

1 For me, *the worst* (bad) part of the book is when the main character dies. It's so sad!
2 Which tickets are ________ (expensive) in the UK: theatre tickets or cinema tickets?
3 Artist Damien Hirst's new exhibition is ________ (good) than his previous ones.
4 I prefer to see films at the cinema because there's a ___ (wide) screen.
5 ________ (scary) character in a film is definitely Damien in the Omen!
6 Is the Eiffel Tower ________ (big) building in Europe?

6 Complete the text with *as/not as ... as* and the adjectives in brackets.

Life of Pi: which was better, the book or the film?
Nobody imagined a film version of *Life of Pi* could ever be [1]*as successful as* (successful) the book, but it was! Of course, there are many differences between the two. For example, the main character, Pi, is [2]________ (young) the character in the book. And in the original novel Pi is [3]________ (happy) he is in the film version – well it is Hollywood after all! Strangely, in the book version of *Life of Pi* the tiger is [4]________ (wild) it is at the end of the film when Pi frees it on a deserted island.
Whichever you personally prefer, critics agree that the story-telling in the film is just [5]________ (good) in the book.

7 Write sentences using the prompts and *too + adjective* or *(not) + adjective + enough*.

1 You never laugh. You're *too serious* (serious).
2 I'm falling asleep. This film is ________ (interesting).
3 Turn the music down. It's ________ (loud).
4 I didn't really enjoy the book. The plot was ________ (predictable).
5 I don't think I'm ________ (talented) to become a professional singer.
6 This painting is not ________ (modern) for the Tate Modern art gallery. It's from 1540!

USE OF ENGLISH

8 Complete the text with the correct answers a–d.

> **STRATEGY | Multiple choice cloze**
>
> Remember that the word you choose must fit grammatically into the sentence and must also have the correct meaning.

The Red Shoes

The Red Shoes is one of the most popular ballet productions by international [1]__ Mathew Bourne, a former professional dancer. It's based on a fairy story by Hans Christian Andersen that describes a young girl's dream to be the world's [2]__ dancer. Bourne, however, treats the story in a(n) [3]__ way by showing us that life can be like art. Thanks to a(n) [4]__ artistic team, the scenes on stage are magical and dream-like. But don't expect a happy [5]__. In this version of the story – it gets very [6]__!

The ballet's music, played by the New Adventures Orchestra, is by the famous [7]__ Bernard Hermann. In the past he worked with director Alfred Hitchcock, famous for his action and mystery [8]__ .

What everyone is saying: 'It's Bourne's [9]__ ballet!' 'Red Shoes is too [10]__ to miss!'

1 **a** audience **b** cast **c** character **d** choreographer
2 **a** great **b** greater **c** greatest **d** too great
3 **a** awful **b** boring **c** delicious **d** original
4 **a** brilliant **b** disgusting **c** old **d** predictable
5 **a** end **b** ending **c** finish **d** finishing
6 **a** angry **b** exciting **c** funny **d** sad
7 **a** composer **b** dancer **c** soundtrack **d** writer
8 **a** films **b** literature **c** painting **d** photographs
9 **a** exciting **b** more exciting **c** most exciting **d** the most exciting
10 **a** bad **b** better **c** good **d** terrible

Use of English > page 172

LISTENING

9 🔊 *3.5* **You are going to hear a review of a film. Complete the sentences.**

1. The Martian is a *science fiction* film.
2. It's set in ________ when a team of astronauts visit the planet Mars.
3. The ________ of the film is Ridley Scott.
4. Joe thinks the film is boring because it's too ________.
5. Joe says the plot is ________.
6. He thinks that the Alien films are ________.

SPEAKING

10 Read the information below and look at the photos. Then, in pairs, do the speaking task.

You are free next weekend and you would like to go out and do something cultural with a friend. Talk to your friend and decide on the best place to go. Look at the pictures which show some ideas to help you.

WRITING

11 You see the following on a website.

> **Our readers' favourite films**
>
> Tell us about your favourite film. Say what type of film it is, who the actors are, who the director is and describe the plot. Tell us why you loved the film.

Write a post about your favourite film.

CREATING SUCCESSFUL SCHOOL PROJECTS

In this week's article, James Maddison, the head teacher of Hilltop Secondary School, gives us some useful tips on how to create a successful school project.

In my experience, the students that plan their projects carefully get the best results. It's a good idea to talk about the key stages of your project with the other people in your team. In my opinion, there are four key stages in a project:

A *Deciding on the project*

Imagine your teacher wants you to do a project on the UK. Clearly, your project can't provide information about every aspect of the UK. So, the first thing for your team to do is to choose which topic you want to focus on. Let's say that your team decides to focus on geography. You can then brainstorm ideas to help you decide which aspects of British geography you want to include, for example, the mountains and the rivers and the major towns and cities.

B *Planning your project*

It's important to plan your work on the project together. It's a good idea for each member of the team to have a different role. Perhaps the most creative person in your team can design the slides? You need to give each person a specific task and agree on a deadline for completing the research and producing the information (factfiles, maps, tables, graphs, video, etc.) for the presentation.

C *Researching the information*

You can talk together about the best ways of finding the information you need for your project. You can use the library and, of course, there's lots of information on the Internet. Perhaps the people in your team can suggest good websites to visit?

D *Presenting the project*

The final stage is to decide in detail what you want to include in the project and how to present this information to your class. Together, you can look at all the information from your research and choose the most important elements. It is a good idea to practise the presentation in your group before you present it to the class.

Working on a school project with your classmates teaches you a lot about teamwork. By following these suggestions you can create successful school projects and develop the teamworking skills everyone needs when they enter the world of work.

1 In pairs, discuss the questions.

1 How often do you do projects at school? Which projects are you working on at the moment?
2 Do you like working on a project on your own or with a team? Say why.

2 Read the article. Then in pairs say which stage A–D you find the most difficult. Say why.

3 Read the article again and complete the chart with words from the text.

A Deciding on the project
- Read the instructions.
- [1]_________ the topic.
- [2]_________ ideas.
- Agree the content of the project.

B Planning your project
- Decide each person's [3]_________ and tasks.
- Agree on a [4]_________.

C Researching the information
- Consult books and the [5]_________.

D Presenting the project
- Decide [6]_________ to present the information.
- [7]_________ your presentation before you present it to the class.

4 In pairs, read these sentences and decide which stage of a project (A–D) in Exercise 3 they belong to.

1 ☐ 'OK, so Jack's job is to create the slides and Sarah's job is to find some good photos of British castles.'
2 ☐ 'In this diagram you can see the organisation of the British parliament.'
3 ☐ 'Yesterday I found a fantastic website that gives a lot of information about the history of cricket.'
4 ☐ 'Space? Let's see, we could include the International Space Station or the Apollo missions to the Moon.'
5 ☐ 'Do we agree that all the information needs to be ready by next Monday?'
6 ☐ 'Why don't we make some posters and a map? We can put them on the walls of our classroom.'

5 What can go wrong when you work on a project in a team? What problems can you face? Discuss in pairs.

6 *3.6* **Listen to Anna and David as they tell Chloe about a presentation they did at school. Then answer the questions.**

1 What was the presentation about?
2 How many people were in the team?
3 Which team members did all the work?
4 What was the problem with Ben?
5 What was the problem with Abby?
6 What problem did they have during the presentation?
7 How did they solve the problem?

7 *3.6* **Read the advice for working in a team on school projects. Did Anna and David follow all the advice? What about Abby? Listen again to check.**

LIFE SKILLS | How to work in a team on school projects

1 Before you start, discuss the project with the other people in your team.
2 Each team member has different skills, so give each person in the team a different role.
3 Listen to other people's ideas and opinions.
4 Use brainstorming to help you to choose the best ideas.
5 Explain things to the other people in your team if they don't understand.

8 In groups of four, discuss your ideas for the project 'A brief guide to an English-speaking country'. Decide on a country, the topics and plan the work for your team. Use the tips from the list below.

1 Choose one of these countries for your project:
Australia Canada New Zealand the USA
2 Choose one of these topics:
culture films food geography sport
3 Brainstorm ideas to decide which aspects of the topic you want to include.
4 Agree what to include in the project.
5 Agree each person's role.
6 Agree a deadline for researching and preparing the information.

9 Do the task below.

LIFE SKILLS | Project

A brief guide to an English-speaking country:
- Prepare your part of the project – research the topic, use factfiles, tables, graphs, maps, etc.
- Create the final presentation with your team.
- Present your team's project to the class.
- Discuss with the class how well you worked as a team, describe any problems you had and say how you solved them.

07 Going to town

VOCABULARY City, transport, travel activities in the city

GRAMMAR *Going to*, Present Continuous for future arrangements, future time expressions **Use of English** > page 173

SPEAKING Asking for and giving directions

WRITING A short message

VIDEO Grammar ▷ Communication ▷ Documentary ▷

SUMMER in the CITY

Emma Do you realise there are only three days until the holidays?

Harry Yes, I can't wait. Are you going to go somewhere nice?

Emma No, I'm not going to go anywhere. I've got no money.

Harry So, what are you going to do this summer?

Emma I'm going to get a summer job in a shop or a café. What about you? Where are you guys going to spend the summer?

Harry We're not going to take any trips this year. Our American cousins are coming to stay with us for a month so we're going to do some sightseeing in London. I'm going to take them to all the usual tourist places but I'd like to do something more original. Any ideas?

Emma Do they like the theatre? I'm going to go to the open-air theatre in Regent's Park again this summer. It's great. You can have a picnic while you watch the show.

Harry Sounds like fun.

Emma And you could visit the British Museum. It's free and they're going to have some awesome exhibitions there.

Harry Great! But they're not going to want to spend all their time doing cultural things so ...

Emma I know! Take them to the lido in Tooting! It's a brilliant outdoor swimming pool! I'm going to go there this weekend with some friends. Why don't you come along?

Harry That's a great idea, except for one thing.

Emma What?

Harry I can't swim.

7A GRAMMAR AND VOCABULARY

1 **SPEAKING Work in pairs. Tell your partner what you usually do in the summer.**

I usually spend time with my friends and I sometimes go away with my family.

2 **3.7 Look at the photo of London and read and listen to the text. What are 'the usual tourist places' in London? Which three suggestions does Emma make?**

Going to

3 **Read the sentences and decide which explanation is correct: a or b. Check your answer in the Grammar box.**

What are you going to do this summer?

I'm not going to go anywhere.

I'm going to get a job in a shop or a café.

We use *going to* + verb to talk about:

a things we are doing now

b things we plan or intend to do in the future.

Going to

We use **going to** + **verb** to talk about future intentions and plans that can change.

+	I'**m going to** watch a film. We'**re going to** get a summer job.
–	He **isn't going to** visit Paris. She **isn't going to** do much sightseeing.
?	**Are** you **going to** have a picnic? Yes, we **are**./No, we **aren't**.
Wh-?	Where **is** he **going to** be this summer? What **are** they **going to** do?

Grammar Reference and Practice > page 167

4 **3.8 Complete the conversation with the correct forms of the words in brackets and *going to*. Then listen and check your answers.**

Emma So where [1]*are you going to take* (you/take) your cousins, Harry?

Harry I'm not sure, but one night [2]______ (we/watch) the open-air show in Regent's Park.

Emma Great! [3]______ (I book) tickets next week. Do you want me to get yours too?

Harry No, don't worry. [4]______ (I/not get) the tickets yet. I want to discuss it with my cousins first. [5]______ (They/do) a lot of sightseeing, so [6]______ (there/not be) time for everything.

Emma OK. [7]______ (My brother/have) a barbecue sometime in the summer. He's got an outdoor pool in his garden. Why don't you all come?

Harry Thanks, Emma! That's a great idea!

5 **Complete the sentences with the correct forms of *going to* and one of the verbs from the box.**

buy ~~do~~ eat not spend not study stay travel

1 'What *are you going to do* this weekend?' 'I'm not sure. I've got no plans.'

2 Anna ______ the weekend at the seaside because she wants to stay at home.

3 My parents ______ a new car this summer and we ______ around Europe.

4 'What ______ tonight?' 'We can have a takeaway if you like.'

5 Jim ______ at university because he wants to get a job straight after school.

6 I ______ in tonight. I'm too tired to go out.

6 **Find the verbs in the conversation in Exercise 2 that go with these nouns.**

1 *go* to an open-air theatre/a lido/a party/the cinema/the beach/the park

2 ______ a museum/a city/family or friends

3 ______ (some) sightseeing

4 ______ a trip

5 ______ a match/a show/a band

6 ______ a meal/a picnic/a coffee/a barbecue/a party

7 ______ a summer job

7 **Write five sentences with *going to* about your plans this weekend. Use the phrases from Exercise 6.**

I'm going to watch a band with my friends on Saturday.

8 **SPEAKING In pairs, talk about your plans from Exercise 7. Try to think of follow-up questions.**

A *I'm going to watch a band with my friends on Saturday.*

B *Who are you going to see?*

A *A band called Murmurs.*

B *I know them! They're going to play at that festival in June.*

20 Read the question and watch the video. Say what the speakers answer. Then, in pairs, ask and answer the question.

What are you going to do this summer?

☐ **I can use *going to* to talk about future intentions and plans.**

A

B

C

D

E

F

MANCHESTER

GETTING HERE

You can get here by:

- **train**
  Arrive at one of the three main train stations: Piccadilly, Oxford Road or Victoria and use a free bus service between them.
- **coach/bus**
  Arrive at Chorlton Street coach station in the city centre.
- **car**
  Drive your car from the M60 motorway straight into Manchester and park in one of the city's car parks.
- **plane**
  Arrive by plane at Manchester Airport and take the bus, the train or a taxi into town.

GETTING AROUND

You can:

- go on foot to most places in the city centre (it only takes about twenty minutes to walk across it).
- ride a bike, moped or motorbike (parking is free).
- go by bus or tram – buy a ticket or a travel card before or when you get on and inform the driver when you want to get off.
- take a trip along the canal by boat or take a water taxi.

1 **SPEAKING** In pairs, look at the words in the box. Which place do you go to most often? Which places do you never go to?

art gallery bank bridge castle church cinema concert hall hospital hotel library market museum park post office sports centre square station supermarket theatre tourist information centre town hall

I often go to the cinema but I never go to the theatre.

2 3.9 Look at the photos and listen. Tick the places in the photos people describe in Manchester. There are two extra places.

1 ☐ 2 ☐ 3 ☐ 4 ☐

3 **SPEAKING** Work in pairs. Tell your partner about your own favourite place in the city. Where do you go with your friends? Where do you go with your family?

4 Read the text about transport in Manchester and complete the table with the verbs from the box.

~~drive~~ get go by ride take go

1*drive* a/your	car
2 ________ on/off a/the	bus/metro/tram/train
3 ________ a/your	bike/moped/motorbike
4 ________	on foot
5 ________	train/coach/bus/plane/ metro/taxi/car
6 ________ a/the	taxi/water taxi/bus/boat/ train/metro

☐ I can talk about places and transport in cities.

5 **Choose the correct words to complete the text message.**

Hi Joe,
Why don't you [1]*drive / take* a bus from Manchester and get [2]*off / on* at Salford Quays? From there you can take a [3]*boat / tram* along the canal and have lunch on board. Then you can go back to Manchester [4]*by / on* coach in time to visit the Imperial War [5]*Church / Museum* and see the 'Life, Art, War' exhibition you're interested in. When I finish college for the day I can come and meet you for dinner at one of the [6]*restaurants / banks* on the Quays. And if you're not too tired, we could watch a show at The Lowry [7]*Station / Theatre* after.
Let me know what you think.
Gemma xxx

6 **3.10 PRONUNCIATION Look at the underlined vowels in the words below and put them in the correct place in the table. Listen and check.**

bike bridge buy drive finish library lido Piccadilly picnic ride river, sightseeing trip visit

/aɪ/	arrive, by, ____, ____, ____, ____, ____, ____, ____
/ɪ/	city, in, ____, ____, ____, ____, ____, ____, ____

7 **SPEAKING In pairs, use the prompts in the box to ask and answer the questions.**

1 Which means of transport do you use to ...?
2 When do you use it?

get to or from school go on holiday
go clothes/food shopping
visit family/friends

I take a bus to the town centre to go clothes shopping, or I sometimes go to London by train.

7C LISTENING

1 **SPEAKING Discuss in pairs. Where do you usually hear announcements? Do you listen to them? Say why.**

2 **3.11 Listen to announcements 1–5. Match them with the places in the box. There is one extra place.**

☐ a coach ☐ a museum ☐ a supermarket ☐ a theatre
☐ a train station ☐ an underground station

3 **3.11 Listen again and choose the correct answers.**

1 What is the problem?
 a Someone can't get their car out of the car park.
 b There's a car in front of the exit to the car park.
 c Two drivers are arguing in the car park.
2 When is someone making this announcement?
 a before the play
 b in the break, between parts of the play
 c after the play
3 Who is the announcement for?
 a passengers with young families **b** station staff **c** all passengers
4 What is the main purpose of the announcement?
 a To thank people for coming to the exhibition.
 b To encourage people to buy something in the shop.
 c To ask people to leave the museum immediately.
5 What is the purpose of the announcement?
 a To give a warning. **b** To give information. **c** To give advice.

4 **3.12 Study Active Listening. Then listen to part of each announcement. Is the missing word a verb or a noun?**

1 *verb* **2** ____ **3** ____ **4** ____ **5** ____

ACTIVE LISTENING | Understanding new words

- Decide what type of word it is, e.g. a noun or a verb.
- Try to write the word. Is it similar to a word in your language?

5 **3.13 Read the sentences and guess the missing word. Then listen and check.**

1 Your car is *blocking* a blue Ford Focus in the shop's car park. Please move it immediately.
2 This evening's performance of *Macbeth* is three hours long, including a 20-minute ______.
3 If you don't feel well, please do not ______ an underground train. Contact a member of station staff for help.
4 Before you leave, please visit our shop. We have a large ______ of books and gifts.
5 Please take all your ______ with you when you leave the coach.

6 **Match the missing words in Exercise 5 with their meanings.**

a ☐ a short break between two parts of a play
b ☐ get on
c ☐ stopping something from moving
d ☐ a group of things you can choose from
e ☐ things you own or are carrying

7 **In pairs, write three public announcements. Make the announcements to your class and guess where you could hear your classmates' announcements.**

☐ **I can understand new words in announcements.**

Lisa Welcome to Manhattan, I'm Lisa, your tour guide. Before we get to the hotel, let me explain what's happening this weekend.

Janet Are we meeting this evening?

Lisa Yes, we're meeting at the hotel reception at eight. Then we're having dinner at Gallagher's, a traditional steak house.

Janet What are we doing tomorrow?

Lisa There are two trips tomorrow. My colleague, Rick, is taking you on an art tour along Museum Mile in the morning, then you're having a picnic lunch in Central Park!

Janet That sounds amazing! What are we doing in the afternoon?

Lisa We're taking a trip to Grand Central Terminal and Times Square. We're going up to the top of the Empire State Building and then we're going around the shops.

Janet Shopping! Fantastic! I'm definitely coming!

Simon Huh! I'm not going to any shops when I'm on holiday in New York!

7D GRAMMAR

1 SPEAKING **Would you like to visit New York City? What would you like to see there? Discuss in pairs.**

2 3.14 **Listen and read the conversation. What places are the tourists going to see?**

Present Continuous: future arrangements

3 **Read the sentences and choose the correct answer. Then study the Grammar box and find more examples of the Present Continuous in the conversation in Exercise 2.**

We're having dinner at Gallagher's.

Rick is taking you on an art tour in the morning.

We use the Present Continuous for future plans and arrangements that we *are* / *aren't* sure about.

Present Continuous: future arrangements

We use the **Present Continuous** to talk about future arrangements.

I'**m flying** to New York on Saturday.

Time expressions: in the morning, next Saturday, this weekend, tomorrow afternoon, tonight.

Grammar Reference and Practice > page 167

WATCH OUT!

I'm going to see *a Warhol exhibition at the Royal Academy.* (That's my intention.)

I'm seeing *a Warhol exhibition at the Royal Academy.* (That's my plan and I've got the tickets.)

4 3.15 **Complete the conversation with the correct Present Continuous forms of the words in brackets. Then listen and check.**

Simon What time [1]*are you leaving* (you/leave) the hotel tomorrow afternoon?

Janet [2]_________ (we/meet) in the hotel reception at about two-thirty. Why?

Simon I can't come. [3]_________ (I/see) Josh in the afternoon.

Janet [4]_________ (Josh /not join) us in Greenwich Village in the evening?

Simon Yes, he is, but [5]_________ (he/take) me in the aerial tram to Roosevelt Island before that.

Janet Really? Well, [6]_________ (you/not go) without me!

Simon [7]_________ (you/come) with us then?

Janet Yes [8]_________ (I/be)!

5 **Look at Janet's diary and write sentences for each day.**

JUNE

Mon	10 p.m. fly home from New York
Tue	7.30 p.m. pizza with Simon
Wed	2 p.m. tennis
Thur	8 p.m. cinema
Fri	shopping with Mum in morning
Sat	Dan's party 8 p.m.
Sun	morning – help Dad in garden

Janet's flying home from New York at 10 p.m. on Monday.

6 SPEAKING **Work in pairs. Write your real or imaginary diary for next week and then arrange a time to meet.**

A *What are you doing on Tuesday evening? Are you free?*

B *No, I'm not. I'm playing football after school on Tuesday. What about Wednesday afternoon?*

A *I'm busy on Wednesday. I'm going to the hairdresser's.*

☐ **I can use the Present Continuous to talk about future plans and arrangements.**

7E SPEAKING

1 Read the conversation and complete the sentence.

Maisy and Scott are meeting at a _________ near _________ underground station at _________.

Maisy Hi, Scott. What time do you want to meet?
Scott Is 12.30 OK? Do you know where the café is?
Maisy 1 p.m. is better. I don't even know the name of the café!
Scott 1 p.m. is fine. It's a new place called Tin Café. It's really near Blackwall underground station.
Maisy OK. I can use my phone. See you there!

2 21 3.16 Watch or listen to the conversation. Where does the woman give Maisy directions to?

a Blackwall underground station only
b Blackwall underground station and Tin Café
c Blackwall and Kingsway underground stations

3 21 3.16 Study the Speaking box. On the map find the bus stop where Maisy asks for directions. Then watch or listen to the conversation again and identify which places (A–E) are Kingsway and Blackwall stations.

SPEAKING | Asking for and giving directions

Asking for directions

Excuse me … /Sorry …
Where's (Blackwall station)?
How do I get to (Blackwall station)?
Can you tell me the way to (the station)?
Where's the nearest (post office)?
Is there (a visitor information centre) near here?

Giving directions

Go/Walk to the end of (Queen Street).
Go/Walk straight on.
Take the first/second road on the left/right.
Go/Walk along (Green Street).
Turn left/right at the (traffic lights).
Go/Walk past (the library).
It's on the left/right.
It's opposite/next to (a supermarket).

4 3.17 Complete the conversations with one word in each gap. Then listen and check.

A Excuse me. Is [1]*there* a good café near here?
B Yes. Go to the [2]_________ of Broad Street. There's a good café on the right. It's [3]_________ to a clothes shop.

A Excuse me. How do I [4]_________ to the castle?
B Go [5]_________ on. [6]_________ left at the sports centre. Then [7]_________ the first road on the right.

A Sorry. Where's [8]_________ nearest park?
B Walk [9]_________ Roman Road. Go [10]_________ the shopping centre and the park is [11]_________ the left.

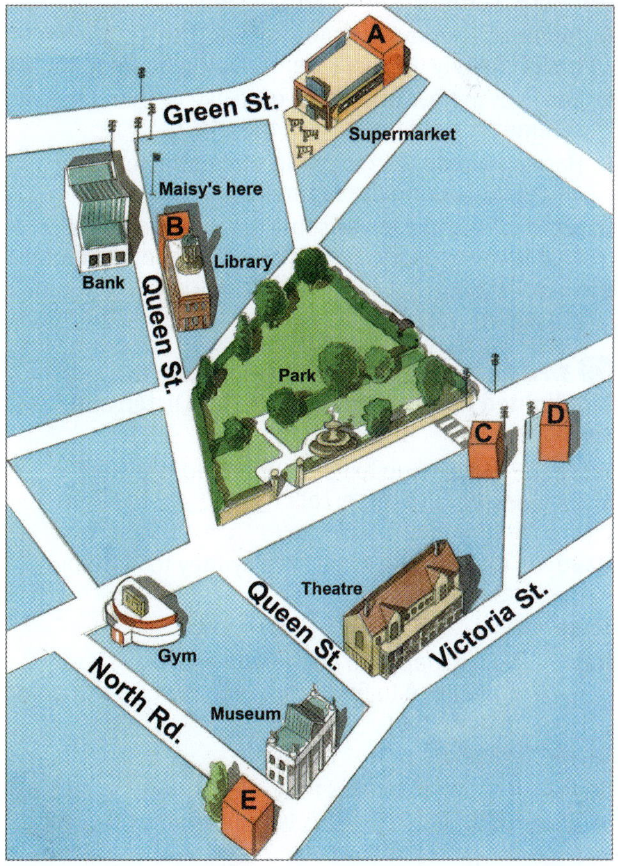

5 3.18 Listen to three conversations. Match places 1–3 with the letters A–E on the map.

1 ☐ post office
2 ☐ visitor information centre
3 ☐ market

6 In pairs, take turns to give directions. Use the map to ask for and give directions:

1 from the museum to the supermarket.
2 from Kingsway underground station to the park.
3 from the supermarket to the gym.

☐ **I can ask for and give directions.**

7F READING AND VOCABULARY

1 **Read the advert and answer the questions.**

1 Who is the advert for?
2 What's the name of the website?
3 What services does it provide?
4 How much does it cost?

2 **Read the travel plans and decide which person you would like to join on their trip. Say why.**

3 **Read the text again and answer the questions.**

1 When is Mark going to San Francisco?
2 Where is Mark going to visit by boat?
3 How is George going to travel?
4 Which cities is he planning to visit?
5 Who is Elena going to stay with in Oxford?
6 How does she plan to get around Oxford?
7 How is Tessa going to save money?
8 What does she want to do in Queensland?

4 **Read the text and match holiday plans 1–4 with travel friends A–E. There is one extra person.**

A Jonathan is studying in Australia and he's planning to travel cheaply for a year before going home to the UK.
B Zoe lives in New York and would like to spend the summer in a different city in the USA.
C Hannah would love to spend some time learning a new skill during the summer.
D Steve would like to see some great artwork and architecture before starting art college in September.
E Yolanda wants to improve her English and see some old architecture.

5 *3.20* **Complete the conversation with the highlighted words from the text. Then listen and check.**

Tessa I'd love to go to Perth. We could [1]*stay* with my friend Lucy there. Let's [2]_________ the train timetables.
Dave I'm not going to go from Sydney to Perth by train!
Tessa OK. I can [3]_________ on my own.
Dave No. I'm happy to go to Perth especially if we don't need to find [4]_________. But I'm not going to buy a train [5]_________.
Tessa Why not?
Dave It's too far. It takes forty-eight hours by train. It's better to [6]_________ a flight. It only takes six hours by plane.
Tessa Cool! Lucy's great. We stayed with the same [7]_________ family in France last year.
Dave What do you want to do this morning? We could take a sightseeing [8]_________ if you like.
Tessa No. Let's [9]_________ bikes! That way we can visit Sydney and get fit at the same time!
Dave Good idea!

***Are you planning a trip** but are nervous about travelling alone?*
***Are you looking for friends** to share a fantastic travel experience with?*
Then 'Let's go!' is the website for you.

We match people, places and interests to help you find the perfect travel friend.
All you need to do is create an online profile and write a brief summary of your travel plans.
The service is absolutely free!

6 **SPEAKING** **In pairs, plan a city trip with places you would like to visit. Then ask and answer questions about your plans with another pair.**

A *Where are you planning to go?*
B *We're planning to visit London.*
A *When are you leaving?*
B *We're leaving in July.*
A *What are you going to do in London?*
B *We're going to …*

7 **REFLECT | Society** **Look at the website and different travel ideas. In pairs, discuss the questions.**

1 1 Do young people in your country usually travel on their own, with friends or family?
2 What do you think are the most interesting places to visit in your country?
3 What's the best way to get around your country?

22 WATCH AND REFLECT **Go to page 156. Watch the documentary *Sydney – the perfect city?* and do the exercises.**

☐ **I can identify specific information in online forum posts and talk about travelling.**

Find a travel friend

Let's go!

3.19

1 San Franciscan Summer

I'm spending July in San Francisco this year! I can't wait! I'm really looking forward to seeing the Golden Gate Bridge although the bridge isn't actually gold, it's red. San Francisco is famous for its historic buildings like the Mission Dolores church and the cable cars that go up and down the beautiful steep streets. You can't visit the city without taking a boat trip to the Island of Alcatraz with its famous old prison. It was impossible to escape from.
Get in touch if you're a history fanatic like me!

Mark

2 A Grand Tour of Europe

In the past rich young British and American people travelled to Europe to admire the works of art and architecture. And guess what? That's what I'm doing this summer! I'm leaving in July, but I need to check the train timetables and buy my Interrail ticket. I'm going to visit Paris, Venice, Florence, Rome and Vienna. I'm going to find cheap accommodation in hostels and I want to book tours for the museums and art galleries before I get there. If you want to come, please contact me ASAP.

George

3 English in Oxford

I'm doing an English course at a school in Oxford for a month next August and I'm staying with a host family. I'm a bit nervous about going on my own, so I'm looking for another Spanish speaker (16–18) to hang out with. I'm going to do some sightseeing – Oxford was the first university city in the UK so there are lots of important cultural sites to visit. And as everyone cycles in Oxford, I'm going to hire a bike to get around. If you are interested, let me know.

Elena

4 An Australian blog

I'm going to travel around Australia for a year and blog about it. To keep costs low. I'm going to book cheap flights and stay with friends in different cities and eat street food. I'm going to start in Sydney and take a tour of the Sydney Opera House – it's an amazing building. It has lots of events every year (ballets, concerts, operas), so I'm going to watch at least one show. I'm also going to visit Queensland because I really want to snorkel in the Great Barrier Reef. Did you know it's the largest living thing on Earth and you can see it from space? Would you like to join me or even be my guide in the cities I visit?

Tessa

7G WRITING | A short message

1 **SPEAKING In pairs, discuss the question. What type of messages do you usually read or write? Use the prompts below to help you.**

computer chat email letter social media message (post-it) note text message

I don't often write emails or letters, but I write text messages and social media messages to my friends and family.

2 **Read messages 1–2. Who are they to and from? What are the messages about? Are they formal or informal?**

1

Kev,
Going to be late tonight – going to parents' evening. Dinner in oven – just need to heat it up for ten minutes.
Don't forget to take dog for walk and do your homework.
See you later,
Mum

2

Laura,
Really sorry. On the bus but going to be late - heavy traffic. Don't wait at home.
Meet me outside cinema at 7.30.
Please buy tickets and popcorn.
Thanks!;)
Phil

3 **Read messages 1–2 again and choose the correct answers a–c.**

Message 1:

a The woman is going to meet her son at the parents' evening.
b The woman can't go to the parents' evening because she is working late.
c The woman is going to be late home because she is going to the parents' evening.

Message 2:

a Phil isn't going to get to the cinema on time.
b Phil and Laura aren't travelling to the cinema together.
c Phil is going to meet Laura at the cinema after he buys the tickets.

4 **Compare the message below and message 1 in Exercise 2. Which kinds of words are missing in the message in Exercise 2? Study the Writing box and check your answers.**

Kev,

I'm going to be late home tonight because I'm going to the parents' evening. There's some dinner in the oven – you just need to heat it up for ten minutes.

Don't forget to take the dog for a walk and do your homework.

See you later,

Mum

WRITING | A short message

In an informal message, you can leave some words out:
the verb to be: am, is, are
determiners: some
subject pronouns: I, you, he, she, it, we, they
there is/there are
articles: the, a, an
conjunctions: because , ...
prepositions: for, in, on, at, ...

5 **Read the message and remove some words to make it shorter.**

Hi Mum,
Thanks a lot for dinner. I loved your lasagne! I took the dog to the park. I'm sorry that I'm not home. I'm at Keira's. We've got some History homework to do. I'm going to get the 10 o'clock bus home.
Love,
Kev

6 **SPEAKING In pairs, take turns to role play this situation: phone your friend and arrange to go shopping together on Saturday afternoon. Agree a time and a place to meet.**

7 **WRITING TASK After your phone call you remember you agreed to help your mum/dad on Saturday afternoon. Write a message to your friend. Then shorten your message – leave out all the words that you can. In your message:**

- apologise for a change in your plans
- explain the reason for the change
- suggest a new plan

☐ **I can write a short message.**

7A GRAMMAR AND VOCABULARY 5.43

at the seaside /ˌæt ðə ˈsiːsaɪd/

book a ticket /ˌbʊk ə ˈtɪkɪt/

do (some) sightseeing /ˌduː (səm) ˈsaɪtˌsiːɪŋ/

get a summer job /ˌget ə ˌsʌmə ˈdʒɒb/

go away (v) /ˌgəʊ əˈweɪ/

go to an open-air theatre/a lido/a party/the cinema/the beach/the park /ˌgəʊ tə ən ˌəʊpən ˌeə ˈθɪətə/ə ˈliːdəʊ/ə ˈpɑːti/ðə ˈsɪnəmə/ðə ˈbiːtʃ/ðə ˈpɑːk/

have a picnic/a barbecue/a party /ˌhæv ə ˈpɪknɪk/ə ˈbɑːbɪkjuː/ə ˈpɑːti/

have a takeaway /ˌhæv ə ˈteɪkəweɪ/

have coffee/a meal /ˌhæv ˈkɒfi/ə ˈmiːl/

have plans /ˌhæv ˈplænz/

look out for sb /ˌlʊk ˈaʊt fə ˌsʌmbɒdi /

stay with sb (v) /ˈsteɪ wɪð ˌsʌmbɒdi /

take a trip /ˌteɪk ə ˈtrɪp/

travel around Europe /ˌtrævəl əˌraʊnd ˈjʊərəp/

visit a museum/a city /ˌvɪzɪt ə mjuːˈziəm/ə ˈsɪti/

visit family/friends /ˌvɪzɪt ˈfæməli/ˈfrendz/

watch a match/a show/a band /ˌwɒtʃ ə ˈmætʃ/ə ˈʃəʊ/ə ˈbænd/

7B VOCABULARY 5.44

airport (n) /ˈeəpɔːt/

art gallery (n) /ˈɑːt ˌgæləri/

bank (n) /bæŋk/

bridge (n) /brɪdʒ/

bus service (n) /ˈbʌs ˌsɜːvɪs/

canal (n) /kəˈnæl/

car park (n) /ˈkɑː pɑːk/

castle (n) /ˈkɑːsəl/

church (n) /tʃɜːtʃ/

cinema (n) /ˈsɪnəmə/

concert hall (n) /ˈkɒnsət hɔːl/

drive (your car) /ˌdraɪv (jə ˈkɑː)/

driver (n) /ˈdraɪvə/

get on/off the bus /ˌget ˌɒn/ˌɒf ðə ˈbʌs/

go back (to Manchester) /ˌgəʊ ˌbæk (tə ˈmæntʃəstə)/

go by boat /by plane /ˌgəʊ baɪ ˈbəʊt/baɪˈpleɪn/

go by train/coach/bus/tram /ˌgəʊ baɪ ˈtreɪn/ˈkəʊtʃ/ˈbʌs/ˈtræm/

go on foot /ˌgəʊ ɒn ˈfʊt/

hospital (n) /ˈhɒspɪtl/

hotel (n) /həʊˈtel/

library (n) /ˈlaɪbrəri/

market (n) /ˈmɑːkɪt/

motorway (n) /ˈməʊtəweɪ/

museum (n) /mjuːˈziəm/

on board /ˌɒn ˈbɔːd/

park (n) /pɑːk/

park (v) /pɑːk/

post office (n) /ˈpəʊst ˌɒfɪs/

quay (n) /kiː/

restaurant (n) /ˈrestərɒnt/

ride a bike/a moped/a motorbike /ˌraɪd ə ˈbaɪk/ə ˈməʊped/ə ˈməʊtəbaɪk/

see an exhibition /ˌsiː ən ˌeksəˈbɪʃən/

shopping centre (n) /ˈʃɒpɪŋ ˌsentə/

sports centre (n) /ˈspɔːts ˌsentə/

square (n) /skweə/

station (n) /ˈsteɪʃən/

supermarket (n) /ˈsuːpəˌmɑːkɪt/

take a taxi/a bus/a tram /ˌteɪk ə ˈtæksi/ə ˈbʌs/ə ˈtræm/

take a water taxi/a boat /ˌteɪk ə ˈwɔːtə ˌtæksi/ə ˈbəʊt/

theatre (n) /ˈθɪətə/

tourist information centre (n) /ˌtʊərɪst ˌɪnfəˈmeɪʃən ˌsentə/

town hall (n) /ˌtaʊn ˈhɔːl/

train/bus station (n) /ˈtreɪn/ˈbʌs ˌsteɪʃən/

travelcard (n) /ˈtrævəlkɑːd/

walk (v) /wɔːk/

7C LISTENING 5.45

attention (n) /əˈtenʃən/

belongings (n) /bɪˈlɒŋɪŋz/

block (v) /blɒk/

board a train /ˌbɔːd ə ˈtreɪn/

exit (n) /ˈegzɪt/

gift (n) /gɪft/

give sb a warning /ˌgɪv ˌsʌmbɒdi ə ˈwɔːnɪŋ/

interval (n) /ˈɪntəvəl/

make an announcement /ˌmeɪk ən əˈnaʊnsmənt/

member of staff /ˌmembər əv ˈstɑːf/

passenger (n) /ˈpæsɪndʒə/

performance (n) /pəˈfɔːməns/

play (n) /pleɪ/

selection (of books) /səˌlekʃən (əv ˈbʊks)/

station staff (n) /ˈsteɪʃ(ə)n stɑːf/

ticket office (n) /ˈtɪkɪt ˌɒfɪs/

underground station (n) /ˈʌndəˌgraʊnd ˌsteɪʃən/

underground train (n) /ˌʌndəgraʊnd ˈtreɪn/

7D GRAMMAR 5.46

aerial tram (n) /ˌeəriəl ˈtræm/

art tour (n) /ˈɑːt tʊə/

fly (v) /flaɪ/

hotel reception (n) /həʊˌtel rɪˈsepʃən/

island (n) /ˈaɪlənd/

tour guide (n) /ˈtʊə gaɪd/

tourist sight (n) /ˈtʊərɪst saɪt/

7E SPEAKING 5.47

ask for/give directions /ˌɑːsk fə/ˌgɪv daɪəˈrekʃənz/

road (n) /rəʊd/

tell sb the way /ˌtel ˌsʌmbɒdi ðə ˈweɪ/

7F READING AND VOCABULARY 5.48

admire (v) /ədˈmaɪə/

architecture (n) /ˈɑːkɪtektʃə/

book a place (on a flight) /ˌbʊk ə ˌpleɪs (ɒn ə ˈflaɪt)/

buy a ticket /ˌbaɪ ə ˈtɪkɪt/

check the train timetable /ˌtʃek ðə ˈtreɪn ˌtaɪmˌteɪbəl/

create a profile /kriˌeɪt ə ˈprəʊfaɪl/

cultural site (n) /ˌkʌltʃərəl ˈsaɪt/

find accommodation /ˌfaɪnd əˌkɒməˈdeɪʃən/

go on your own / gəʊ ˌɒn jər ˈəʊn/

hire a bike /ˌhaɪər ə ˈbaɪk/

hostel (n) /ˈhɒstl/

keep costs low /ˌkiːp ˌkɒsts ˈləʊ/

on Earth /ˌɒn ˈɜːθ/

opera house (n) /ˈɒpərə haʊs/

prison (n) /ˈprɪzən/

rich (adj) /rɪtʃ/

snorkel (v) /ˈsnɔːkəl/

space (n) /speɪs/

stay with a host family /ˌsteɪ wɪð ə ˌhəʊst ˈfæməli/

take a tour of the city /ˌteɪk ə ˌtʊər əv ðə ˈsɪti/

travel cheaply /ˌtrævəl ˈtʃiːpli/

work of art /ˌwɜːk əv ˈɑːt/

7G WRITING 5.49

letter (n) /ˈletə/

on time /ˌɒn ˈtaɪm/

parents' evening (n) /ˈpeərənts ˌiːvnɪŋ/

social media message (n) /ˌsəʊʃəl ˈmiːdiə ˌmesɪdʒ/

text message (n) /ˈtekst ˌmesɪdʒ/

Remember More > page 174

VOCABULARY AND GRAMMAR

1 Look at the pictures and write the words.

1  *museum*

2  ________

3  ________

4  ________

5  ________

6  ________

7  ________

8  ________

2 Complete the sentences with one word in each gap.

1 We always *take* a taxi to the airport – it's expensive but it's more convenient.
2 I usually ________ a bike to school – It's cheap and good for the environment!
3 Lots of people ________ a car to work every day and end up in traffic jams.
4 In small cities it's usually quick and easy to go to places on ________.
5 Sometimes the bus driver doesn't let you ________ on the bus if it's really full.
6 I'm so excited! I'm going to Paris by ________ next weekend and I love flying!

3 Match each person's situation with the best suggestion(s) about what to do.

[1] get a summer job ☐ do some sightseeing
☐ go to the beach ☐ have a sandwich
☐ visit a museum ☐ visit friends

1 I haven't got any money to go on holiday.
2 I want to get to know this city.
3 I'm hungry.
4 I don't want to stay home alone!
5 I want to do something cultural this summer.
6 I just want to have fun!

4 Choose the correct words to complete the text.

ARE YOU LOOKING FOR AN ADVENTURE HOLIDAY?

[1]*Book / Rent* a seat on the Orient Express and travel across Europe to Asia in style.
Trains depart all year round, just [2]*check / look* the online timetable for details.
Journeys are flexible so you can leave the train to [3]*go / take* a tour of cities on the way.
And we can also help you [4]*find / stay* overnight accommodation.
So what are you waiting for? Train tickets go fast so [5]*buy / sell* yours now!

5 Complete the conversation with the correct form of *going to* and the verbs in brackets.

Rose What [1]*are you going to do* (do) today?
Jim I [2]________ (watch) the match on TV, what about you?
Rose I [3]________ (clean) the house. And you [4]________ (help). We agreed, remember?
Jim [5]________ (you go) to the shops after?
Rose No, I [6]________ (not go) because Lily can't come. She [7]________ (visit) her mother in hospital.
Jim Oh! Did I tell you Rob and Jenny [8]________ (come over) after the match?
Rose Really? OK, then [9]________ (you/help) me with the housework, right?
Jim Of course I am!

6 Complete the sentences with the correct Present Continuous forms of the verbs in brackets.

1 Harry [1]*is swimming* (swim) at 9 a.m. on Saturday morning.
2 Maisy [2]________ (have) a guitar lesson on Sunday.
3 They [3]________ (go) shopping in the afternoon.
4 On Sunday in the morning they [4]________ (clean) the house.
5 They [5]________ (not watch) football on Saturday.
6 In the afternoon Susan [6]________ (visit) her grandparents.
7 They [7]________ (not go) to the cinema this weekend.

USE OF ENGLISH

7 Choose the correct words a–c to complete the texts.

1 *Please make sure you **clear your rubbish away** if you __ a barbecue on the beach.*

a get **b** have **c** make

2 RESPECT OTHERS AT ALL TIMES AND BE QUIET WHEN USING THE __.

a library **b** market **c** station

3 Follow the signs and go straight __ for the metro.

a off **b** iup **c** on

4 PLEASE RING THE BELL WHEN YOU WANT TO GET __ THE BUS.

a from **b** off **c** out

5 The __ is a great place to see opera, ballet and listen to classical music.

a concert hall **b** town hall **c** sports centre

6 Queue here to __ tickets to travel today.

a shop **b** find **c** buy

Use of English > page 173

READING

8 **Read the text s and match people 1–4 with activities A–E. There is one extra activity.**

STRATEGY | Multiple matching

In this task you need to match descriptions of people with different texts. Start by reading the descriptions and underlining important information. Then do the same with the texts.

A

I'm going to an arts exhibition in a gallery opposite Brighton football stadium on Sunday. There are going to be lots of different artists and sculptors showing their creations and giving talks. I'm definitely going to go so if you want to come with me, let me know.
Sara

B

My mum's a big fan of the opera and she bought four tickets so we could all go and see *Carmen* at the Royal Opera House in Covent Garden this Saturday. Unfortunately, my brother's got the flu so he can't come with us. This morning my mum said, 'Why don't you ask one of your friends to come, instead?'. Is anyone interested?
Amy

C

On Sunday I'm going to the British Museum with a group of friends. They've got a special exhibition about Ancient Egypt. They're organising a guided tour where they tell you all about their amazing collection of Egyptian statues and sculptures. It's going to be fascinating! Let me know if you're interested.
Ben

D

We're studying Shakespeare's *Romeo and Juliet* at school this term. Yesterday our English teacher told us that they're performing it at the open-air theatre in Regent's Park at the moment. So, a few of us are going to try and get tickets for Saturday evening. I just hope it doesn't rain – you never know with the British weather!
Mia

E

The new football season starts this weekend and I'm going with my dad to the Chelsea–Liverpool match in London. Both teams were really good last year so I think it's going to be an amazing game. Dad says I can invite two friends because it's my birthday on Saturday, so get in touch if you want to come.
Danny

1

☐ David loves music and enjoys going to all types of concerts. He doesn't know much about classical music but he's interested in trying new things.

2

☐ Matt is an American teenager who is staying in London with his English cousin, Sam. Both Matt and Sam like playing and watching all kinds of sport.

3

☐ Phoebe is studying Literature and Drama at school and would love to become an actress one day. She doesn't have any plans for this weekend.

4

☐ Laura is very keen on history and loves watching documentaries. She also enjoys reading about past civilisations like the Romans and the Greeks. She'd like to study Archaeology at university.

SPEAKING

9 **In pairs, take turns to ask for and give directions. Use the map below. Student A: you are at the station and you want to go to the theatre. Student B: you are at the station and you want to go to the cinema.**

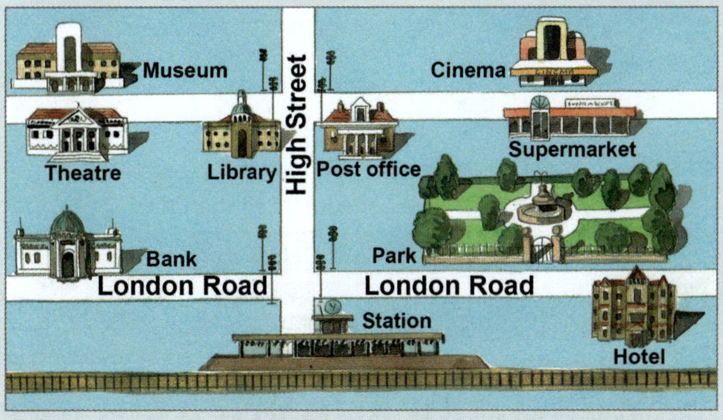

WRITING

10 **Read the task below.**

A friend is arriving in your town by train tomorrow. You are going to meet him/her at a café in the town centre. Write a short email and tell him/her how to get from the station to the café.

Write a an email.

08 Smart future

VOCABULARY Gadgets, computers, science
GRAMMAR *Will* for predictions about the future **Use of English** > page 173
SPEAKING Opinions
WRITING A notice
VIDEO Grammar ▷ Communication ▷ Documentary ▷

TOMORROW'S WORLD A guide to the next fifty years

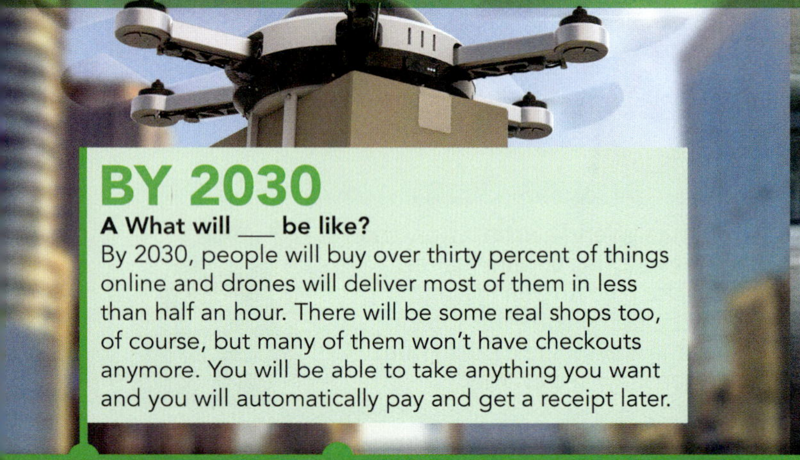

BY 2030
A What will ___ be like?
By 2030, people will buy over thirty percent of things online and drones will deliver most of them in less than half an hour. There will be some real shops too, of course, but many of them won't have checkouts anymore. You will be able to take anything you want and you will automatically pay and get a receipt later.

BY 2050
C Where will we ___?
By 2050, the population of the world will be 9.6 billion and seventy-five percent of people will live in cities, often in huge 'smart' apartment buildings, over ten kilometres tall. Virtual reality will be a big part of our everyday lives. For example, most people in cities won't need to leave their homes. Houses won't even need windows – 'virtual windows' will look completely real.

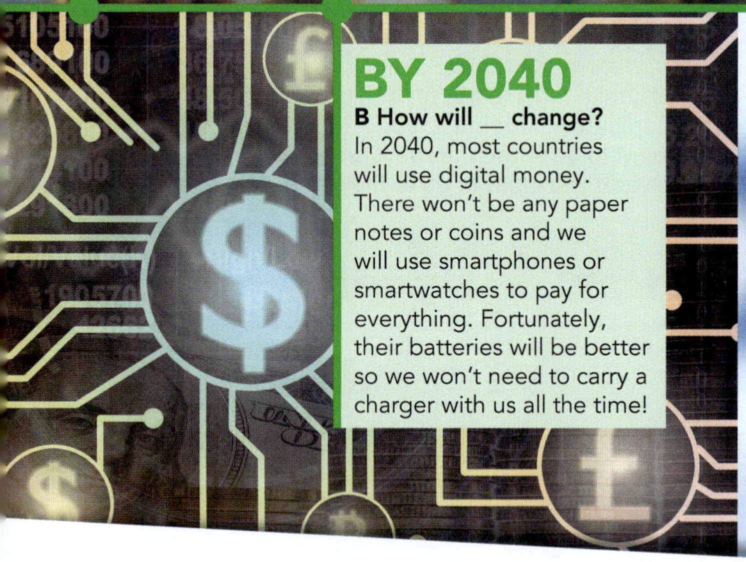

BY 2040
B How will __ change?
In 2040, most countries will use digital money. There won't be any paper notes or coins and we will use smartphones or smartwatches to pay for everything. Fortunately, their batteries will be better so we won't need to carry a charger with us all the time!

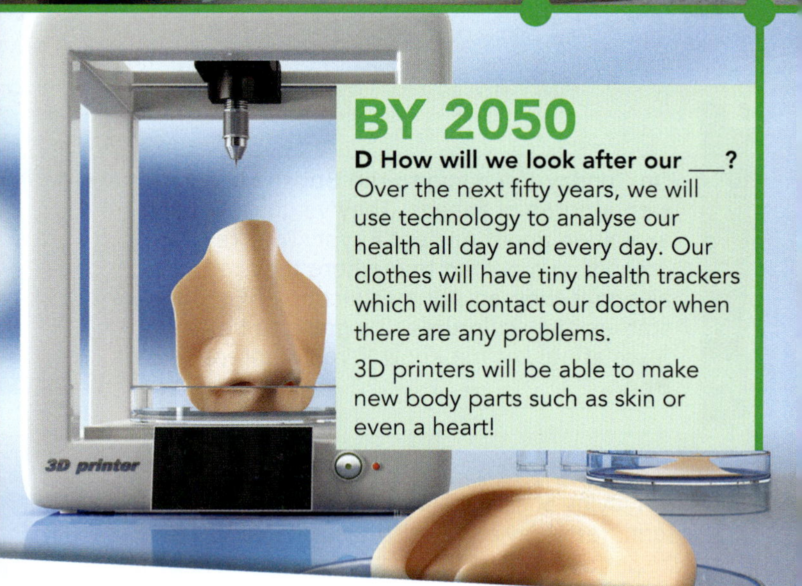

BY 2050
D How will we look after our ___?
Over the next fifty years, we will use technology to analyse our health all day and every day. Our clothes will have tiny health trackers which will contact our doctor when there are any problems.
3D printers will be able to make new body parts such as skin or even a heart!

8A GRAMMAR AND VOCABULARY

1 **SPEAKING Use a dictionary to check the meaning of the words from the box. Then, in pairs, discuss the questions.**

3D printer charger drone health tracker smartphone smartwatch tablet computer virtual reality (VR) headset wireless headphones

1 Which of these gadgets do you use?
2 Which is your favourite? Say why.
3 Which gadget would you like to own? Say why.

2 **In pairs, read the texts and compete headings A–D with the words from the box.**

health live money shopping

3 **What do you think of the predictions? Which are more/less probable? Which are better/worse for people? Discuss in pairs.**

Will

4 **Read the sentences and choose the correct answers in the rules.**

By 2030, drones will deliver most things in less than half an hour.

By 2040, there won't be any paper notes or coins.

Where will we live?

1 We use *will/won't* to talk about
  a future plans.
  b future predictions.

2 We use
  a *will/won't* + *to* + infinitive
  b *will/won't* + infinitive

5 **Study the Grammar box and check your answers to Exercise 4.**

Will	
We use *will* to make predictions about the future.	
+	In a few years I **will** (**'ll**) **leave** home.
–	In twenty years people **will not** (**won't**) **use** paper money or coins.
?	**Will** you **study** languages at university? Yes, I **will**. / No, I **won't**.
Wh-?	When **will** you **leave** home?
Time expressions: in the next few years, in ten months, next year, by 2050	
Grammar Reference and Practice > page 168	

6 **Study *Watch out!* and complete the sentences with *will* or *won't*. Then, in pairs, say if you agree or disagree with the predictions.**

1 In ten years many homes *will* have a robot assistant to help clean, cook and do other chores.

2 In the next twenty years computers _________ become as creative as humans. They will be able to create works of art on their own.

3 By 2050, petrol cars _________ exist any more and all transport will be electric.

4 In the next fifty years thanks to 3D printers, scientists _________ be able to make many human body parts.

5 In 100 years thousands of scientists _________ live on the Moon and tourists will go there on holiday.

6 By 2200 people _________ need to study languages because English will be the only language.

7 In the next 200 years we _________ make contact with people from another planet.

WATCH OUT!

Present: *We **can** travel all over the world.*

Future: *In the future we **will be able to** go on holiday without leaving our homes.*

7 **3.21 PRONUNCIATION Listen and choose the sentence you hear.**

1 **a** He will be late. **b** He'll be late.
2 **a** It will be cold. **b** It'll be cold.
3 **a** We will leave soon. **b** We'll leave soon.
4 **a** They won't like it. **b** They don't like it.

8 **3.22 Listen and complete the sentences.**

1 *I'll* be there at six.
2 _________ need any money.
3 _________ help us.
4 _________ love virtual reality.

9 **Complete the predictions with *will/won't* and a verb from the box to make them true for you. Then write seven questions to ask your partner.**

be ~~buy~~ drive go learn live move start

1 In the next few weeks I *will buy* a new smartphone.
Will you buy a new smartphone in the next few weeks?
2 In the next two years I _________ how to play the guitar.
3 I _________ to university in the next five years.
4 In 20 years I _________ an electric car.
5 I _________ at my parents' house in 2040.
6 In fifty years I _________ a grandparent.
7 In the future I _________ to another country.
8 Next year I _________ some new subjects at school.

10 **SPEAKING In pairs, ask and answer the questions you wrote in Exercise 9. Try to add another question to find more information.**

A *Will you buy a new smartphone in the next few weeks?*
B *Yes, I will.*
A *Where will you buy it?*

23 Read the question and watch the video. Say what the speakers answer. Then, in pairs, ask and answer the question.

How will we live in the future?

☐ **I can use *will/won't* to make predictions about the future.**

Second-hand computer equipment Buy cheaper, sell faster!

1 *desktop computer*, 4.2GHz, 16GB RAM **Price**: €499

2 ________, for PC/ Laptop **Price**: €45

3 ________ **Price**: €25

4 ________ **Price**: €5

5 ________, **Price**: €25

6 ________ **Price**: €149

7 ________, 500GB **Price**: €99

8 ________, **Price**: €35

61cm, LED 9 ________ monitor **Price**: €199

8B VOCABULARY | Computer equipment

1 Complete descriptions 1–9 with the words from the box.

~~desktop computer~~ hard disk laptop battery scanner screen speakers USB cable wireless keyboard wireless mouse

2 Which items of computer equipment in Exercise 1 do you have in your room? Discuss in pairs.

3 Complete the sentences with the verbs from the box.

~~charge~~ print scan switch off turn up type

1. How often do you need to *charge* the battery on your phone?
2. Do you ________ your computer when you go to bed or do you leave it on all night?
3. Can you ________ without looking at the keyboard?
4. Do you ________ your speakers and listen to loud music when you're home alone?
5. Have you got a printer that can ________ and ________?

4 3.23 **Listen to a man answering the questions in Exercise 3. What are his answers? Then ask and answer the questions in pairs.**

5 Match the verbs with the icons.

attach copy ~~delete~~ download install save

1 *delete*

2 ________

3 ________

4 ________

5 ________

6 ________

6 Choose two words or phrases that go with each verb.

1. delete *a file / a hard disk / an email*
2. save *the Internet / your changes / a document*
3. copy *some text / a file / a keyboard*
4. attach *a website / a USB cable to your phone / a file*
5. install *an app / a printer / a document*
6. download *some music / a laptop / an app*

7 SPEAKING In pairs, answer the questions.

1. What do you do with emails and text messages after you read them?
2. Do you usually download music or listen to it online? Say why.
3. How many apps did you install on your phone last week? What were they?
4. Do you check your phone after going to bed? Is it a good idea? Say why.

☐ I can talk about computers.

8C GRAMMAR

1 Look at the pictures of gadgets. What do you think they do?

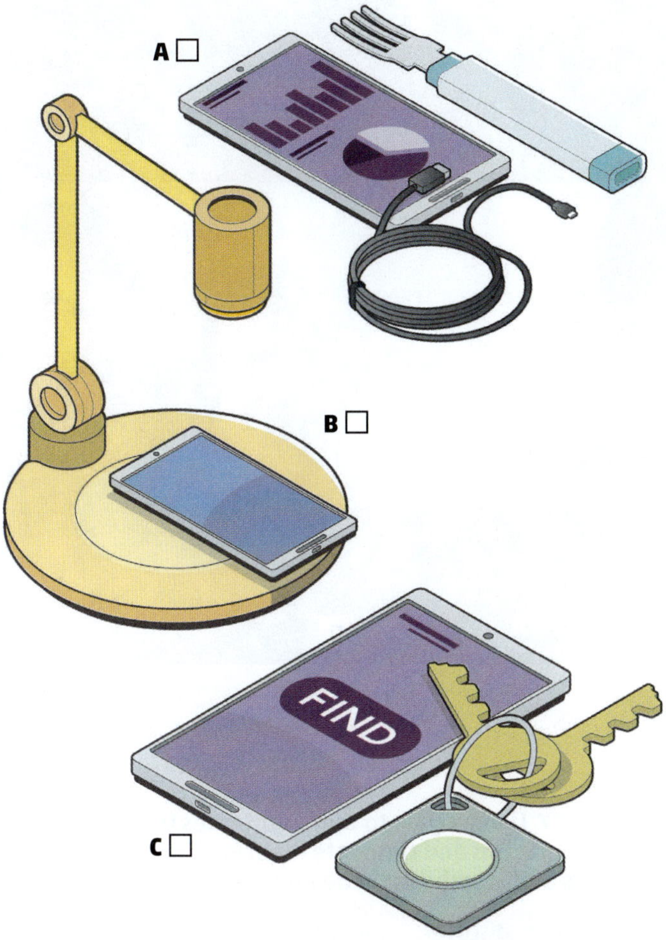

A ☐ B ☐ C ☐

2 🔊 3.24 Listen and match the conversations to each gadget.

Adverbs of manner

3 🔊 3.24 Match the beginnings and endings of the sentences from the conversations. Then listen again and check.

1 [c] The tracker beeps quietly at first
2 ☐ It's brilliant!
3 ☐ I could charge my phone
4 ☐ Check your phone
5 ☐ My mum says
6 ☐ Eating slowly
7 ☐ I eat too quickly

a and sometimes I get a stomach ache.
b can charge wirelessly.
c and then it starts beeping loudly.
d really easily with this gadget.
e It works really well.
f can help you lose weight.
g that I always eat too fast.

4 Look at the underlined adverbs in Exercise 3. Then choose the correct words to complete rules 1–4. Study the Grammar box to check.

1 We add *-ly* to most *adjectives* / *verbs* to make adverbs.
2 For adjectives ending in *-y*, we change *-y* to *-i* / *-e* and add *-ly*.
3 The adverbs *good* and *fast* are *regular* / *irregular*.
4 We often put adverbs at the *beginning* / *end* of a sentence.

Adverbs of manner

We use **adverbs of manner** to describe how we do things.

Adjective	Adverb
loud	loud**ly**
slow	slow**ly**
safe	safe**ly**
beautiful	beautiful**ly**
easy	eas**ily**
Irregular	
good	**well**
fast	**fast**
hard	**hard**

Grammar Reference and Practice > page 168

5 Change the adjectives in the box to adverbs and complete the sentences.

bad careful good healthy ~~perfect~~ polite urgent

1 My brother speaks English *perfectly*. He lived in London for ten years.
2 I did very ________ in my last exam. I need to get a better mark this time.
3 Can I borrow your phone? I need to call someone ________.
4 You need to read this ________. It's very important.
5 Can I have a salad? I'm trying to eat ________.
6 I like Thomas. When I see him, he always smiles ________.
7 Well done! You played really ________.

6 🔊 3.25 Listen and complete the sentences with the adverb form of the adjectives from the box.

~~confident~~ dangerous happy hard loud quick

1 She is speaking *confidently*.
2 Someone is screaming ________.
3 He is studying ________.
4 Someone is typing ________.
5 The baby is smiling ________.
6 The man is driving ________.

7 Complete the sentences with the correct forms of the words in brackets. Use the adjective or adverb.

1 My sister plays the guitar really *well* although she is not a ________ musician. (good, professional)
2 He isn't a ________ driver. He always drives too ________ (careful, fast)
3 I've got a very ________ exam tomorrow. I have to study ________ tonight. (important, hard)
4 My computer wasn't ________ but it starts up really ________ (cheap, slow)

8 In pairs, take turns to mime an action in the manner of adverbs from this lesson. Guess what your partner is doing.

Are you riding a bike dangerously?

☐ **I can use adverbs to talk about the way we do things.**

A

B

C

D

8D LISTENING AND VOCABULARY

1 SPEAKING **In pairs, describe photos A–D. What are the people doing in each photo?**

2 3.26 **Listen to four conversations. Match them with photos A–D.**

1 ☐ **2** ☐ **3** ☐ **4** ☐

3 3.26 **Listen to the conversations again and choose the correct answers.**

1 What does the girl think the problem is with the computer?
 a The keyboard isn't working properly.
 b The hard disk is broken.
 c They need to charge the battery.

2 How did the girl feel about her experience with a virtual reality headset?
 a Frightened because everything looked so real.
 b Excited about trying it one more time.
 c Surprised about the quality of the picture.

3 The two friends agree that smart speakers are
 a useful.
 b good fun at parties.
 c cheap.

4 What does the girl think about time travel?
 a She loves films about travelling in time.
 b She believes that one day we will be able to travel in time.
 c She is very interested in the science of time travel.

4 3.27 **Listen again to these sentences from the conversations and complete them with the correct forms of the verbs from the box.**

develop discover experiment invent produce ~~test~~

1 Mum knows how *to test* the hard disk.
2 Well, lots of companies _________ headsets now.
3 You need to _________ with questions.
4 Perhaps scientists _________ something new and amazing about physics.
5 Then they'll be able _________ a time machine.
6 I think a time machine is a lot harder _________ than the Internet.

5 **Choose the correct verbs to complete the predictions.**

In the next ten years ...

1 astronomers will *develop* / *discover* life on another planet.
2 IT companies will *experiment* / *produce* very cheap 3D video phones.
3 we will stop *inventing* / *testing* cosmetics on animals.
4 scientists will continue to *experiment* / *produce* with animals.
5 companies will *develop* / *test* video games that are even more and more realistic.
6 somebody will discover / *invent* a new, better alternative to the Internet.

6 SPEAKING **In pairs, say why you agree or disagree with the predictions in Exercise 5. Then use the verbs in Exercise 4 to make your own predictions.**

I think scientists will discover new sources of energy.

☐ **I can identify the main points in a conversation and talk about technology.**

8E SPEAKING

1 **Read the article below. What is 'the Internet of things'? Does it make our lives easier? Discuss in pairs.**

IN THE AVERAGE UK HOME, around eight devices connect to the Internet. In the next few years, experts think that number will increase dramatically.
You can already buy 'smart' versions of many everyday objects. For instance, there are already 'smart' lights, fridges and even mirrors! These gadgets are part of 'the Internet of things'. You can control them with an app on your mobile phone and some work with 'voice assistants' – you just say your instructions.

2 *24* *3.28* **Watch or listen. How does Charlie turn on the lights/the TV? How does he play some music? What goes wrong?**

3 *24* *3.28* **Study the Speaking box. Complete the conversation with a word or phrase in each gap. Then watch or listen again to check.**

VA = Voice Assistant

Mia Charlie, I'm not saying the Internet of things is rubbish. But personally I [1]*think* it will make our lives easier.
Max [2]__________ with Mia. Now let's go inside.
Charlie I'm sorry but I [3]__________.
Max It's dark. Turn the lights on. Wow, Charlie! You turned the lights on with your phone!
Charlie Yes, Max. We've got 'smart' lights.
Mia Yeah, but who wants to take their phone out, start the app … It takes too long.
Charlie You're [4]__________, Mia. So what about this? Voice Assistant, turn on the TV.
VA I'm turning on the TV.
Mia/Max Awesome!
Charlie Voice Assistant, play a song.
VA Here's one of your favourite songs.
Max Cool. Voice Assistant, turn it up! I can't hear because of the TV.
VA I'm turning up the TV.
Charlie No! Not the TV! Voice Assistant, turn it off.
VA I'm turning off the lights.
Max Um, Charlie. I can't see anything.
Charlie Well, obviously it doesn't work perfectly, but in [5]__________, we'll use these gadgets a lot in the future.
Mia Really? I'm [6]__________ about that.

SPEAKING | Opinions

Giving opinions
(Personally,) I think … | In my opinion, …
(Personally,) I don't think … | I'm sure that …

Agreeing	**Disagreeing**
Yes, I agree.	(I'm sorry but) I don't agree.
You're right.	That's (probably) true but …
Exactly.	I'm not sure (about that).
I agree with him/her/you.	I don't think so.
I think so too.	

4 *3.29* **In pairs, choose the correct words to complete the conversations. Then listen and check.**

A [1]*I'm sure / Personally*, I think that in ten years' time most cars will be electric.
B I'm not sure [2]*about / with* that. They're too expensive.
A Yes, for now, but they will get cheaper very quickly.

A [3]*In my opinion / Exactly*, technology will become one of our biggest problems.
B I [4]*think / don't think* so too. Lots of people won't have jobs.
A You're [5]*right / sure*. And no jobs means no money!

A I'm [6]*agree / sure* that in five years' time virtual reality will be part of everyday life.
B Yes, I [7]*agree / think*. Virtual reality is amazing now. Imagine it in five years' time!
A [8]Exactly! / *Personally*. It'll be amazing!

A [9]*I don't think / That's true* our planet is the only one with life.
B I agree [10]*with you / you*. One day we'll find another one.
A [11]*That's / You're* probably true but I won't be alive!

5 **Work in groups of three. Read the statements. Take turns to give your opinion, agree and disagree.**

1. Many young people spend too much time online.
2. Every home will have a voice-controlled assistant.
3. Everyone in the world needs free Internet access.
4. We will all have personal robots in the future.

☐ **I can express, agree and disagree with opinions.**

8F READING AND VOCABULARY

1 SPEAKING **In pairs, look at the photos on page 109. What do you think is happening? Think of ways in which robots can help us in our daily lives.**

2 **Read the article quickly. Does the author think that computers and robots will become as intelligent as humans one day?**

3 **Look at the text extract below. What do you think the underlined pronouns 'they' refer to?**

Will computers become as intelligent as the human brain one day? In some ways <u>they</u> are already smarter than us. <u>They</u> can solve problems quickly and without making mistakes. And <u>they</u> don't need to eat or sleep, of course.

4 **Study Active Reading and then check your answers to Exercise 3.**

ACTIVE READING | Understanding pronouns

A pronoun replaces a noun. When you are not sure what a pronoun refers to:

- read the sentence with the pronoun carefully.
- read the sentences before and after the one with the pronoun to find the noun or nouns.
- decide if the noun matches the pronoun – for example, *it* cannot refer to a person; *they* cannot refer to a singular noun.

5 **Read the article. Match sentences A–F with gaps 1–4 in the text. Use the underlined words to help you. There are two extra sentences.**

A <u>They</u>'ll be able to recognise how you are feeling.
B <u>They</u> say that eighty-seven percent of the time their machine understands our emotions correctly.
C <u>They</u> can write original music and stories and even invent new technology.
D The company sells <u>them</u> for less than $2,000.
E One interesting idea is to use <u>them</u> in online education.
F For example, <u>it</u> looks happy when it sees you in the morning.

6 **Read the text again and answer the questions.**

1. What do humans need that computers don't need?
2. Which country does *Affectiva* come from?
3. Which company makes Pepper?
4. How long did it take to sell the first 1,000 Peppers?
5. Who will computers help by understanding their emotions?

7 **Look at the highlighted adjectives and phrases in the text. Which ones are positive? Which are negative? Which can be both positive and negative? Put them in the correct column of the table.**

Positive	Negative	Both
in a good mood		

8 **Complete the sentences for you. Then, in pairs, compare your sentences.**

1. I feel angry when …
2. I'm usually in a good mood when …
3. I get worried when …
4. I am usually in a bad mood when …
5. I am always bored …
6. I feel amazed when …
7. I get scared when …

9 REFLECT | Society **Read the article. Then, in pairs, discuss the questions.**

A recent survey suggests that many teenagers now prefer to communicate online than in person – face-to-face. In the survey, fifty percent of teenagers said they feel more confident when they can type messages to friends. They also prefer texting because it's quick and easy, and it gives them more time to think.
In another survey, nearly half of families with children said they text each other when they're at home!

1. Do the survey results surprise you? Do you prefer communicating online or in person?
2. What are the advantages and disadvantages of texting friends instead of talking to them face-to-face?

25 WATCH AND REFLECT **Go to page 157. Watch the documentary *Microchipping* and do the exercises.**

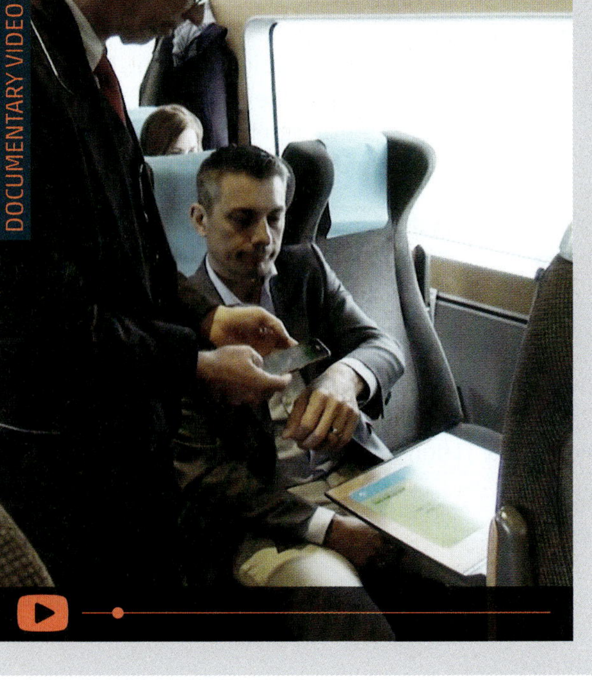

☐ **I can identify the structure of a text and talk about feelings and communication.**

COMPUTERS AND ROBOTS WITH EMOTIONAL INTELLIGENCE

3.30

Will computers become as intelligent as the human brain one day? In some ways they are already smarter than us. They can solve problems quickly and without making mistakes. And they don't need to eat or sleep, of course. But the human brain has other abilities that we can't give computers – at least, not yet! For instance, humans are creative. [1]___ Humans can also feel and recognise emotions. We know, for example, when another person is in a good or in a bad mood. And this ability is very important in interaction with other people.

A

Now scientists are studying how computers can read human emotions. *Affectiva*, a US company, is developing software that uses cameras to look at human faces. The company collected over six million videos of people from seventy-five different countries to use in their software. However, it isn't always possible to identify someone's emotion from their face. That's why researchers at a US university developed a computer that can hear your heart and your breathing wirelessly. [2]___

A Japanese company, *SoftBank Robotics* already produces and sells a robot called Pepper that can recognise human emotions. Pepper analyses both your face and the sound of your voice. It knows when you are happy, surprised or amazed and tries to help when you are sad, worried or angry. Pepper can also show its own emotions. [3]___ It even gets scared in the dark! But are we ready for a robot like Pepper in our daily lives? It seems some people are. The company sold the first 1,000 Peppers in just one minute.

What about the future? How will computers that understand our emotions be useful? [4]___ Computers will soon be able to recognise when students are finding a subject too easy or too difficult, or even when they're bored. They can use this information to change the activities students do – to help them learn.

And when will this all happen? Some computer scientists believe that within fifteen years computers will understand our emotions perfectly. Can you imagine this? Your smartphone will know more about your feelings than your best friend!

B

B

I'm selling my Samson Sports fitness tracker. It's only six months old and it's in perfect condition. I got it from my brother when he bought a new one but I never use it. Send me an email if you're interested.
Jake

1 SPEAKING **In pairs, discuss the questions.**

1. What kind of things do you often lose?
2. What was the last thing you lost? What happened?
3. What do you do with old gadgets, such as smartphones? Do you sell them to other people or swap them with friends?

2 Read notices A and B. Match them with the statements below.

1. ☐ someone wants to find something.
2. ☐ someone wants to sell something.

3 Read the notices again. Answer the questions.

1. Which notice is better at attracting your attention, A or B? Say why.
2. Is there any information that is not necessary in notice A or B?
3. Is there any important information missing from notice A or B?

4 Study the Writing box and check your answers.

WRITING | A notice

To attract people's attention, you can:
- write a big heading, e.g.: LOST! FOR SALE!
- include an accurate photo of the item you lost/want to sell.

Make your notice clear and easy to read:
- use bullet points.
- don't include unnecessary information.

Include all the necessary information:
- write a simple description of the object (colour, name, etc.).
- say where and when you lost the object (LOST!).
- give your name and contact details.
- offer a reward (LOST!) or give the price (FOR SALE!).

5 The writer of notice A included these sentences. Do you think they are useful? Say why.

> 'PLEASE HELP! THESE HEADPHONES WERE A BIRTHDAY PRESENT AND MY FAVOURITE POSSESSION!'

6 Rewrite notice B. Use the tips in the Writing box. Add any necessary information.

7 3.31 **Listen and complete the texts with one word in each gap.**

1. Lucy wants to sell her [1] *laptop*. It's a [2] ________ with a 13 inch screen. It originally cost [3] ________ but she is selling it for [4] ________. It's [5] ________ years old and is in [6] ________ condition.
2. Robert lost his [7] ________ today. It's a Samson [8] ________. He left it in a [9] ________ on Upper Street at about [10] ________ p.m. He wants to offer a reward of [11] ________.

8 WRITING TASK **Choose one of the situations in Exercise 7 and write a LOST! or FOR SALE! notice.**

- Use the Writing box to help you.
- Add any other necessary information, e.g. a contact number or email address.

 ☐ **I can write a short notice.**

8A GRAMMAR AND VOCABULARY 5.50

3D printer (n) /ˌθriː ˌdiː ˈprɪntə/
analyse (v) /ˈænəlaɪz/
automatically (adv) /ˌɔːtəˈmætɪkli/
charger (n) /ˈtʃɑːdʒə/
checkout (n) /ˈtʃekaʊt/
coin (n) /kɔɪn/
deliver (v) /dɪˈlɪvə/
drone (n) /drəʊn/
electric car (n) /ɪˌlektrɪk ˈkɑː/
future (n) /ˈfjuːtʃə/
gadget (n) /ˈgædʒɪt/
health tracker (n) /ˈhelθ ˌtrækə/
make contact with sb /ˌmeɪk ˈkɒntækt wɪð ˌsʌmbɒdi /
Moon (n) /muːn/
note (n) /nəʊt/
part of the body/body part /ˌpɑːt əv ðə ˈbɒdi/ ˈbɒdi pɑːt/
petrol car (n) /ˈpetrəl kɑː/
planet (n) /ˈplænɪt/
robot (n) /ˈrəʊbɒt/
scientist (n) /ˈsaɪəntɪst/
smartphone (n) /ˈsmɑːtfəʊn/
smartwatch (n) /ˈsmɑːtwɒtʃ/
tablet computer (n) /ˌtæblɪt kəmˈpjuːtə/
virtual reality (VR) headset (n) /ˌvɜːtʃuəl riˌæləti (ˌviː ˈɑː) ˈhedset/
wireless headphones (n) /ˌwaɪələs ˈhedfəʊnz/

8B VOCABULARY 5.51

attach a cable to your phone /əˌtætʃ ə ˌkeɪbəl tə jə ˈfəʊn/
attach a file /əˌtætʃ ə ˈfaɪl/
charge (v) /tʃɑːdʒ/
computer equipment (n) /kəmˈpjuːtə ɪˌkwɪpmənt/
copy some text/a file /ˌkɒpi səm ˈtekst/ə ˈfaɪl/
delete a file/an email /dɪˌliːt ə ˈfaɪl/ən ˈiː meɪl/
desktop computer (n) /ˌdesktɒp kəmˈpjuːtə/
download music/an app /ˌdaʊnˌləʊd ˈmjuːzɪk/ ən ˈæp/
hard disk (n) /ˌhɑːd ˈdɪsk/
install an app/a printer /ɪnˌstɔːl ən ˈæp/ə ˈprɪntə/
laptop battery (n) /ˈlæptɒp ˌbætəri/
PC (n) /ˌpiː ˈsiː/
print (v) /prɪnt/
save a document/your changes /ˌseɪv ə ˈdɒkjəmənt/jə ˈtʃeɪndʒɪz/
scan (v) /skæn/
scanner (n) /ˈskænə/
screen (n) /skriːn/
speakers (n) /ˈspiːkəz/
switch off /ˌswɪtʃ ˈɒf/
tech-free (adj) /ˌtek ˈfriː/
turn up /ˌtɜːn ˈʌp/
type (v) /taɪp/
USB cable (n) /ˌjuː es ˈbiː ˌkeɪbəl/
wireless keyboard/mouse /ˌwaɪələs ˈkiːbɔːd/ ˈmaʊs/

8C GRAMMAR 5.52

badly (adv) /ˈbædli/
confidently (adv) /ˈkɒnfɪdəntli/
dangerously (adv) /ˈdeɪndʒərəsli/
do well in an exam /ˌduː ˌwel ɪn ən ɪgˈzæm/
fast (adj, adv) /fɑːst/
happily (adv) /ˈhæpəli/
hard (adj, adv) /hɑːd/
healthily (adv) /ˈhelθili/
key ring (n) /ˈkiː rɪŋ/
lose (v) /luːz/
loudly (adv) /ˈlaʊdli/
perfectly (adv) /ˈpɜːfɪktli/
politely (adv) /pəˈlaɪtli/
press a button /ˌpres ə ˈbʌtn/
safely (adv) /ˈseɪfli/
slowly (adv) /ˈsləʊli/
start up /ˌstɑːt ˈʌp/
tracker (n) /ˈtrækə/
urgently (adv) /ˈɜːdʒəntli/
well (adv) /wel/

8D LISTENING AND VOCABULARY 5.53

broken (adj) /ˈbrəʊkən/
develop (v) /dɪˈveləp/
discover (v) /dɪsˈkʌvə/
excited (adj) /ɪkˈsaɪtɪd/
experiment with sth (v) /ɪkˈsperəmənt wɪð ˌsʌmθɪŋ/
frightened (adj) /ˈfraɪtnd/
invent (v) /ɪnˈvent/
produce (v) /prəˈdjuːs/
surprised (adj) /səˈpraɪzd/
test (v) /test/
time machine (n) /ˈtaɪm məʃiːn/
time travel (n) /ˈtaɪm ˌtrævəl/
travel in time /ˌtrævəl ɪn ˈtaɪm/

8E SPEAKING 5.54

alive (adj) /əˈlaɪv/
imagine (v) /ɪˈmædʒɪn/
Internet access (n) /ˈɪntənet ˌækses/
make life easier /ˌmeɪk laɪf ˈiːziə/
personal robot (n) /ˌpɜːsənəl ˈrəʊbɒt/
start an app /ˌstɑːt ən ˈæp/
turn the lights on/off /ˌtɜːn ðə ˌlaɪts ˈɒn/ˈɒf/
voice assistant/voice-controlled assistant (n) / ˈvɔɪs əˌsɪstənt/ˌvɔɪs kənˌtrəʊld əˈsɪstənt/

8F READING AND VOCABULARY 5.55

amazed (adj) /əˈmeɪzd/
angry (adj) /ˈæŋgri/
bored (adj) /bɔːd/
breathing (n) /ˈbriːðɪŋ/
communicate face-to-face/in person / kəˌmjuːnɪkeɪt ˌfeɪs tə ˈfeɪs/ɪn ˈpɜːsən/
communicate online /kəˌmjuːnɪkeɪt ˌɒnˈlaɪn/
computer scientist (n) /kəmˌpjuːtə ˈsaɪəntɪst/
excited (adj) /ɪkˈsaɪtɪd/
happy (adj) /ˈhæpi/
heart (n) /hɑːt/
human brain /ˌhjuːmən ˈbreɪn/
in a good/bad mood /ɪn ə ˌgʊd/ˌbæd ˈmuːd/
interaction (with other people) /ˌɪntərˌækʃən (wɪð ˌʌðə ˈpiːpəl)/
recognise (v) /ˈrekəgnaɪz/
researcher (n) /riˈsɜːtʃə/
sad (adj) /sæd/
scared (adj) /skeəd/
software (n) /ˈsɒftweə/
solve problems /ˌsɒlv ˈprɒbləmz/
stressed (adj) /strest/
surprised (adj) /səˈpraɪzd/
understand/recognise/read/identify/show emotions /ˌʌndəˌstænd/ˌrekəgnaɪz/ˌriːd/ aɪˌdentɪfaɪ/ˌʃəʊ ɪˈməʊʃənz/
worried (adj) /ˈwʌrid/

8G WRITING 5.56

fitness tracker (n) /ˈfɪtnəs ˌtrækə/
in perfect condition /ɪn ˌpɜːfɪkt kənˈdɪʃən/
notice (n) /ˈnəʊtɪs/
possession (n) /pəˈzeʃən/
reward (n) /rɪˈwɔːd/
swap (v) /swɒp/

Remember More > page 174

VOCABULARY AND GRAMMAR

1 Match 1–7 with a–g to make the names of computer equipment and gadgets.

1 [b] desktop	a battery
2 ☐ fitness	b computer
3 ☐ hard	c cable
4 ☐ laptop	d disk
5 ☐ USB	e headset
6 ☐ virtual reality	f headphones
7 ☐ wireless	g tracker

2 Complete the instructions with the correct words from the box.

attach document save screen smartphone ~~switch on~~

HOW TO EMAIL A DOCUMENT USING YOUR NEW SMART PRINTER

[1] *Switch on* your computer, tablet or [2]________.

Place your [3]________ under the scanner.

Check you are happy with the scan on your device [4]________.

[5]________ the file, [6]________ it to your email and send.

3 Match the adjectives in the box with the situations 1–6.

angry bored excited interested surprised ~~nervous~~

1 You've got an important exam. *nervous*
2 You receive an unusual present.
3 Someone is rude to you.
4 There is something good on TV.
5 It's raining and there's nothing to do.
6 You're about to go on holiday.

4 Complete the conversation with *will* and the correct form of the verbs in brackets.

Harry Where [1]*will you live* (you/live) in ten years?
Gracie [2]_________ (I/move) to London with friends, but [3]_________ (we/not have) a house – we'll get a flat. What about you?
Harry [4]_________ (I/be) a famous scientist, so [5]_________ (I/not stay) in one place but travel all over the world!
Gracie Cool! And do you think [6]_________ (you/drive) a big sports car?
Harry No, because [7]_________ (people/will use) public transport or walk everywhere in the future.
Gracie So how [8]_________ (you/travel)?
Harry (I/fly) [9]_________ everywhere by plane, of course!

5 Write predictions about yourself using the verbs in the box and time expressions.

become buy find go learn start

1 by 2025
2 in the next three years
3 in six months
4 next year
5 in the future
6 in the next few weeks

6 Choose the correct words to complete the sentences.

1 Stay *safe* / *safely*! Never drive too *quick* / *quickly*!
2 This is a message for Chris: please contact the office *urgent* / *urgently*!
3 John did *good* / *well* in his exams.
4 My sister makes friends very *easy* / *easily*.
5 Read all the exam questions *careful* / *carefully*.
6 'Can you speak French?' 'Yes, I can speak it *perfect* / *perfectly*!'
7 Sh! You are talking very *loud* / *loudly*!
8 I plan to eat more *healthy* / *healthily* food this year!

USE OF ENGLISH

7 Choose the correct words a–d to complete the text.

IN THE NEXT TEN YEARS ...

Scientists will further [1]__ eye-control technology for all our devices and gadgets.
There will be a 3D [2]__ in every house, so we can make food, medicines and things for the home.
Artificial intelligence will [3]__ very important in all aspects of our lives. And we will get most of our entertainment and information through [4]__ reality headsets.
Someone will [5]__ some new smart clothes. These will change colour or shape when it's too hot or cold.
We won't be [6]__ about our personal information online because [7]__ be so much information about everyone online we won't [8]__ stop it.
In fact, technology will progres s so [9]__ , that we will be [10]__ by all the changes.

	a	b	c	d
1	a develop	b discover	c experiment	d invent
2	a computer	b keyboard	c mouse	d printer
3	a become	b exist	c find	d go
4	a wireless	b fast	c visual	d virtual
5	a do	b plan	c learn	d test
6	a angry	b excited	c interested	d worried
7	a there will	b there won't	c will there	d won't there
8	a able to	b be able to	c can	d can be
9	a easily	b hard	c quickly	d slowly
10	a amazed	b bored	c happy	d stressed

8 **Complete the second sentence so that it means the same as the first one. Use no more than three words in each gap.**

STRATEGY | Transformations

Make sure you read the first sentence carefully and understand the meaning. The second sentence must be as close to that meaning as possible.

1. My brother loves listening to music at full volume on his speakers.
   My brother loves *turning up the* volume on his speakers to listen to music.
2. There are new apps on my phone.
   I __________ on my phone yesterday.
3. My school will have a new art room next year.
   Next year, there __________ a new art room in my school.
4. I'm optimistic about getting a place at university.
   I hope I __________ a place at university.
5. Our class didn't do very well in the test and the teacher was angry.
   We did very __________ test so the teacher was angry.

Use of English > page 173

LISTENING

9 3.32 **Listen and choose the correct answers.**

1. The teacher thinks that Jack is tired because
   a he read a book until midnight.
   b he was online until midnight.
   c he went to bed late.
2. The app is for people who want to
   a know the best way to get to school.
   b listen to music.
   c live healthily.
3. The scientist thinks that in twenty years' time electric cars will
   a be able to go faster.
   b have better batteries.
   c be cleaner.
4. The boy thinks that his personal robot will be able to
   a do the housework for him.
   b go to the supermarket for him.
   c have a conversation with him.

SPEAKING

10 **Look at the photos. In pairs, take turns to describe what you can see in the photos and answer the questions below.**

1. What are the students doing?
2. What class do you think this is?
3. Talk about other things in the photograph.

WRITING

11 **Write an email to a friend to tell him/her about the gadget you decided to buy for your brother/sister. Include the following information:**

- what the gadget is
- why you want to buy this gadget
- what your brother/sister will be able to do with it
- ask your friend what he/she thinks of the idea for the gadget

LIFE SKILLS How to use the Internet in a safe way

1 Jed, 16
The other day I sent a message to Amy, a girl in my class, asking her to go to the cinema. Only, it wasn't me! Someone pretended to be me. I think it was my friend, Steven, because I once told him my password. I think he sent the message to Amy as a (not very funny) joke. It was so embarrassing when I saw Amy in class the next day. I explained what happened and said I was very sorry. She didn't think it was very funny. [1]____

2 Chloe, 16
It was my sixteenth birthday last Saturday so I had a party with a few of my friends at my house. Unfortunately, one day last week I told some friends about the party on social media and gave them my address. My parents went out for the evening. At ten o'clock a large group of students arrived at the party. They were from my school but they weren't my friends. They were very loud and badly behaved and they played a stupid game in the hall. When my parents got home they were very angry because the house was a mess and the big mirror near the front door was broken. [2]____

3 Will, 15
Last week, I posted a selfie of me and my best friend Ben on my social media site. We were with some friends in the park and it was a really cool photo. Well, it was a really cool photo of me. I looked great! But it was a terrible photo of Ben. He looked completely ridiculous! Now, he's really angry with me and won't answer his phone when I call him. It was really stupid of me to post that photo but I did it without thinking. [3]____

1 In pairs, discuss the questions below.

1. What do you use the Internet for?
2. Which social networking sites do you use?
3. What are the good things about using social media?
4. What problems can you have when you use social media?

2 Read the forum posts and match gaps 1–3 with sentences A–C. Then, in pairs, say which of these problems you had.

A My dad told me to change my privacy settings so that only my close friends can see my posts in the future.
B Anyway, I'm going to change my password and I won't share it with anyone ever again.
C I'll be more careful when I share photos online in the future.

3 3.33 **Listen to someone talking about staying safe online. Complete her advice with the words from the box. Then match tips a–d to forum entries 1–3 opposite. There is one extra tip.**

check cyberbully horrible identity online passwords post ~~settings~~ share social strangers

a Think about your privacy [1]*settings*. It isn't a very good idea if people you don't know – complete [2]_________ – can see what you're posting [3]_________, so please [4]_________ your settings carefully.
b Think carefully before you [5]_________ a photo. Would the other people in the photo be happy to see it on [6]_________ media?
c Keep all your [7]_________ secret. Don't [8]_________ them with anyone. That way you can protect your [9]_________.
d Never say anything [10]_________ about another person online. Don't be a [11]_________. And if someone is horrible to you, tell your parents or your teacher.

4 3.33 **Listen again and check your answers.**

5 Read the advice in the box below. Are you a smart Internet user? In groups, say how often you follow each piece of advice – always, sometimes or never.

A *Do you ever share your passwords?*
B *No, I don't.*
C *Sometimes. My sister knows one of my passwords so that she can post things on my site.*

LIFE SKILLS | How to use the Internet in a safe way

1. Don't share your password with other people.
2. Don't share personal information online.
3. Be nice to other people when you're online.
4. Check your privacy settings on social media sites.
5. Be careful when you post photos on the Internet.

6 In pairs, look at the situations below and say what advice you can give each person.

1. Once I told my brother my Facebook password and yesterday he sent a message from me to a boy at my school. The message said, HAPPY VALENTINE'S DAY! It was really embarrassing!
2. There's a girl in my class who's always horrible to me. She always tells other people that I'm stupid. So last week I sent a message to her. I wrote, 'No one in our class likes you because you're so unfriendly'.
3. I got a message on Facebook from someone I don't know this morning. He said he liked all my photos and he wants to meet me after school.
4. Once I went to a party dressed as Dracula. I posted a photo on Facebook and now all my teachers call me 'Dracula'. It's so annoying!

7 REFLECT | Values In groups of four, discuss these statements. Do you agree with them? Say why.

1. When you post messages to people on social media, imagine you are speaking to them face-to-face.
2. Respect other people when you are online.
3. A person that you only know online isn't a real friend.
4. When you post a comment or a photo on social media, it will be online forever.

8 Do the task below in pairs.

LIFE SKILLS | Project

A With your partner, agree a personal action plan for how you will use social media sites in the future. Write the action plan on a piece of paper.
B Go online and make any necessary changes to your social media account(s).
C Tell the rest of the class what action you took to improve your safety online.

INTERNET SAFETY ACTION PLAN
1 I will change my passwords.
2 I won't ...
3
4
5

09 Fit and healthy

VOCABULARY Sports, equipment, body and health

GRAMMAR *Must/mustn't, have to/don't have to, should/shouldn't*
Use of English > page 173

SPEAKING Talking about illness

WRITING An online forum post

VIDEO Grammar ▷ Communication ▷ Documentary ▷

UNUSUAL SPORTS

Fed up with football? Bored with basketball? Tired of tennis? Well, don't worry because in this week's blog post we're looking at some unusual sports and they're great fun!

Cycle ball, or radball, is basically playing football on a bike in a gym. There are two players in each team. They have to hit the ball with their heads or the front wheels of their bikes. They mustn't put their feet on the ground at any time. The goalkeepers can use their hands to defend but the other players mustn't touch the ball with their hands. It's simple and fun but you must be good at riding a bike if you want to play radball.

When you go kayaking, you usually look for water. But snow kayakers have to find some snow. It's great fun but you must be fit and strong to do this sport. That's because you have to carry your kayak to the top of a hill before you can start and kayaks are heavy! Do you have to have any particular skills to kayak down a hill? Well, you don't have to be a good skier, although it probably helps if you are, but you must like snow. If you aren't afraid of going very, very fast, check it out. It's so cool!

9A GRAMMAR AND VOCABULARY

1 SPEAKING In pairs, ask and answer the questions.

1. What's your favourite sport?
2. How often do you play it?
3. Is it a popular sport in your country? Say why.

2 Look at the photos of two sports. Do you know what they are and what is unusual about them? Read the text and check your answers.

Must/mustn't/have to/don't have to

3 Read the examples and complete the sentences with *must*, *mustn't*, *have to* or *don't have to*.

You must be good at riding a bike.
You don't have to be a good skier.
Snow kayakers have to find some snow.
They mustn't put their feet on the ground.

1. We use ________ / ________ when something is necessary.
2. We use ________ when something isn't necessary.
3. We use ________ when something isn't allowed.

Must/mustn't/have to/don't have to

must/have to = it's necessary

You **must** be really fit to do this sport.
They **must** have a healthy diet.
You **have to** run fast.
She **has to** be a very good swimmer.
Does he **have to** practise every day?
Do you **have to** know the rules?

don't have to = it isn't necessary

You **don't have to** know the rules.
He **doesn't have to** use special equipment.

mustn't = it isn't allowed

They **mustn't** touch the ball with their hands.

Grammar Reference and Practice > page 169

4 3.34 Complete the conversation with the correct words. Listen and check.

Jules What are you reading, Alex?
Alex It's a blog post about unusual sports, this article's about Octopush.
Jules Is that when someone [1]*has to / have to* fight an octopus?
Alex No, it's like underwater hockey in a swimming pool.
Jules Wow! You [2]*don't have to / have to* be good at swimming to do that.
Alex Yes, you [3]*must / mustn't* hold your breath for a long time too.
Jules Do you [4]*have to / have* know the rules of hockey?
Alex No, you [5]*don't have to / mustn't* be an expert hockey player but you [6]*don't have to / mustn't* be afraid of the water.
Jules It's not for me then!

5 Complete the swimming pool rules with *must/mustn't* and the verbs in the box.

eat have ~~leave~~ push run use

VICTORIA POOL RULES

You [1]*must leave* your clothes and shoes in the changing room.
You [2]________ a shower before entering the pool.
You [3]________ or drink in the pool area, only in the canteen.
You [4]________ other people into the pool.
You [5]________ around the swimming pool.
Small children [6]________ the pool with an adult.

6 Put the words from the box in the correct column of the table.

~~aerobics~~ athletics ~~basketball~~ ~~climbing~~ cycling hockey horse riding judo karate mountain biking rugby skateboarding swimming tennis volleyball yoga

do	go	play
aerobics	*climbing*	*basketball*

7 Write two things you don't have to do and two things you mustn't do when you practise one of the sports from Exercise 6. Then guess your partner's sport.

A *You don't have to do this with other people. You don't have to use special equipment. You mustn't talk when you do this.*
B *Is it yoga?*

8 SPEAKING Discuss in pairs. Would you like to be an elite sportsperson? Say why.

26 Read the question and watch the video. Say what the speakers answer. Then in pairs, ask and answer the question.

What do you have to do to be a professional sportsperson?

☐ **I can use *must, mustn't, have to, don't have to* to talk about necessity.**

9B LISTENING AND VOCABULARY

1 **SPEAKING In groups of four, ask and answer questions to find out who likes sport the most.**

I play basketball three times a week, I go to football matches every weekend and I watch a lot of sport on TV. What about you?

2 **In groups, work out the meaning of the highlighted words in the quiz. Then do the quiz and check your answers on page 175.**

QUIZ WHAT DO YOU KNOW ABOUT SPORT?

1 **How high is a tennis net in centimetres?**
a 50 cm **b** 91 cm **c** 140 cm

2 **The first trophy for the FIFA World Cup was called the Jules Rimet Trophy. Who was Jules Rimet?**
a a lawyer and president of FIFA
b a French footballer
c the sculptor of the trophy

3 **Do you use a bat or a racket in these sports?**
tennis badminton table tennis baseball cricket

4 **Which player always wears gloves in a football team?**

5 **How wide is a football goal in metres?**
a 5.5 m **b** 7.3 m **c** 9.1 m

6 **Think of three sports that you usually have to wear a helmet for.**

7 **When did people start using swimming goggles?**
a the 14th century **b** the 18th century
c the 20th century

8 **What is the best colour for a life jacket?**
a grey **b** black **c** orange

3 **SPEAKING Which of the things in the quiz have you got at home? How often do you use them? Discuss in pairs.**

4 **You are going to listen to four conversations. Study Active Listening. Then look at the photos in Exercise 6. Which words do you predict you will hear?**

1 mountain biking, bike, gloves, ...

ACTIVE LISTENING | Predicting before listening

Before you listen:

- Read the questions and look at the pictures carefully.
- Try to predict some words you will hear.

5 **4.1 In pairs, compare your lists. Then listen to the conversations and check. How many words did you and your partner guess correctly?**

6 **4.1 Listen to the four conversations again. Choose the correct answers.**

1 What does Simon need to borrow?

A

B

C

2 What did Carla's team win?

A
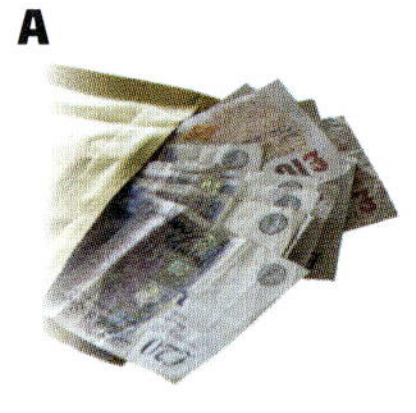
B

C

3 Which activity did Jack not want to do on Sunday?

A

B

C

4 What does Seb have before swimming competitions?

A

B

C

7 **REFLECT | Society In pairs, discuss the questions.**

1 Do cyclists have to wear a bike helmet in your country? Is it a good idea?
2 Do you always wear a bike helmet when you cycle? Why? Why not?

☐ **I can identify specific information in a conversation and talk about sport.**

9C VOCABULARY | Body

1 **SPEAKING Look at the photos and say what sports they show. Then answer the questions in pairs.**

1 Do you like these sports? Say why.

2 Which sport do you think is harder? Say why.

2 **Match items 1-20 in the photos with the words from the box. Which word is not in the photos? What does it mean?**

☐ ankle ☐ arm ☐ back ☐ body ☐ ear ☐ elbow ☐ eye [1] face ☐ finger ☐ foot ☐ hand [12] head ☐ knee ☐ leg ☐ mouth ☐ neck ☐ nose ☐ shoulder ☐ stomach ☐ toe ☐ wrist

3 **Read Emma's post on social media. What does she want to find out?**

4 **Read Rachel and Rick's comments. What sports are they talking about? How did they answer Emma's question?**

5 **4.2 PRONUNCIATION Listen and mark the words in the box with /ɪ/ or/iː/. Can you think of any other words you know in English with these sounds?**

	fit	feet	finger	knee	teeth	wrist
/ɪ/	✓					
/iː/		✓				

6 **Check you understand the adjectives below. Then for each one find an opposite adjective in the text.**

Adjective	Opposite
narrow	1 ______
round	2 ______
weak	3 ______
fat	4 ______ 5 ______

7 **SPEAKING Choose a different sportsperson. In pairs, describe his/her body. Use the texts and the adjectives from Exercise 6 to help you.**

SPORTS FORUM

EMMA: Hi all! I just wondered... How is your body different if you're a professional sportsperson?

RACHEL: Marathon runners are often slim. I run a lot every day and I have a flat stomach and thin arms. My friend is not thin and she's a great runner too! But we have to have strong legs. When you run long distances, it's important to wear very good running shoes to protect your feet, toes and ankles.

RICK: Tennis players usually have wide shoulders and a strong back. Also, we play with one arm so it's stronger than the other one. For example, I play with my left hand so my left arm, hand and even my wrist and the fingers are stronger.

What should you do
to get fit?

1 DO IT EVERY DAY

- Exercise should be part of your daily routine like brushing your teeth or doing your homework.
- You shouldn't take the lift, you should walk up the stairs.
- You shouldn't go to school by car. Instead, you should walk or cycle.
- If you have to take the bus, you should get off a couple of stops from school and walk (or run) the rest of the way.
- You shouldn't spend so much time in front of screens. You should get outside more.
- When you listen to music, you shouldn't sit still. You should get up and dance.

2 MAKE SURE IT'S FUN

You [1]*should* do a sport but you [2]________ do one you dislike. If you like being with people, you [3]________ try a team sport or join a gym. If you like your own company, you [4]________ choose an individual sport. But the main thing is you [5]________ have fun.

NO PAIN, NO GAIN?

[6]________ exercise hurt? Whatever exercise you do, it [7]________ be something that makes you breathe hard. You [8]________ stop as soon as it gets hard but you [9]________ do too much, either.

TAKE CARE OF YOURSELF

You [10]________ always warm up before you start. You [11]________ use cheap sports equipment.

9D GRAMMAR AND VOCABULARY

1 SPEAKING **What do you do to get fit? Discuss in pairs.**

2 **Read Part 1 of the leaflet. In pairs, say how often you follow the recommendations in the leaflet.**

I don't do exercise every day, only at weekends or in PE class. What about you?

Should/shouldn't

3 **Read the sentences from the leaflet and decide if grammar explanations 1–3 are true or false.**

What should you do to get fit?
Exercise should be part of your daily routine.
You shouldn't take the lift.

1 ☐ We use *should/shouldn't* to say something is a good idea.
2 ☐ We use *should/shouldn't* to give advice.
3 ☐ *Should/Shouldn't* have different forms for different persons.

4 **Study the Grammar box to check your answers to Exercise 3. Then find more examples of *should* and *shouldn't* in the leaflet.**

Should/shouldn't

We use ***should/shouldn't*** to say something is a good idea or to give advice.

	I • You • He • She • It • We • They
+	I **should do** regular exercise.
–	You **shouldn't eat** too much.
?	**Should** we **drink** more water? Yes, we **should**./No, we **shouldn't**.

Grammar Reference and Practice > page 169

5 **Complete Part 2 of the leaflet with *should* or *shouldn't*. Then, in pairs, say if you agree or disagree with the recommendations in the leaflet.**

6 **Read the health problems below and work out the meaning of the highlighted expressions.**

1 I ran 10 kilometres and now my feet hurt and I've got a backache.
2 I spent all weekend in my room gaming and now I feel sick and I've got a headache.
3 I went snowboarding yesterday and now I've got a temperature and a sore throat.
4 I spent hours watching TV series and eating chocolate and now I've got a toothache and my stomach hurts.

WATCH OUT!

*My arm **hurts**. I'**ve got** a backache.*

7 SPEAKING **In pairs, think of advice to health problems in Exercise 6. Use *should/shouldn't* and the prompts below.**

do more sport go for a walk go to bed with a hot drink
not eat so much not play video games so much
not run so far next time see a doctor/dentist
take some aspirin warm up before you start
wear a hat and a scarf next time wear better trainers

☐ **I can use *should* and *shouldn't* to give an opinion or advice.**

9E SPEAKING

1 **In pairs, describe the photo. What do you think is going to happen?**

2 **27 4.3 Read and watch or listen. Why does Martin want to catch his sister's illness?**

Thursday morning ...

Mum Jo, what's the matter?
Jo I feel sick and my stomach hurts.
Mum Come here ... Let me see ... Oh, dear! You've got a temperature. You shouldn't go to school today.
Martin I wasn't well last week and I went to school.
Mum You only had a cold. Jo, you should try to eat something.
Jo Martin, do you want my cereal? I can't eat it.
Martin No, thanks. I don't want to be sick. And I've got exams next week. Actually, ...
Jo What are you doing?
Martin I'm going to eat your cereal! Maybe I'll be in bed next week too. Then I can't do my exams!
Jo Martin!
Martin Get well soon!

Friday afternoon ...

Martin How are you feeling, Jo?
Jo I feel a lot better. I'll be fine for Jake's party, I think.
Martin What?
Jo You look terrible, Martin. Are you feeling alright?
Mum Let's see ... You've got the same thing as Jo.
Martin But I'm meeting friends later. And Saturday is Jake's party!
Mum Sorry, Martin. You must go to bed. Jo's illness only lasted two days. You'll be OK for your exams next week!
Martin Oh, no!

3 **27 4.3 Study the Speaking box. Use the prompts to write sentences about Martin and Jo's health problems and the results. Watch or listen again and check.**

1 Martin/last week
2 Jo/Thursday
3 Martin/Friday

SPEAKING | Talking about illness

Asking about someone's health

What's the matter?
How are you feeling?
Are you feeling alright?
What's wrong?

Describing how you're feeling/symptoms

I don't feel well.
I feel sick.
I can't sleep.
I've got (a sore throat).
My (stomach) hurts.
I feel (a lot) better.

Showing sympathy

I hope you feel better soon.
Get well soon.

Giving advice

You should (try to eat some breakfast).
You shouldn't (go to school today).
You must (go to bed).
Why don't you ...?

4 **4.4 Study the Speaking box again. Then put the conversation in the correct order. Listen and check.**

a ☐ **Doctor** OK. I'll just have a look. Well, the ear seems to be healthy. Does anything else hurt?
b ☐ **Doctor** I see. Can I look? Say 'Ah'.
c ☐ **James** It's my left ear. It really hurts.
d ☐ **James** Ah.
e ☐ **Doctor** Which side? Or is it both?
f ☐ **Doctor** You're welcome. I hope you feel better soon.
g ☐ **James** Hi Doctor. I've got earache. It's really bad.
h ☐ **James** I've got a sore throat too.
i [1] **Doctor** Sit down, James. How are you feeling today?
j ☐ **James** Ah, OK. I'll call my dentist this afternoon. Thanks Doctor.
k ☐ **Doctor** OK. Ah. There's a problem with the tooth at the back. You must see a dentist, James.

5 **Complete the short conversations with the phrases from the box.**

eat anything sweet go to the hospital ~~lie on the floor~~ sit down take a paracetamol

A My back hurts.
B Why don't you [1]*lie on the floor*?

A I've got a headache
B You should [2]__________.

A My arm hurts and I can't move it.
B You must [3]__________.

A I have toothache.
B You shouldn't [4]__________.

A My legs feel weak.
B Why don't you [5]__________?

6 **In pairs, take turns to role play the situations. Student A, go to page 175. Student B go to page 176. Then change roles.**

☐ **I can ask and talk about health and illness.**

9F READING AND VOCABULARY

1 SPEAKING **In pairs, look at the pictures. What do you think is difficult when you live or work in space?**

2 **Read the text and check your answers. Did you learn anything new?**

3 **Read the text again and choose the correct answers.**

1 You must have an easy-going personality in space because
a it's hard to study science.
b it helps you stay physically fit.
c you need to stay friends with others.
d you may be on your own a lot.

2 What must you experience to prepare for space?
a Long distance walking
b Zero gravity
c Bad weather
d Extreme team sports

3 Sleeping in space is hard because it's often
a dirty.
b light.
c hot.
d dark.

4 What happens to you in space at first but then stops?
a You feel weak.
b You grow.
c Your head hurts.
d Your skin turns brown.

5 Which activity don't astronauts do inside the spaceship?
a Gymnastics
b Baseball
c Basketball
d Golf

6 Which sentence gives the best summary of the text?
a What you need to know to become an astronaut.
b A step-by-step guide to space travel.
c The history of life in space.
d Why don't young people today want to become astronauts?

4 **Match the highlighted words from the text with definitions 1–6.**

1 It's a red liquid that moves oxygen around your body. You can't live without it. *blood*
2 It's an organ that moves blood around your body. It's the symbol of love.
3 They help you move your arms and legs. If you train a lot they get bigger.
4 They're hard and sportspeople sometimes break them.
5 This covers and protects the whole of your body.
6 You think and remember with this.

5 SPEAKING **In pairs, ask and answer the questions.**

What should you do to have:

- strong muscles/bones?
- a happy mind?
- a healthy heart?
- healthy skin?

You have to do yoga or go to the gym to develop strong muscles.

6 REFLECT | Society **What is important for good teamwork? In pairs or small groups, discuss the question.**

agree with others be creative be flexible
do what you want follow the rules listen to others
respect people solve problems take turns

A *In my opinion, you should agree with others.*
B *I don't agree! Sometimes people have really crazy ideas you don't have to accept!*

▷ *28* WATCH AND REFLECT **Go to page 158. Watch the documentary *Life in zero gravity* and do the exercises.**

q&a So you want to go to space?

4.5

CAN ANYONE BE AN ASTRONAUT?
Of course, not. For a start, if you want to be an astronaut, you have to be able to speak English, the international language of space. You don't have to have a Science degree but most astronauts do. Most of them are pilots too. Life in a spaceship is physically and mentally hard so you must have a healthy body and mind. You need to be easy-going, patient, and helpful to spend so much time in a small space with other people.

WHAT'S THE TRAINING LIKE?
Candidates have to train for a year to learn how to stay healthy and safe. They practise space walking and living in zero gravity. They train in extreme conditions with limited equipment and food to learn how to solve problems and to work in a team. Everyday tasks like eating, washing and sleeping can be complicated on a spaceship. There is no running water so you have to wash with wet tissues; it's hard to enjoy the dry food that astronauts have to eat. And to sleep you must cover your eyes because the sun rises every 90 minutes on the International Space Station (ISS). You also have to attach yourself to something so you don't fly away!

WHAT HEALTH PROBLEMS DO ASTRONAUTS HAVE?
Life in zero gravity causes changes to our bodies. Bones and muscles become thin and weak so you must do a lot of exercise in space to stay fit and to help the heart move blood around your body. Astronauts often get backache because you actually grow in space – up to 8 centimetres! It's also common to have headaches and to feel sick, especially at the beginning. You have to take vitamins to replace fresh fruit and vegetables. But you don't have to put on sun cream because space suits protect your skin from radiation.

CAN YOU PLAY SPORTS IN SPACE?
According to NASA, astronauts on board the ISS spend most of their time working and exercising (they do a lot of gymnastics). But they also enjoy playing sports like baseball and basketball. One time, an astronaut even hit golf balls into space while space walking. As you can imagine, playing ball games in zero gravity is not the same as on Earth but it's still fun!

ARE YOU STILL INTERESTED?
So now you know. If you want to go to space, study hard, learn to fly and take care of your body and mind.

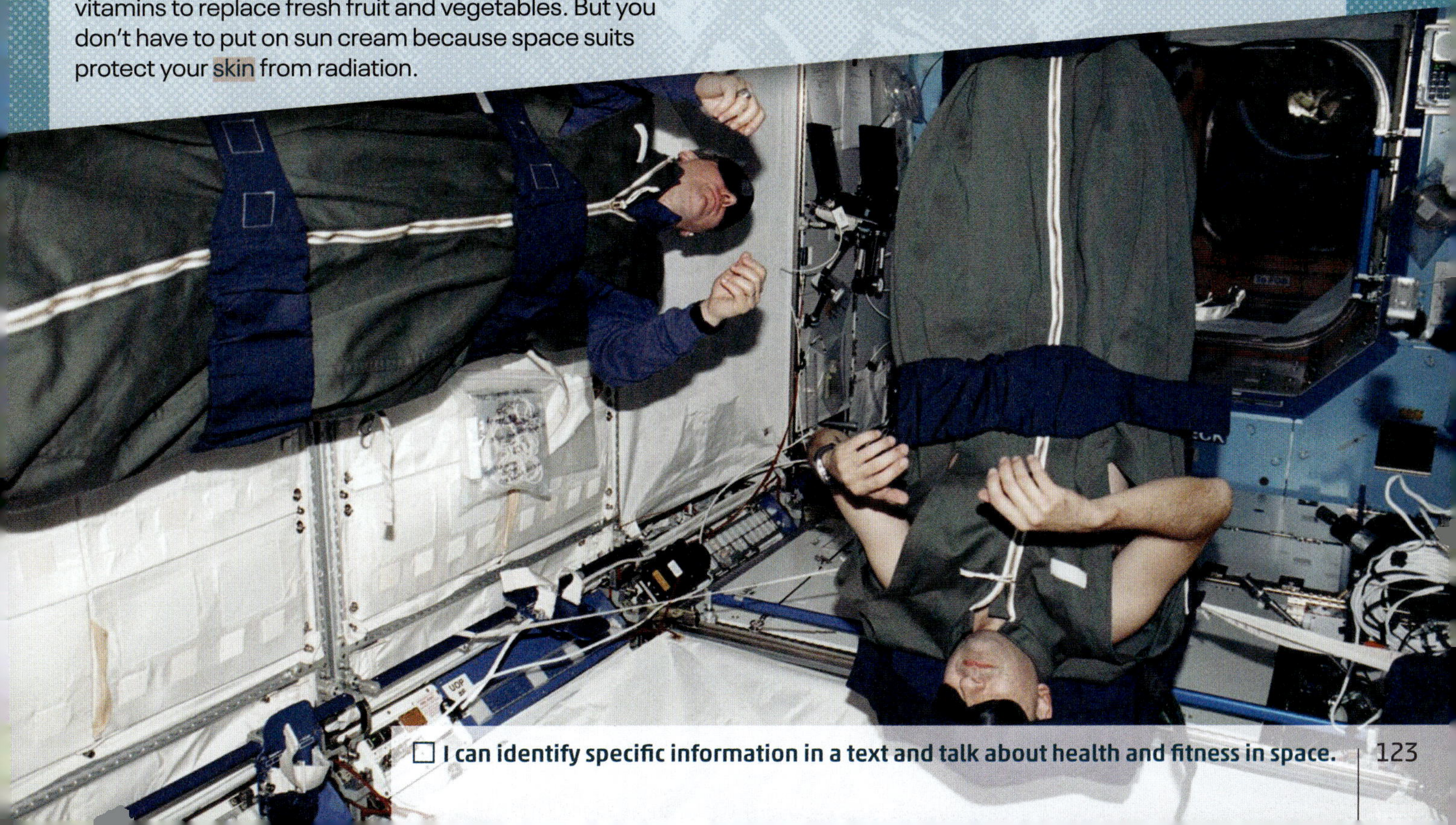

☐ **I can identify specific information in a text and talk about health and fitness in space.**

9G WRITING | An online forum post

1 SPEAKING **Which of the things below worry you about your health and fitness?**

bad diet   problems concentrating   feeling tired/no energy   no exercise/fresh air   not enough/too much sleep   stress   too much technology

I worry about my bad diet, but I don't worry about stress.

2 **Read the online posts and match them with the problems from Exercise 1.**

SPEAK OUT! | STUDENT FORUM

Libby (16)

I never manage to go to bed early during the week even when I know I have to get up for school in the morning. This **also** means I often miss the bus to school. And when I'm in class and I know I must concentrate properly – I can't, so the teachers complain **too**. The truth is I find it hard to fall asleep, but I don't really understand why! I know I shouldn't use my phone or tablet late at night but I always do. I **also** have no energy during the day which is really annoying! Have you got experience of being a zombie **too**? Help!

Tom (17)

My problem is I don't get enough exercise or fresh air and my diet is bad [1]_________!
I know I shouldn't miss breakfast but I often do, so I'm always hungry by the morning break. At college you don't have to go far for unhealthy food – there are self-service machines with lots of sugary snacks and fizzy drinks [2]_________. There is [3]_________ a fast food café where my friends and I go for lunch. We can [4]_________ walk to the local shops to buy healthier food but they're quite far away so we don't do that very often. I [5]_________ tried preparing my food at home but I kept forgetting to bring it to college with me! PLEASE give me some advice on how to become a better and healthier me!

3 **Read Libby's post again and complete the rules with *too* or *also*.**

1. We use the linking word _________ before the verb (but after the verb *to be*).
2. We use the linking word _________ at the end of the sentence.

4 **Read Tom's post and complete it with *too* and *also*.**

5 **Study the Writing box. Read the examples from Libby and Tom's posts. Find more examples.**

WRITING | An online forum post

Give details about the problem:
I never manage to go to bed early during the week.
This means I usually miss breakfast so I'm tired but I'm **also** hungry.
It **also** means I often miss the bus to school.
I **also** have problem concentrating in class.

Say how you feel about it:
I feel bad and the teachers complain **too**.
I'm **also** annoyed because I have no energy.
The truth is I find it hard to fall asleep.

Say how you tried to solve the problem(s):
I also tried preparing my food at home.

Ask for advice:
Have you got experience of being a zombie **too**? Help!

6 WRITING TASK **Write a post on the student forum. In your post:**

- explain what the problem is.
- say how it makes you feel.
- ask for advice.

☐ **I can write an online forum post.**

9A GRAMMAR AND VOCABULARY 5.57

aerobics n /eə'rəʊbɪks/
athletics n /æθ'letɪks/
basketball n /'bɑːskətbɔːl/
climbing n /'klaɪmɪŋ/
competitive adj /kəm'petətɪv/
cycling n /'saɪklɪŋ/
defend v /dɪ'fend/
goalkeeper n /gəʊl'kiːpə/
gymnastics n /dʒɪm'næstɪks/
hit the ball (with your head) /hɪt ðə bɔːl (wɪð jə hed)/
hockey n /'hɒki/
horse riding n /hɔːs 'raɪdɪŋ/
hurt yourself v /hɜːt jɔː'self/
judo n /'dʒuːdəʊ/
karate n /kə'rɑːti/
kayaker n /kaɪækə/
kayaking n /kaɪækɪŋ/
mountain biking n /'maʊntɪn 'baɪkɪŋ/
rugby n /'rʌgbi/
skateboarding n /'skeɪtbɔːdɪŋ/
snow n /snəʊ/
swimming n /'swɪmɪŋ/
tennis n /'tenɪs/
underwater n /ˌʌndə'wɔːtə/
volleyball n /'vɒlibɔːl/
win v /wɪn/
yoga n /'jəʊgə/

9B LISTENING AND VOCABULARY 5.58

alarm clock n /ə'lɑːm klɒk/
baseball / cricket bat n /'beɪsbɔːl / 'krɪkɪt bæt/
cyclist n /'saɪkləst, 'saɪklɪst/
field n /fiːld/
FIFA World Cup n /'fiːfə wɜːld kʌp/
football goal n /'fʊtbɔːl gəʊl/
football team n /'fʊtbɔːl tiːm/
footballer n /'fʊtbɔːlə/
gloves n /glʌvz/
goalkeeper n /'gəʊlˌkiːpə/
helmet n /'helmɪt/
life jacket n /laɪf 'dʒækɪt/
swimming goggles n /'swɪmɪŋ 'gɒgəlz/
table tennis bat n /'teɪbəl 'tenɪs bæt/
tennis / badminton racket n /'tenɪs / 'bædmɪntən 'rækɪt/
tennis net n /'tenɪs net/
towel n /'taʊəl/
trophy n /'trəʊfi/

9C VOCABULARY 5.59

ankle n /'æŋkəl/
arm n /ɑːm/
back n /bæk/
body n /bɒdi/
ear n /ɪə/
elbow n /'elbəʊ/
eye n /aɪ/
face n /feɪs/
fat adj /fæt/
flat adj /flæt/
finger n /'fɪŋgə/
foot (pl. feet) n /fʊt/fiːt/
hand n /hænd/
hard adj /hɑːd/
head n /hed/
knee n /niː/
leg n /leg/
mouth n /maʊθ/
narrow adj /nærəʊ/
neck n /nek/
nose n /nəʊz/
round adj /raʊnd/
shoulder n /'ʃəʊldə/
slim adj /slɪm/
soft adj /sɒft/
stomach n /'stʌmək/
strong adj /strɒŋ/
toe n /təʊ/
tooth (pl. teeth) n /tuːθ/tiːθ/
weak adj /wiːk/
wide adj /waɪd/
wrist n /rɪst/

9D GRAMMAR AND VOCABULARY 5.60

feel sick /fiːl sɪk/
go to the dentist /gəʊ tə ðə 'dentɪst/
have a headache / toothache / backache / stomach ache / earache /hæv eɪ 'hedeɪk / 'tuːθ-eɪk / 'bækeɪk / 'stʌmək eɪk/
have a sore throat /hæv eɪ sɔː θrəʊt/
have a temperature v / hæv eɪ 'temprətʃə/
have an earache /hæv ən 'ɪəreɪk/
hurt v /hɜːt/
see a doctor /siː eɪ 'dɒktə/
take some aspirin /teɪk səm 'æsprɪn/

9E SPEAKING 5.61

feel alright /fiːl ˌɔːl'raɪt/
feel weak /fiːl wiːk/
have a cold v /hæv eɪ kəʊld/
illness n /'ɪlnəs/
symptom n /'sɪmptəm/

9F READING AND VOCABULARY 5.62

astronaut n /'æstrənɔːt/
blood n /blʌd/
bone n /bəʊn/
candidate n /'kændədət/
dry food n /draɪ fuːd/
extreme conditions n /ɪk'striːm kən 'dɪʃ ənz/
grow v /grəʊ/
health problems n /helθ 'prɒb ləmz/
heart n /hɑːt/
International Space Station n /ˌɪntə'næʃənəl speɪs 'steɪʃən/
liquid n /'lɪkwɪd/
mind n /maɪnd/
muscle n /'mʌsəl/
organ n /'ɔːgən/
pilot n /'paɪlət/
protect something from (radiation) v /prə'tekt 'sʌmθɪŋ frəm (ˌreɪdi'eɪʃən)/
running water n /'rʌnɪŋ 'wɔːtə/
skin n /skɪn/
space suit n /speɪs suːt/
space travel n /speɪs 'trævəl/
survive v /sə'vaɪv/
train to be (an astronaut) v /ˌtreɪn tə ˌbi (ən 'æstrənɔːt)/
zero gravity n /'zɪərəʊ 'grævəti/

9G WRITING 5.63

bad diet n /bæd 'daɪət/
fizzy drink n /'fɪzi drɪŋk/
fresh air n /freʃ eə/
stress n /stres/
sugary snacks n /'ʃʊgəri snæks/

Remember More > page 174

VOCABULARY AND GRAMMAR

1 Complete the sports collocations.

~~aerobics~~ climbing cycling hockey judo karate kayaking rugby swimming tennis volleyball yoga

do *aerobics*, ________, ________, ________
go ________, ________, ________, ________
play ________, ________, ________, ________

2 Complete the sentences with the words from the box.

bat gloves goggles life jacket ~~net~~ trophy

1 You must hit the ball over the *net* in tennis.
2 You should wear swimming ________ under water – they help you see better.
3 Goalkeepers have to wear ________ in football and hockey to protect their hands.
4 Which country has got the World Cup ________ now?
5 You have to play cricket with a ________ not a racket!
6 You shouldn't go kayaking without a ________.

3 Look at the pictures and write the parts of the body.

1 *ankle*

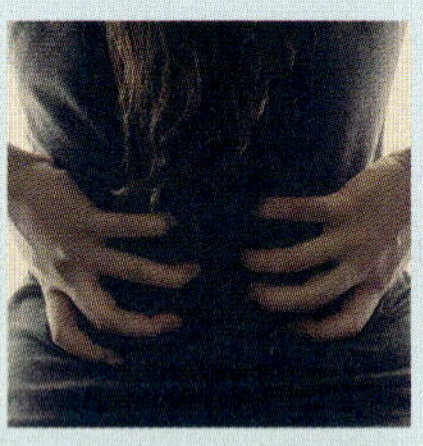
2 ________

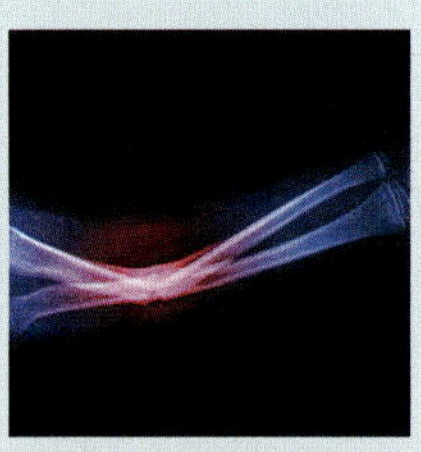
3 ________

4 ________

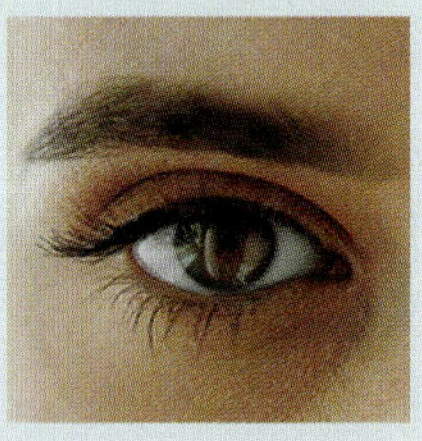
5 ________

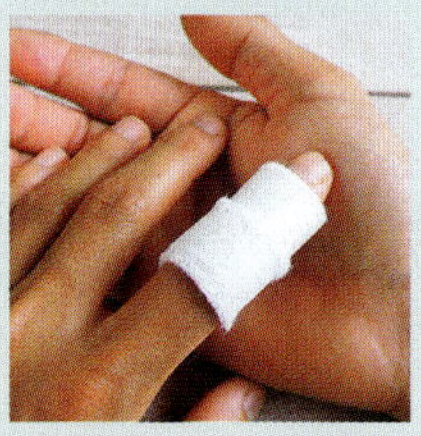
6 ________

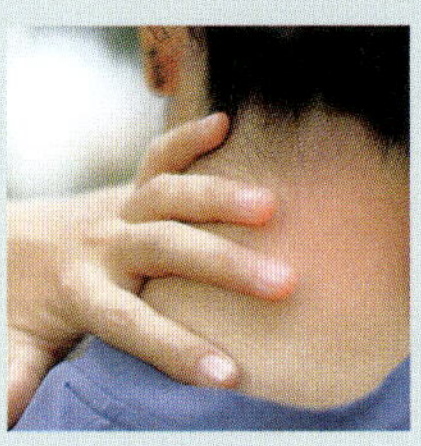
7 ________

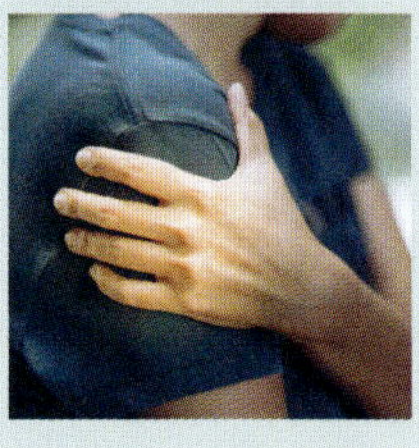
8 ________

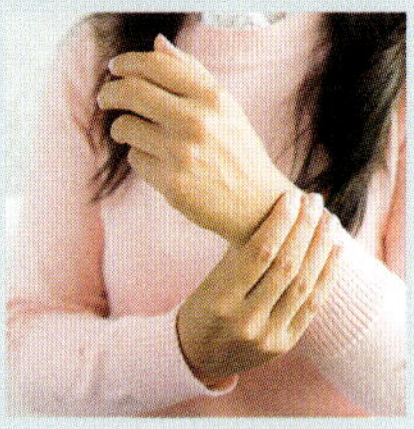
9 ________

4 Complete the conversation with one word in each gap.

Megan You look terrible, Owen! Are you feeling [1]*alright*?
Owen No, I don't feel very [2]________.
Megan What's the [3]________?
Owen My stomach [4]________.
Megan Your face feels hot. Have you got a [5]________?
Owen No, but I feel [6]________. I really can't eat!
Megan Maybe you should go to the [7]________.
Owen Good idea. I hope I feel [8]________ soon!

5 Choose the correct words to complete the school gym rules.

RULES FOR USING THE SCHOOL GYM

1 You *must* / *mustn't* bring bags into the gym. Someone could fall over them and get hurt.
2 You *don't have* to / *mustn't* wear special gym clothes, just comfortable clothes.
3 You *have to* / *don't have to* wait for the teacher before entering the gym for safety reasons.
4 You *don't have to* / *mustn't* play on the equipment at any time.
5 You *have to* / *mustn't* help others to use the equipment if you can.
6 You *must* / *don't have to* put everything away at the end of the lesson, ready for the next class.

6 Read the problems and write suggestions using *should* or *shouldn't*.

1 I can't sleep at night.
2 I need to lose weight.
3 I'm stressed about my exams.
4 I'm hungry all the time.
5 I don't like fruit and vegetables.
6 I often get hurt during football practice.

USE OF ENGLISH

7 Complete the text with one word in each gap.

WHAT SHOULD YOU DO IF YOU FIND A PERSON ON THE GROUND

First you [1]*should* say something to see if the person can hear you, but you [2]________ move them.

To check if they are breathing, you [3]________ to put your ear near their face and listen carefully.

If they are not breathing, gently push their [4]________ back to let air come in through their nose and mouth.

Next, go down on your [5]________ next to the person and put your two [6]________ over their heart.

Push down hard thirty times and then breathe into their [7]________ twice.

You [8]________ repeat the process until the ambulance arrives.

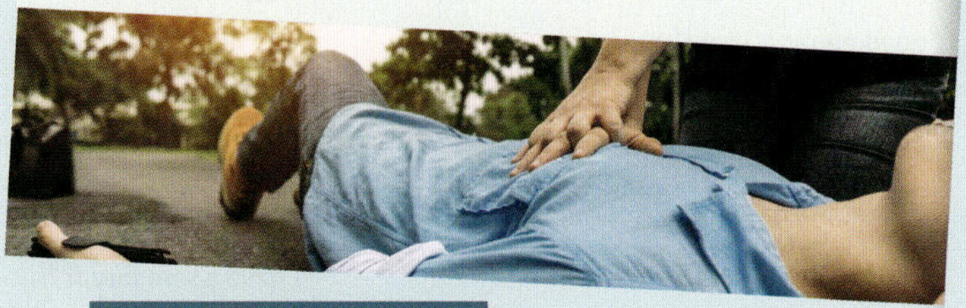

Use of English > page 173

READING

8 **Read the text. Match sentences A–H with gaps 1–5 in the text. There are three extra sentences.**

STRATEGY | Gapped text

Read the text ignoring the gaps to understand its general meaning. Then try to choose the missing information to complete the text. Pay special attention to the words that come before and after the gaps.

A Alistair Brownlee is fitter than his brother, Jonny.
B He wants to win another gold medal at the next Olympic Games.
C Jonny finished second in the Olympic Games in Rio de Janeiro in 2016.
D What kind of training does Alistair do to prepare for triathlons?
E Sometimes, I even do the three sports on the same day!
F In a triathlon you have to do three sports, one after the other.
G He isn't going to take part in the triathlon at the next Olympic Games.
H After doing this, they go to the running track, where they usually run for about seventy-five minutes.

SPEAKING

9 **Look at the photo showing a sports star with an injury. In pairs, take turns to describe what you can see in the photo and answer the questions below.**

1 What's the matter with the footballer?
2 How is he feeling?
3 What's going to happen next?

WRITING

10 **Do the task below.**

Write a short story about someone who has a sports injury. Include the following information:

- where the person was and when it happened
- how he/she got the injury
- the part of the body he/she hurt
- what happened after he/she got the injury

my dream is … to do a marathon

I like keeping fit so I cycle to work during the week. I go running on Saturdays and I go swimming on Sundays. [1]___ My dream is to take part in a triathlon. It's one of the hardest sporting competitions in the world. [2]___ First, you have to swim 1.5 kilometres, then you have to cycle forty kilometres and, finally, you have to run ten kilometres.

Last week, I decided to find out how to prepare for one. I know that you have to be incredibly fit to compete in triathlons. So the first thing I did was to find out everything about the world's best ever triathlete: Alistair Brownlee, the British athlete who won gold medals at the Olympic Games in both 2012 and 2016.

[3]___ Every day he trains with his younger brother, Jonny, who is also a top triathlete. They get up at 6.15, have a quick breakfast of muesli or cereals and at 7.00 they go to the pool, where they swim for one and a half hours. [4]___ Then they work out in the gym for an hour or so before having a break for lunch – usually a sandwich or a bowl of pasta – at around 12.30. In the afternoon they start training again, riding their bikes for three hours in the countryside near the town of Leeds in the north of England.

Clearly, Alistair is a very determined person. [5]___ He knows that the only way he will be able to be an Olympic champion again is to train for five or six hours every day, follow a special diet and go to bed early every night so that he doesn't feel tired when he trains the following day.

Alistair is one of the most successful British athletes of all time and he works extremely hard to maintain his physical fitness. He is my real hero!

10 Our planet, our hands

VOCABULARY Geographical features, animals, environment, weather

GRAMMAR Present Perfect with *ever* and *never*, Present Perfect with *already*, *just* and *yet* **Use of English** > page 173

SPEAKING Giving and reacting to personal news

WRITING An article

VIDEO Grammar ▷ Documentary ▷ Communication ▷

WILDTIME PROJECTS

If you care about animals and the environment, join us! We're looking for volunteers!

Help in Thailand

Keep the deserts in Australia healthy

Clean up beaches in Scotland

10A GRAMMAR AND VOCABULARY

1 SPEAKING **Look at the photos. Which project looks the most interesting? Say why.**

2 **Which of these geographical features can you see in the photos?**

beach coast ~~desert~~ forest hill island jungle lake mountain ocean river rocks sand sea valley waterfall

3 **Complete the sentences with words from Exercise 2.**

1. The Atacama is the driest *desert* in South America.
2. The Pacific is the largest ________ in the world. It's half the size of world's open water supply.
3. The world's highest ________ is Angel Falls in Venezuela. The water falls almost 1,000 metres!
4. About 250 people live on the ________ of Tristan da Cunha in the South Atlantic. Their nearest neighbours are 2,400 kilometres away!
5. Uluru or Ayers Rock is a large ________ in Northern Australia which is almost 350 metres high.

4 **In groups, take turns to think of one of the geographical features in Exercise 2. Then give clues to your partners to help them guess what it is.**

A *You often find this next to a valley.*
B *Is it a mountain?*
A *No, it isn't. It's similar but it isn't as high as a mountain.*
C *Is it a hill?*
A *Yes, your turn.*

5 **4.6 Listen to the interview and answer the questions.**

1. Who is Cassie talking to?
2. Which project does Cassie want to volunteer for?
3. Does Cassie like animals? How do you know?
4. What useful experience has Cassie got for this project?
5. When did she go to Thailand and what did she do there?
6. Why should Cassie speak to Simon?
7. Was Cassie successful in her interview?

Present Perfect with *ever* and *never*

6 4.7 **Read and listen to an extract from the interview. Look at the underlined sentences and choose the correct words in the sentences below.**

Maisie In your application it says you've volunteered at a zoo in the UK.
Cassie That's right.
Maisie When did you start?
Cassie I started two years ago. I haven't worked with elephants but I've worked with other animals. I've done lots of things. I've cleaned their cages, I've given them their food and ...
Maisie OK, now, this is a three-month project. Have you ever lived abroad without your family?
Cassie No, I haven't. I've never been abroad alone but I've travelled a lot with my family. In fact, we went to Thailand last year.
Maisie Oh, you've visited Thailand! Where did you go?
Cassie We visited the islands in the south. We spent a lot of time at the beach.
Maisie Well, there aren't any beaches in this project. It's in a village over 500 kilometres from the sea, on a river in the middle of the jungle!
Cassie Yes, I know. A friend of mine has volunteered on your project. Simon Tench? He's told me all about it. It sounds amazing.

1 We form the Present Perfect with the correct form of *have* / *be* and the past participle of a verb.
2 We use the Present Perfect to describe *experiences* / *everyday* activities.
3 We *use* / *don't use* past time expressions (e.g. last year, two weeks ago, yesterday) with the Present Perfect.
4 We use *ever* / *never* in questions and *ever* / *never* in negative sentences.

7 **Study the Grammar box and check your answers.**

Present Perfect with *ever* and *never*

We use the **Present Perfect** to talk about past experiences in our life when we do not say exactly when they happened.

	I • You • We • They	He • She • It
+	I **have** (**'ve**) **visited** Spain.	He **has** (**'s**) **seen** a jungle.
–	We **have not** (**haven't**) **stayed** on an island. They **have** (**'ve**) **never visited** Thailand.	He **has not** (**hasn't**) **volunteered**.
?	**Have** you (**ever**) **climbed** a mountain? Yes, I **have**./No, I **haven't**.	**Has** she (**ever**) **worked** with children? Yes, she **has**./No, she **hasn't**.

Past participles of regular verbs end in *-ed*.
There is a list of irregular past participles on page 171.

Grammar Reference and Practice > page 170

8 **Complete the sentences with the correct affirmative Present Perfect forms of the verbs in brackets.**

1 You *have met* (meet) my sister before.
2 My parents ________ (live) in another country.
3 My brother ________ (lose) two phones.
4 Sam and I ________ (try) Thai food.
5 I ________ (ride) on an elephant.

9 **Complete the sentences with the correct Present Perfect forms of the words from the box.**

never/travel ever/drive never/do visit ~~write~~

1 I *have written* three songs.
2 We ________ yoga.
3 Sara ________ many foreign countries.
4 **A** ________ your parents ________ in the UK?
B Yes, ________.
5 I ________ to the US.

10 **Write questions in the Present Perfect. Use the verbs from the box. More than one answer is sometimes possible.**

climb see sleep swim visit volunteer

1 in a forest?
2 in a lake?
3 a mountain?
4 a country in Asia?
5 on a project abroad?
6 a waterfall?

1 Have you ever slept in a forest?

WATCH OUT!

We use the Present Perfect to ask about experiences and the Past Simple to ask for more details, e.g. When? Where? etc.

A *Have you ever been to Thailand?* **B** *Yes, I have.*
A *Where did you go?* **B** *I went to Bangkok.*

11 **SPEAKING In pairs, ask and answer the questions in Exercise 10. Ask for more details.**

12 **Form new pairs and use your notes from Exercise 11 to talk about your partner's experiences.**

Anna has lived in Thailand. She spent a year there when she was four but she can't remember much about it.

29 **Read the unfinished sentence and watch the video. Say how the speakers finish the sentence. Then in pairs, finish the sentence for yourselves.**

I have never ...

☐ **I can use the Present Perfect to talk about experiences.**

Which animals ...

1 are the most dangerous to humans?
a sharks **b** mosquitoes **c** snakes

2 can predict the weather?
a ants **b** lions **c** flies

3 can jump up waterfalls?
a sharks **b** crocodiles **c** salmon

4 can't recognise themselves in a mirror?
a dolphins **b** dogs **c** penguins

5 are the same as they were 30 million years ago?
a whales **b** crocodiles **c** tigers

6 communicate by dancing?
a monkeys **b** flies **c** bees

7 can't jump?
a elephants **b** ducks **c** bees

10B VOCABULARY | Animals and animal body parts

1 **How many animals can you write in 60 seconds? Make a list and then compare it with your partner's list.**

2 **SPEAKING Look at the words in the box. Are there any animals you wrote in Exercise 1? Which can you see in the photos?**

ant bee crocodile dolphin duck elephant fly lion monkey mosquito penguin salmon shark snake tiger whale

3 **4.8 Do the quiz. Then listen and check.**

4 **SPEAKING In pairs, ask and answer the questions.**

1. Which animals in Exercise 1 live in your country?
2. How many of the animals have you seen in the wild?
3. Have you ever had a pet? What was it?

5 **Write the animals in Exercise 1 in the correct column. Then add two more animals you know to each column.**

Birds	Fish	Insects	Mammals	Reptiles
		ant		

6 **Match descriptions 1–7 with animals from Exercise 2.**

1. This is a type of cat. It has orange and black **fur**. *tiger*
2. This animal has **wings** and can fly.It makes honey.
3. This reptile has four legs, a huge mouth, with sharp **teeth**.
4. This animal uses its **tail** to help it climb trees.
5. This animal's **skin** is very thick on its body but very thin on its huge ears.
6. This bird uses its **feathers** to keep dry in the water.
7. This is the most common bird in Antarctica. It has no teeth but uses its **beak** to catch fish.

7 **4.9 PRONUNCIATION Look at the underlined vowels in the words below and put them in the correct place in the table. Listen and check.**

~~beak~~, bee, feather, head, lake, mosquito, penguin, snake, tail, teeth, weather, whale

/iː/	/e/	/eɪ/
beach *beak*	desert	dangerous

8 **SPEAKING Take turns to choose an animal from your table in Exercise 5, then describe it to your partner. How many animals can you guess in one minute?**

A *This animal has grey skin and lots of sharp teeth.*
B *A shark!*

☐ **I can talk about animals.**

10C GRAMMAR

SAVE THE PLANET

We're doing a lot to protect the environment: recycling, saving water, etc. But we haven't done enough yet. So what have you done to save the planet? Post your answers in the comments.

A  I've <u>just</u> come back from volunteering on a conservation project in Greece. I think I saw more plastic bags in the sea than fish! This must stop!

B  Our teacher asked us to calculate how much electricity we waste at home. So I'm looking for all the things that are on but we aren't using. I've <u>already</u> turned off six lights, a TV, and a computer in our house and I haven't checked all the rooms yet!

C  We've <u>just</u> finished doing this survey on recycling at our school. It's a really good way to make people think and there are prizes! Have you done it at your school <u>yet</u>?

D  We've <u>already</u> picked up almost fifty kilograms of rubbish from our local beach and it's only lunchtime! How much will we collect by the end of the day?

1 Read the messages on social media. Which person (A–D):

1 ☐ wants more people to answer some questions?
2 ☐ is doing some homework on an environmental topic?
3 ☐ is doing some volunteer work right now?
4 ☐ got home from a trip abroad a short time ago?

Present Perfect with *already*, *just* and *yet*

2 Look at the underlined words in the posts and answer the questions.

1 We use __________ in affirmative sentences for things that happened a short time ago.
2 We use __________ in affirmative sentences to say something happened earlier than we expected.
3 We use __________ at the end of negative sentences and questions to talk about something we expect to happen.
4 We put __________ and __________ after the auxiliary verb *have*.

3 Study the Grammar box and check your answers to Exercise 2.

Present Perfect with *already*, *just* and *yet*

We use the **Present Perfect** to talk about things that happened in the past but are important now.
We often use the **Present Perfect** with *already*, *just* and *yet*.

+	I**'ve just got** home. We**'ve already seen** three dolphins.
–	We **haven't been** into the jungle **yet**.
?	**Have** you **asked** Dad **yet**?

Grammar Reference and Practice > page 170

WATCH OUT!

The past participle of the verb *go* is *gone* or *been*:
*They've **gone** to the UK.* (= They are in the UK or travelling there at the moment.)
*They've **been** to the UK.* (= They went to the UK and they returned.)

4 🔊 ***4.10*** **Choose the correct words to complete the sentences.**

1 A Let's go out tonight.
B I can't. I've *already / just* got back from holiday.
2 A Have you finished your project *just / yet*?
B No! I've *just / yet* started.
3 A This is my friend, Tom.
B Hi, Tom. I think we've *already / just* met – at Carla's party.
4 A Where are you? I've *already / just* been here for ten minutes.
B Sorry. We haven't left home *already / yet*.

5 Write sentences and questions in the Present Perfect and the words in brackets.

1 My sister / pass / her driving test. (just)
2 She / go / to Thailand. (already)
3 the match / start? (yet)
4 My friends and I / finish / our exams. (already)
5 I / win / a competition. (just)
6 We / not / leave / school. (yet)

6 SPEAKING In pairs, ask and answer questions about your partner's day using the Present Perfect and *already*, *just* and *yet*. Add information using the Past Simple.

- (do) any homework?
- (post) any photos, questions or comments online?
- (plan) your weekend?
- (download) any apps on your phone?
- (read) the news?

A *Have you done any homework yet?*
B *Yes, I've already done Maths. I did it at lunchtime. But I haven't done English yet.*

☐ **I can use the Present Perfect to talk about past events that are important now.**

Say 'no' to PLASTIC BAGS

4.11

Close your eyes for a second and imagine a beautiful tropical beach. Now, imagine the same beach covered in ugly plastic waste. Terrible, isn't it? Well, that picture inspired sisters Isabel and Melati Wijsen from the island of Bali to start an environmental campaign to stop plastic pollution. And now their campaign has spread across the world.

Bali is one of 17,000 islands in Indonesia. It is a popular tourist destination which is famous for its weather, beaches, mountains and forests, as well as wildlife, such as birds, monkeys, dolphins and sharks. But every year, during the wet season, wind pushes a 100 tonnes of plastic from the sea onto the beaches. It takes hundreds of people and thirty-five lorries to remove it all. The next day it's back again.

After a school lesson about world leaders, Isabel and Melati started thinking. How could they, as schoolchildren, make a difference to the world? The girls wrote a list of Bali's problems and agreed that plastic pollution was the most important. They found out that Rwanda, a very poor country in Africa, decided to ban plastic bags in 2008. The girls agreed this is what they wanted to happen in Bali. But to do that, they needed help. So they started *Bye Bye Plastic Bags* (BBPB) – a campaign to stop plastic bags polluting the beautiful beaches of Bali.

The first thing they tried to do was to collect a million signatures from supporters. Soon they realised this could take a long time and they were impatient for action. So once they had 100,000 signatures, they presented the petition to the local government and asked for a meeting. While they waited, the girls, and other volunteers on the campaign, gave presentations at schools, markets and festivals. Eighteen months later, the government agreed to meet them. In the meeting, the government promised to encourage the people of Bali to stop using plastic bags. The campaign wasn't over but now everyone knew about it.

Isabel and Melati were only ten and twelve when they started their campaign in 2013. Since then they've spent almost all their free time on BBPB. They've travelled all over the world and they've spoken at over 150 events. They've talked to a lot of important people about their campaign and they've won several environmental awards. The ban on plastic bags was officially announced on Bali in 2019 by the Governor of the island. But not only on Bali is BBPB active: with almost 50 global teams all over the world *Bye Bye Plastic Bags* has grown into a global NGO (non-governmental organisation) led by young people. The story of Isabel and Melati has inspired other teenagers to take similar actions.

10D READING AND VOCABULARY

1 SPEAKING Look at the photo on page 132. Discuss the questions.

1 What is the environmental problem in the photo?
2 Where do you think this is?

2 In pairs, read the Plastic Facts information and say what these numbers correspond to.

20 450 100,000 a million 5 trillion

3 Read the article quickly. What would be a good introduction?

A In this article, we meet two sisters from Bali, Indonesia, to learn about how school has changed their lives.
B For Isabel and Melati Wijsen, their lives are a balance of school and environmental campaigning. Here we learn how they do it.
C You don't have to wait to be an adult to make a difference to the world. Here we meet two young people with big ideas.

4 Read the article again and choose the correct answers.

1 What do we know about Bali from the article?
 a The weather on the island is always good.
 b The island produces a lot of plastic.
 c Tourism is important to the island.
 d It's the largest island in Indonesia.
2 Isabel and Melati decided to start a campaign against plastic bags because
 a they learned about another country's successful campaign.
 b it was part of a project at school.
 c they are the biggest form of plastic pollution in Bali.
 d it was an easy problem to solve.
3 Why didn't the girls collect more signatures?
 a They didn't want to wait.
 b The government said it was unnecessary.
 c They didn't have enough volunteers
 d They needed more time for other parts of the campaign.
4 In the writer's opinion, what is the most important thing the girls have done?
 a They've had meetings with world leaders.
 b They've encouraged other people to start BBPB campaigns.
 c They've found the time to work on the campaign.
 d They've changed the law in Indonesia.

5 Match the highlighted words in the article and Plastic Facts information with definitions 1–6.

1 Stop people using something. *ban*
2 People who help or agree with you.
3 An organised plan to do something.
4 Animals in their natural environment.
5 The negative, dirty results of industry and transport.
6 Break down into tiny pieces.

PLASTIC FACTS

- **Scientists believe there are more than 5 trillion pieces of plastic in the sea.**
- **A plastic bag takes twenty years to decompose and a plastic bottle can take about 450 years.**
- **Every year, plastic pollution in our oceans kills around 100,000 sea mammals and over a million sea birds and fish.**

6 Complete the questions with the words from Exercise 5. Then, in pairs, ask and answer the questions.

1 Is there a similar environmental *campaign* to BBPB in your country?
2 Have you heard that it can take an orange skin six months to __________? Why do you think it is not ok to throw it on the ground?
3 What would you like to __________ in your country?
4 What's the best way to persuade people to become __________ of a campaign to keep your town clean?
5 Is plastic __________ a big problem where you live?
6 What __________ is in danger where you live?

7 SPEAKING In pairs, think about the article you read and discuss these questions.

1 How often do you buy bottled water? What do you do with the bottle after drinking it?
2 What can we do to use less plastic packaging?

30 WATCH AND REFLECT Go to page 159. Watch the documentary *Helping hands* and do the exercises.

☐ **I can understand specific information in a longer text and talk about the environment.**

10E LISTENING AND VOCABULARY

1 SPEAKING **How often do you check the weather forecast? Where do you usually check it?**

2 4.12 **You are going to hear four conversations. Match situations A–D with questions 1–4 in Exercise 3. Then listen and check.**

A a podcast about the weather
B a conversation between two friends
C a conversation between a parent and a child
D a weather forecast

3 4.12 **Listen to the four conversations again. For each question, choose the correct answer A, B or C.**

1 What will the weather be like next week?
a very different from last week
b better than last week
c as rainy as last week

2 What does Sally advise Jack to do?
a take appropriate clothing for the weather
b be careful of the hot sun
c look up the weather forecast again

3 What does Clare think is the most important reason for giving storms names?
a It encourages safety.
b It helps with communication.
c It makes storms more interesting.

4 What do Mark and his mum agree about?
a He should take a light jacket to school.
b He can decide what to take later.
c He doesn't need to take a coat today.

4 **Match the words in the box with the cities on the weather map. Then in pairs, ask and answer questions about the weather forecast.**

cloudy foggy ~~rainy~~ snowy stormy sunny windy

A *What's the weather like in London?*
B *It's rainy.*
A *What's the temperature?*
B *It's eight degrees.*

5 **Match the nouns in the box with the adjectives in the table.**

~~cloud~~ fog rain snow storm sun wind

Adjective	Noun
cloudy	1 *cloud*
stormy	2 ________
rainy	3 ________
windy	4 ________
foggy	5 ________
sunny	6 ________
snowy	7 ________

6 **Complete the sentences with the correct nouns or adjectives from Exercise 5.**

1 It's really hot today. You shouldn't sit in the *sun* for a long time.
2 Dad doesn't want to drive today. It's too ________ and he can't see.
3 I hate ________ weather because I'm afraid of lightning.
4 Be careful! The ________ is so strong I almost fell over.
5 The ________ is really heavy and I forgot my umbrella.
6 This morning was beautiful but the sky is a bit ________ now.
7 There was so much ________ so we went skiing.

7 SPEAKING **Discuss the questions.**

1 What's the weather like today? How is it different from last week?
2 What's your favourite season: spring, summer, autumn or winter? Say why.
3 Have you ever had really bad weather during a holiday? What did you do?

8 REFLECT | Society **In pairs, read the text and discuss the questions.**

1 Why do the British talk about the weather so often?
2 Do people often talk about the weather in your country too? If not, what do people prefer talking about?

The British love talking about the weather. According to a survey 94 percent of British people say they have had a conversation about the weather in the last six hours. The average adult posts at least one comment about it on social media every week. And each person spends eleven minutes every week checking the forecast on TV or on their phones. What is the reason for this obsession? One reason is that British weather is never boring. It's difficult to predict and it often changes during the day. But many British people admit that the topic is simply an easy one to discuss with anyone – especially people we don't know very well.

☐ **I can understand the context and identify specific information in a conversation and talk about weather.**

10F SPEAKING

1 In pairs, look at the notice and answer the questions.

1 What is the notice about?
2 What do students have to do?
3 What can students win?

> **GO GREEN!**
>
> **POSTER COMPETITION**
>
> **Theme: Supporting the environment in everyday life**
> We're looking for artists and designers with a passion for the environment. Design a poster and win!
>
> **PRIZES**
> First prize of £500 for your school to spend on environmental projects. The top five posters will appear in schools all over the country.
>
> **More details at www.gogreenposters.org**

2 *31* *4.13* **Watch or listen to Part 1 of the story. Who is going to design a poster for the competition?**

3 *32* *4.14* **Watch or listen to Part 2. What did Liam, Ava and Karen win? Is Liam happy at the end? Say why.**

4 *32* *4.14* **Study the Speaking box and read the dialogue. Then watch or listen to Part 2 again and choose the words and phrases you hear.**

Ms. Turner Guys! Guys! I've got some [1]*good / fantastic* news! I've just heard the results of the *Go Green!* competition. Two students from our school have won prizes.
Liam [2]*That's amazing news! / Oh, wow!* Who won?
Ms Turner Well, Karen Taylor's poster is one of the top five. Well done, Karen. Your poster will be in schools all over the country.
Liam [3]*Good for you, / I'm really happy for you*, Karen!
Ava Yes, congratulations! So …
Ms Turner [4]*Unfortunately, / I'm sorry, but* you didn't win this time, Ava.
Liam [5]*Oh, no! / That's awful.*
Ms. Turner Liam! You've won £500 for the school!
Liam Oh, wow! I've never won anything before! I'm sorry, Ava.
Ava No. [6]*Don't worry. / Never mind.* I'm really happy for you Liam.
Ms Turner Liam. [7]*Bad luck! / More good news!* The head teacher would like you to give a speech to the school next week – with some ideas on how to spend the money.
Liam A speech? In front of the whole school?

COMMUNICATION VIDEO

SPEAKING | Giving and reacting to personal news

Giving good news
Good news!
I've got some good/fantastic/great news.
I've just heard (the results of the *Go Green!* competition).

Giving bad news
I'm afraid I've got some bad/terrible/awful news.
I'm sorry, but …
Unfortunately, …

Responding to good news
That's great/amazing (news). | Oh, wow!
Congratulations! | Well done!
I'm really happy for you. | Good for you!

Responding to bad news
That's terrible/awful (news). | Bad luck!
Oh, no! | Don't worry.
Never mind.

5 *4.15* **Listen to four people giving news and choose the best response. Then listen and check.**

1 **a** That's amazing news.
b Never mind.
c Congratulations!
2 **a** Good for her.
b That's awful!
c I'm really happy for you.
3 **a** Don't worry.
b Oh, no!
c Oh, wow!

6 Write three pieces of news, using the topics below.

- you / your family / your friends / your school
- an event in your or another country

7 In groups, share your news and respond to the news you hear. Then repeat the news you've heard to other students.

☐ **I can give and react to good and bad news.**

10G WRITING | An article

1 **SPEAKING In pairs, look at photos A and B and the notice at the top of the website. Then, answer the questions.**

1 Do you have any of these environmental problems in your area?
2 What other types of environmental problems are there?
3 Which problem would you like to write about?

2 **Read the article. Does the article answer all the questions in the notice on the website?**

3 **Study the Writing box and read the article again. Does the writer follow all the advice?**

WRITING | An article

- Add an interesting title to encourage the reader to read the article.
  MY WORLD IS NOT YOUR RUBBISH BIN
- Introduce the topic.
  I live in ... / There are several typical environmental problems ... / One of the biggest problem is ...
- Use the next two or three paragraphs to answer each question.
  Why is it a problem? Firstly, rubbish is unhealthy ... / Finally, it costs ...
  What can young people do about it? Young people need to start a local campaign.
- Give examples where possible.
  For example, rubbish encourages ... / For instance, at our school we organised a petition.
- Add a short conclusion and finish with an interesting sentence.
  In my opinion, / To sum up, / In conclusion, / I'm sure we could ... / Our planet is in our hands.

4 **Read the notice below. Which of the titles a–c is best for an article like this?**

ARTICLES WANTED!
What things do you do in your daily life that are good for the environment? What could you do that you haven't done yet? What should we do to encourage young people to help save the planet from pollution?

a Leave home half an hour earlier and ... save the planet!
b My Green Day!
c You're never too young to do this.

5 **Look at the phrases in the box. Which of them are things you do every day? Which are things you could do in an environmental campaign?**

walk or cycle to school | give talks | grow food at home | make a video | organise meetings | pick up rubbish | recycle waste | design posters | save water | turn off lights | use less packaging | volunteer on a wildlife project

6 **WRITING TASK Write your article. Use the tips in the Writing box and the ideas in Exercise 5 to help you. Write your article in response to the notice in Exercise 4.**

A

ARTICLES WANTED!

Which local environmental problem are you most interested in?
Why is it a problem?
What can young people do about it?

Write an article that answers these questions and send it to us. We'll print the most interesting articles on our website.

THIS MONTH'S WINNER:
MY WORLD IS NOT YOUR RUBBISH BIN

I live in a huge city with two million people so there are several typical environmental problems, such as traffic and air pollution. For me, one of the worst problems is rubbish on the streets.

Firstly, rubbish on the streets is unhealthy for both humans and wildlife. For example, rubbish attracts animals like rats and they spread diseases. Other animals can easily eat something dangerous in the rubbish and die. A lot of rubbish goes down rivers and adds to the pollution in the sea. Finally, it costs a lot of money to clean up our rubbish. We could spend this on many more useful things.

Young people need to set an example for the next generation and always put their rubbish in the bin – if possible, a recycling bin. They could also start a local campaign to encourage other people to recycle. For instance, at our school we organised a petition to put more bins on the streets. We got 2,000 signatures!

In my opinion, it's not that difficult to solve the problem of rubbish. I'm sure we could all do a lot more to improve the situation. Our planet is in our hands!

B

 ☐ **I can write an article.**

10A GRAMMAR AND VOCABULARY 5.64

abroad (adv) /ə'brɔːd/
beach (n) /biːtʃ/
coast (n) /kəʊst/
desert (n) /'dezət/
elephant (n) /'eləfənt/
forest (n) /'fɒrɪst/
hill (n) /hɪl/
island (n) /'aɪlənd/
jungle (n) /'dʒʌŋgəl/
lake (n) /leɪk/
mountain (n) /'maʊntɪn/
ocean (n) /'əʊʃən/
open water (n) /'əʊpən'wɔːtə(r)/
river (n) /'rɪvə/
rocks (n) /rɒks/
sand (n) /sænd/
sea (n) /siː/
valley (n) /'væli/
waterfall (n) /'wɔːtəfɔːl/

10B VOCABULARY 5.65

ant (n) /ænt/
beak (n) /biːk/
bee (n) /biː/
bird (n) /bɜːd/
body part (n) /'bɒdi pɑːt/
crocodile (n) /'krɒkədaɪl/
dolphin (n) /'dɒlfɪn/
duck (n) /dʌk/
elephant (n) /'eləfənt/
feather (n) /'feðə/
fish (n) /fɪʃ/
fly (n) /flaɪ/
fur (n) /fɜː/
honey (n) /'hʌni/
insect (n) /'ɪnsekt/
lion (n) /'laɪən/
mammal (n) /'mæməl/
monkey (n) /'mʌŋki/
mosquito (n) /mə'skiːtəʊ/
penguin (n) /'peŋgwɪn/
reptile (n) /'reptaɪl/
salmon (n) /'sæmən/
shark (n) /ʃɑːk/
sharp (adj) /ʃɑːp/
skin (n) /skɪn/
snake (n) /sneɪk/
tail (n) /teɪl/
thick (adj) /θɪk/
tiger (n) /'taɪgə/
tooth (pl. teeth) (n) /tuːθ/tiːθ/
whale (n) /weɪl/
wings (n) /wɪŋz/

10C GRAMMAR 5.66

do a survey /duː ə'sɜː(r)veɪ/
do volunteer work /ˌduː ˌvɒlən'tɪə wɜːk/
environmental (adj) /ɪnˌvaɪrən'mentl/
plastic bag (n) /ˌplæstɪk 'bæg/
post a comment/a photo/a question /ˌpəʊst ə 'kɒment/ə 'fəʊtəʊ/ə 'kwestʃən/
recycling (n) /riː'saɪklɪŋ/

10D READING AND VOCABULARY 5.67

ban (v) /bæn/
bottled water (n) /ˌbɒtld 'wɔːtə/
campaign (n) /kæm'peɪn/
decompose (v) /ˌdiːkəm'pəʊz/
kill (v) /kɪl/
local government (n) /ˌləʊkəl 'gʌvəmənt/
plastic packaging (n) /ˌplæstɪk 'pækɪdʒɪŋ/
plastic pollution (n) /ˌplæstɪk pə'luːʃən/
plastic/glass bottle (n) /ˌplæstɪk/ˌglɑːs 'bɒtl/
present (v) /prɪ'zent/
promise (v) /'prɒmɪs/
recycle (v) /ˌriː'saɪkəl/
reduce waste /rɪˌdjuːs 'weɪst/
research (n) /rɪ'sɜːtʃ/
sign a petition /ˌsaɪn ə pə'tɪʃən/
signature (n) /'sɪgnətʃə/
spread (v) /spred/
supporter (n) /sə'pɔːtə/
tourism (n) /'tʊərɪzəm/
wet season (n) /'wet ˌsiːzən/
wildlife (n) /'waɪldlaɪf/
wind (n) /wɪnd/
world leader (n) /ˌwɜːld 'liːdə/

10E LISTENING AND VOCABULARY 5.68

advise (v) /əd'vaɪz/
appropriate (adj) /ə'prəʊpriət/
bad weather (n) /ˌbæd 'weðə/
cloud (n) /klaʊd/
cloudy (adj) /'klaʊdi/
degree (n) /dɪ'griː/
fall over (v) /ˌfɔːl 'əʊvə/
fog (n) /fɒg/
foggy (adj) /'fɒgi/
heavy rain (n) /ˌhevi 'reɪn/
lightning (n) /'laɪtnɪŋ/
rainy (adj) /'reɪni/
season (n) /'siːzən/
sky (n) /skaɪ/
snow (n) /snəʊ/
snowy (adj) /'snəʊi/
storm (n) /stɔːm/
stormy (adj) /'stɔːmi/
sun (n) /sʌn/
sunny (adj) /'sʌni/
temperature (n) /'temprətʃə/
topic (n) /'tɒpɪk/
umbrella (n) /ʌm'brelə/
weather forecast (n) /'weðə(r) 'fɔː(r)kɑːst/
wind (n) /wɪnd/
windy (adj) /'wɪndi/

10F SPEAKING 5.69

appear (v) /ə'pɪə/
design (v) /dɪ'zaɪn/
give a speech /ˌgɪv ə 'spiːtʃ/
go green /ˌgəʊ 'griːn/
good news /ˌgʊd 'njuːz/
passion for sth (n) /'pæʃən fə ˌsʌmθɪŋ/

10G WRITING AND VOCABULARY 5.70

air pollution (n) /'eə pəˌluːʃən/
attract (v) /ə'trækt/
grow food /ˌgrəʊ 'fuːd/
rat (n) /ræt/
rubbish bin (n) /'rʌbɪʃ bɪn/
set an example /ˌset ən ɪg'zɑːmpəl/
spread diseases /ˌspred dɪ'ziːzɪz/
traffic pollution (n) /'træfɪk pə'luːʃ(ə)n/
win a prize /ˌwɪn ə 'praɪz/

Remember More > page 174

10 Revision

VOCABULARY AND GRAMMAR

1 Look at the map and label the geographical features.

2 Choose the correct words to complete the sentences.

1 *Ants* / *Bees* make honey from flowers.
2 We're going down to the lake to feed the *whales* / *ducks*.
3 A *shark* / *whale* is a mammal not a fish.
4 *Elephants* / *Monkeys* can jump high and climb trees.
5 Big cats like *lions* / *penguins* hunt for food in a group.
6 A *dolphin* / *salmon* can be a sea fish or a river fish.
7 Don't worry, it won't bite you. It's just a *fly* / *mosquito*!
8 People are scared of *snakes* / *sharks* because of the way they move across the ground.

3 Read the descriptions and write the correct words.

1 Monkeys use this to hold on to trees so they can use their hands to eat fruit. *tail*
2 A bird uses this to pick up and eat food.
3 This is black and yellow on tigers.
4 Penguins have black and white ones.
5 Bees move these quickly to fly.
6 Animals use these to bite with.
7 This covers the bodies of all mammals.

4 Complete the conversation with the words from the box.

cloudy foggy rainy ~~snowy~~ stormy sunny windy

Jay When is the best time to visit India, Myra?
Myra Probably November to February but it depends where you go. It's [1] *snowy* in the Himalayan Mountains in winter, but in the south it's usually [2] ________, but not too hot.
Jay Is there a [3] ________ season?
Myra Yes, there is. From June to October it can be very wet and [4] ________ with lightning and …
Jay And what about from March to May? What's the weather like then?
Myra That's summertime in India and it's much too hot to do anything. The sky is blue, it's never [5] ________. It can be a bit [6] ________ by the sea, which is nice when it's so hot.
Jay I bet you don't have any [7] ________ days in India when you can't see anything!
Myra Oh, no, you get lots in big cities like Mumbai or Delhi because of the traffic pollution! We call it 'smog'.

5 Write Present Perfect questions with *ever* using the prompts. Then answer the questions.

1 you / swim / Pacific Ocean?
Have you ever swum in the Pacific Ocean?
2 you / see / dolphins?
3 you / fly / in a helicopter?
4 you / volunteer / wildlife project?
5 you / ever / visit / jungle?
6 you / ride / elephant?

6 Write six sentences about family and friends with *never* and the Present Perfect form of the verbs from the box.

drive lose meet try sleep write

7 Complete the sentences with *just*, *yet* or *already*.

1 Have we arrived *yet*?
2 Oh, no, we've ________ missed the last bus home!
3 I've ________ seen this film twice before.
4 You don't need to download the app again. I've ________ done it.
5 You can't drive ________. You're too young!
6 'Have you heard about the accident?' 'Yes, I've ________ heard about it on the news!'

USE OF ENGLISH

8 **Choose the correct words a-d to complete the text.**

> **STRATEGY | Multiple choice cloze**
>
> Remember that the word you choose must fit grammatically into the sentence and must also have the correct meaning.

WILDLIFE IN THE DESERT

[1]__ are dry areas. They never have much rain but they aren't all full of sand. There are also [2]__ polar deserts – these are full of ice. And there are cool deserts near the coast – the water from the sea cools the temperature.
It's not easy to see the wildlife in the desert [3]__ there are some animals that live there. Many birds live in the desert. They can use their [4]__ to fly up high when it is very hot. Big mammals, such [5]__ elephants and lions also live in the desert because they can move to cooler places. Reptiles like snakes can live there too. They need to keep cool, [6]__ during the day they go underground. They come out at night [7]__ they must look for food. Insects can also survive in [8]__ conditions. Little ants with very long [9]__ quickly work together to carry food underground.

	a	b	c	d
1	**a** deserts	**b** jungles	**c** valleys	**d** islands
2	**a** hot	**b** tropical	**c** cold	**d** warm
3	**a** firstly	**b** also	**c** and	**d** but
4	**a** beaks	**b** fur	**c** tails	**d** wings
5	**a** as	**b** for example	**c** that	**d** too
6	**a** because	**b** but	**c** so	**d** also
7	**a** just	**b** because	**c** often	**d** that
8	**a** that	**b** a	**c** this	**d** these
9	**a** beaks	**b** feathers	**c** legs	**d** teeth

9 **Complete the second sentence using the word in bold so that it means the same as the first one. Use no more than three words including the word in bold.**

1. I've never been to Australia, but I'd like to go. **YET**
   I haven't *visited Australia yet*, but I'd like to go.
2. They announced the flight two minutes ago. **JUST**
   They ____________ the flight.
3. Congratulations on winning the competition! **HAPPY**
   You've won the competition! I ____________ you!
4. Are they away now or haven't they left? **ALREADY**
   Have they ____________ their holiday?
5. Which plants and animals do we need to protect today? **DANGER**
   Which plants and animals ____________ today?

Use of English > page 173

LISTENING

10 4.16 **You will hear Tom telling Sophie about his trip to South Africa. For each question, choose the correct answer a-c.**

> **STRATEGY | Multiple choice task**
>
> When you're not sure which option to choose, use the method of elimination: start by crossing out the answer which is definitely wrong, then the one which you think is probably wrong, until there is only one option to choose.

1. Tom went to South Africa
   a for a holiday.
   b to study at a university.
   c to work as a volunteer.
2. In South Africa Tom worked
   a in a safari park.
   b in a monkey hospital.
   c in a school.
3. At the animal hospital there were
   a only monkeys.
   b a lot of different animals.
   c monkeys and a few other animals too.
4. During his trip to South Africa Tom took lots of photos of
   a monkeys
   b horses.
   c lions, rhinos and giraffes.
5. When Tom was in South Africa
   a it wasn't very warm at night.
   b it was very hot during the day.
   c it was cloudy most of the time.
6. What did Tom dislike about the trip?
   a There were too many mosquitoes.
   b He had to sleep in a tent.
   c He had to share a bedroom with other people.

SPEAKING

11 **In pairs, discuss the questions.**

1. What can you and your friends do to help to protect the environment?
2. What are the most serious environmental problems in your country?
3. What should the government do to make the cities in your country cleaner?
4. Have you ever signed a petition? What was it for?

WRITING

12 **Write a short article about the problems where you live. Say what the government should do to protect the environment. Remember to:**

- add an interesting title to encourage the reader to read the article
- introduce the topic
- write two or three paragraphs
- give examples where possible
- add a short conclusion

MAKING SENSE OF MEMORY

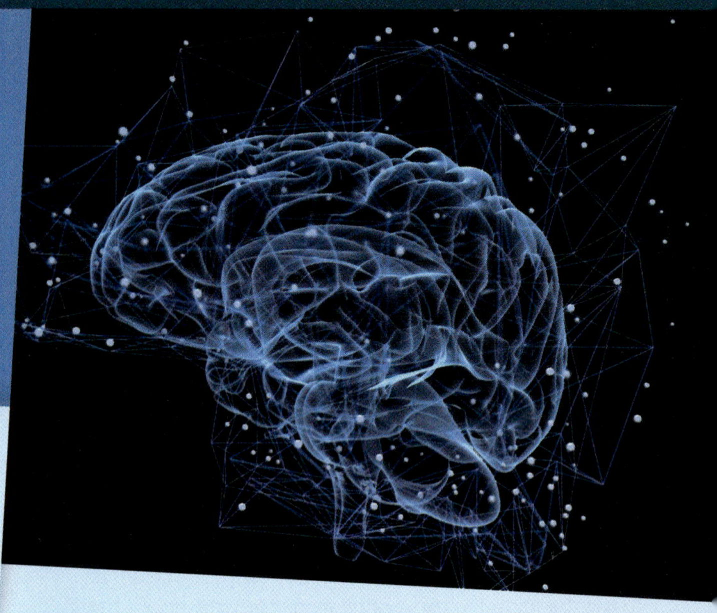

1 ☐ How do you remember the information you need when you take a test or an exam? The answer, of course, is that you use your memory. But what is memory and how does it work? In your everyday life it's important to create new memories, store them in your brain and then recall them when you need them. For example, when you cycle to school, you need to remember the rules of the road and how to get to school from your house. And when school finishes, you must remember exactly where you left your bike that morning.

2 ☐ Our brain uses three main processes in order to create memories. First, it encodes the information that you see, hear, smell or taste into a form that your mind can understand. Then it stores the information in your short-term or long-term memory. Later, when you need the information, you can recall it from your memory. This is similar to the way your computer works. It encodes the data in a language the computer can understand and stores it in a file on the hard disk. Later you can open the file when you need the information.

According to scientists, there are three stages of memory:

3 ☐ This is the earliest stage of memory and happens when you first experience something. At this stage we store information about things that we see for no more than half a second and information about things that we hear for three to four seconds. In order to remember any of this information, we must go to the next stage.

4 ☐ This is the information we are currently thinking about. When we pay attention to sensory memories, we create short-term memories. These memories usually last for twenty to thirty seconds. An example of this is when someone tells you their phone number and you need to remember it while you look for a pen and some paper.

5 ☐ If information is important to us, it becomes part of our long-term memory. In theory we can store very large amounts of data in our brains forever. We can access some of this information easily, but, as everyone knows, some of it can be difficult to remember.

6 ☐ So why do we have problems remembering things? Sometimes this is because we don't encode the information properly. For example, you know what a ten-euro note looks like. You can remember the colour and you know that it looks different from a five-euro note. But can you draw a picture of it? If you can't, it's because you didn't encode it into your memory. Another reason is that sometimes we find it hard to recall the information from our long-term memory. Fortunately, there are a number of ways you can improve your ability to remember things. One technique is to use mnemonics – these help you to remember things when you take tests or exams.

GLOSSARY

sensory – connected with the four senses (sight, hearing, smell or taste)
recall – remember something from the past
encode – put information into a different form for storing
store – put things in a special place for use in the future
short/long-term – something that lasts for a short/long time

1 In pairs, take turns to do these memory tests.

- Write five numbers and show the list to your partner for five seconds. Can he/she write them down?
- Tell your partner about everything you did after school yesterday until you went to sleep. Give as much detail as possible. Can he/she repeat it in the correct order?

2 Which of these things are easy or difficult for you to remember: words, images, numbers, position of objects, order of things? Discuss in pairs.

3 Read the article and match headings A–G with paragraphs 1–6. There is one extra heading.

A Long-term memory
B How do we 'make' memories?
C Sensory memory
D What is memory?
E The effects of age on memory
F Remembering isn't always easy
G Short-term memory

4 **In pairs, answer the questions.**

1 How can you remember things better?
2 What techniques can we use?

5 **4.17 Listen to five students' tips for remembering information and match people 1–5 with pictures A–E.**

1 Chloe ________
2 David ________
3 Ed ________
4 Zoe ________
5 Alan ________

A

B

C

D

E

6 **Complete the advice below with the words from the box.**

acronyms acrostics chunks loci rhymes

LIFE SKILLS | How to improve your memory

One of the ways to improve memory is to use mnemonics.

1 Use ________: when you use this technique, you imagine placing the things you want to remember along a route you know well or in a room or building you're familiar with.
2 Use ________: this technique can help you to remember phone numbers, bank account numbers and lists.
3 Use ________: they contain the first letters of the words or ideas you need to remember.
4 Use ________: here is an example that can help you with your English spelling: I before E, except after C, but only when the sound is E.
5 Use ________: these are sentences that help you remember information in the correct order. The words contain the first letter of the words or ideas you need to remember.

7 **Which of the techniques in Exercise 6 would you use to remember the following? In pairs, create a mnemonic to help you remember each piece of information. Use each mnemonic from Exercise 6 once only.**

1 the colours of the rainbow: red, orange, yellow, green, blue, indigo, violet
2 a bank account number, for example: 748255260
3 the year that the first astronauts landed on the Moon: 1969
4 the points of the compass in clockwise order: north, east, south and west
5 the names of all my teachers

8 **Which of the six mnemonics in Exercise 6 have you used before? Tell your partner about a mnemonic you have used to help you remember information in your studies.**

9 **Do the task below.**

LIFE SKILLS | Project

A In pairs, use three of the techniques described to create a mnemonic to help you remember an important piece of information in three different school subjects.
B Present one of your mnemonics to the class.
C Vote for the best five mnemonics created by your class.

CULTURE SPOT 1 British food

A

B

C

D

E

BRITISH FOOD

WE ASKED JEFF COLLINS, AN AMERICAN FOOD JOURNALIST LIVING IN LONDON, TO TELL US WHAT KIND OF FOOD THE BRITISH EAT THESE DAYS.

4.18

Ed So, what's the food like in the UK?

Jeff Well, in my experience, it's generally very good. These days British people like eating Indian, Chinese, Thai or Italian food, so there's plenty of variety. For example, for dinner British families often cook Asian dishes, like curries and stir-fries or they sometimes make spaghetti Bolognese or lasagne.

Ed And why do you think they eat so much international food?

Jeff I think it's because when British people go on holiday they usually go abroad, to countries where it's warm and sunny, like France, Spain, Italy and Greece. When they're in these places they try all kinds of different food. They eat the same meals as the locals. Also, because in the 1960s and 1970s thousands of immigrants arrived and brought with them their own traditional food. Now you can find Indian, Chinese, Thai, Greek, Italian and Spanish restaurants in every town in the UK – there's so much choice!

Ed So, what typical British dishes can you find in the UK these days?

Jeff Well, if they go out to a pub for lunch on Sundays, people usually have a Sunday roast – that's roast beef, lamb or chicken with Yorkshire pudding, vegetables and gravy. For me it's the perfect Sunday lunch!

Ed And do the British still have bacon and eggs for breakfast?

Jeff Well, yes, they do, but not every day. Sometimes people have a full English breakfast at the weekends, either at home or in a café.

Ed And what about fish and chips? Are you a fan?

Jeff Yes, absolutely! I don't have it very often, but there's a fantastic fish-and-chip shop near where I live, so sometimes I get a takeaway on my way home from work. Fish and chips go nicely with another British speciality, a strong cup of tea.

Ed And finally, are there any other British specialities you can recommend?

Jeff Yes, there are. If you come to the UK, you should try a cream tea.

Ed A cream tea? What's that?

Jeff Well, it's a scone – a kind of cake – that you eat with strawberry jam and cream. You usually have it in the afternoon with a cup of tea. It's delicious!

FACT BOX Popular British dishes

- The most popular food for British people to cook at home is a Chinese stir-fry.
- The British eat nearly 400 million portions of fish and chips every year.
- A full English breakfast contains more than 1,000 calories.

1 In pairs, answer the questions.

1 Imagine a British friend is coming to your country. Can you recommend five typical dishes from your country for them to try?
2 Can you name any typical British foods or drinks? Use the photos on page 142 to help you.
3 Read the introduction to the interview. Who is Jeff Collins?

2 In pairs, match dishes 1–5 with photos A–E. Read the text to check.

1 [C] fish and chips
2 [ ] cream tea
3 [ ] stir-fry
4 [ ] roast beef
5 [ ] English breakfast

3 Choose the correct words a–c to complete the sentences.

1 When British people are on holiday they usually eat
 a British food.
 b the local dishes.
 c better food than in the UK.
2 People in the UK sometimes have bacon and eggs
 a on Saturdays or Sundays.
 b every morning.
 c for lunch on Sundays.
3 When Jeff has fish and chips he also has
 a a cup of cold milk.
 b a cup of tea.
 c a cup of coffee.
4 A cream tea is
 a a cup of tea with cream.
 b a cake.
 c a cup of tea with a special cake.

4 In pairs, answer the questions.

1 Which of the dishes that Jeff describes would you like to try? Say why.
2 Which of the dishes wouldn't you like to try? Why not?

5 *4.19* Listen to Julia talking to Adam about her trip to the UK. Complete the sentences.

1 When Julia was in the UK she ate both British and *international* food.
2 She stayed in the home of a British _________.
3 In a kedgeree there is rice, _________, onions, _______ and peas.
4 Julia thought that the _________ crumble and custard was _________.
5 You make custard with _________, _________ and sugar.
6 Julia also tried _________ and mash.
7 British people usually have gravy with their roast _________.

6 Complete the sentences with the words from the box.

dessert dish ingredients ~~main course~~ meal starter takeaway

1 For my *main course* I had roast beef, Yorkshire pudding and vegetables.
2 When we were in London we had a fantastic three-course _________ in a Thai restaurant.
3 The _________ of a typical English breakfast are eggs, bacon, sausages, fried bread and baked beans.
4 Paella is a popular Spanish _________ made with rice and sea food.
5 For my _________ I'd like the tomato soup.
6 Would you like apple pie and ice cream for _________?
7 I don't want to cook this evening, so let's get a _________. How about a pizza?

7 REFLECT | Culture In groups, answer the questions.

1 What is a traditional breakfast in your country? Does it include any of the same ingredients as an English breakfast?
2 What is a typical Sunday lunch or dinner in your country?
3 What are the most popular 'takeaway' foods where you live? Can you find fish and chips in your country?
4 Which international foods does your family eat?
5 Do you think people eat fewer traditional dishes these days?

GLOSSARY

calorie - a unit for measuring the amount of energy that food can produce
custard - a sweet sauce made of milk, sugar, eggs and flour
immigrant - a person who comes to a country to live there

CULTURE SPOT 2 *English or British?*

The Giant's Causeway

The Edinburgh Festival

4.20

Northern Ireland is separated from the other countries in the UK by the Irish Sea. It is the smallest country in the UK and a third of its 1.9 million people live in the capital city, Belfast. Northern Ireland is a country of hills, mountains, lakes and a dramatic coastline. Lough Neagh is the largest inland lake in the UK and the Giant's Causeway on the northern coast is a UNESCO World Heritage Site.

Scotland Most of the UK's mountains are in the Scottish Highlands, including Ben Nevis, the highest mountain in the UK at 1,345 meters. Scotland is the only place in the UK where you can go skiing. It is also famous for its beautiful lochs (lakes) and for the hundreds of islands around its coast. There are 790 of them and only 130 are populated! Scotland is very popular among tourists, who are fascinated by traditions, such as the Highland Games, Scottish dancing, men wearing kilts and, of course, bagpipes. Every year over one million people visit Edinburgh and most of them come in August, when the city is home to 'The Fringe', the biggest festival of theatre and the arts in the world.

The Gower Peninsula near Swansea

The Roman Baths in the city of Bath

Wales is famous for its mountains, rivers and spectacular beaches and is a popular destination for people who like walking, mountain-biking, canoeing or surfing. There are also lots of historic castles you can visit, as well as the beautiful 12th century cathedral in St Davids, the smallest city in the UK. The population of Wales is just over three million and about 500,000 people speak Welsh, as well as English. The Welsh for 'Good morning' is 'Bore da'. Wales also has the railway station with the longest name in the world: Llanfairpwllgwyngyllgogerychwyrndrobwllllan tysiliogogogoch.

England You can find mountains in the north of England, but in the rest of the country there are low hills or the land is quite flat. England is part of the island of Great Britain and you are never more than seventy miles from the sea. There are hundreds of beautiful beaches around the coast but it isn't often warm enough to swim, except in summer, and the sea is always cold.
London welcomed over nineteen million visitors from other countries in 2016 and large numbers of tourists also visited the historic cities of Oxford, Cambridge, York, Bath and Stratford-upon-Avon, where Shakespeare was born. Make sure you don't miss Stonehenge, a prehistoric monument that is over 4,000 years old.

FACTFILE UNITED KINGDOM AND NORTHERN IRELAND

AREA: 242,495 km^2
POPULATION: 67 million
COUNTRIES: England, Wales, Scotland and Northern Ireland
CAPITAL CITY: London
CURRENCY: pound sterling (£)

FACTFILE ENGLAND

CAPITAL CITY: London, population 9,2 million
FLAG: St George's Cross
SYMBOL: the English Rose

FACTFILE WALES

CAPITAL CITY: Cardiff, population 474,000
FLAG: the Welsh Dragon
SYMBOL: the Leek

FACTFILE SCOTLAND

CAPITAL CITY: Edinburgh, population 530,000
FLAG: St Andrew's Cross
SYMBOL: the Thistle

FACTFILE NORTHERN IRELAND

CAPITAL CITY: Belfast, population 340,000
FLAG: St Patrick's flag
SYMBOL: the Shamrock

GLOSSARY

bagpipes - a traditional Scottish musical instrument
coast - the area where the land meets the see
hill - an area of land that is higher than the land around it
kilt - a type of skirt traditionally worn by Scottish men
sink - disappear under the surface of water

1 Look at the *Factfile* and answer the questions in pairs.

1 How many countries are there in the United Kingdom (UK)?
2 How many people live in the UK?
3 Which currency do they use in the UK?
4 What are the capital cities and symbols of Wales, Scotland and Northern Ireland?
5 What is the population of London?

2 Read the text quickly and decide what these numbers refer to.

1 1.9 milion
2 500,000
3 1,345
4 790
5 1 million
6 70
7 19 million
8 4,000

1 It's the population of Northern Ireland.

3 Read the text again and decide if statements 1–6 are true or false.

1 ☐ The Giant's Causeway is the name of a lake in Northern Ireland.
2 ☐ Wales is a good place to go for activity holidays.
3 ☐ Many people in Wales speak Welsh and English.
4 ☐ There aren't many mountains in Scotland.
5 ☐ A lot of tourists visit Edinburgh every summer.
6 ☐ Shakespeare was born in London.

4 In pairs, answer the questions. Which country in the UK would you most like to visit? Say why.

5 *4.21* **Listen to Sarah talking to Paul about her holiday in the UK. Complete the table.**

Country	Town/Place	Activities
England	[1] *London*	They visited [2] ________ and art galleries. They went to a [3] ________ called *Mamma Mia*.
	Bath	They visited the [4] ________.
[5] ________	Gower Peninsula	They went swimming and [6] ________.
Northern Ireland	[7] ________	They visited the [8] ________ Museum.
Scotland	Edinburgh	They went to the Edinburgh [9] ________. They saw a funny [10] ________ and a musical.

6 REFLECT | Culture In groups, answer the questions.

1 Compare your country to the UK. Think about the area, the geography and the population of the country and its capital city.
2 Which is the highest mountain in your country? Which is the longest river?
3 Which are the most popular cities or places for tourists to visit in your country?
4 Which festivals do tourists go to in your country?

LITERATURE SPOT 1 *The Sisterhood of the Travelling Pants*

FACT BOX *Ann Brashares*

Ann Brashares wrote *The Sisterhood of the Travelling Pants* in 2001. It was the first of a series of five Sisterhood books. The book follows the adventures of four school friends as they spend the summer holidays apart, sharing a pair of jeans which fits them all despite their different sizes.

1 **In pairs, read the information in the Fact Box and answer the questions.**

1 Do you know any books by Ann Brashares or films based on her books? Which ones have you read or watched?
2 Do you usually read books before or after watching their film adaptations? Say why.
3 What are your favourite TV series? Say why.

2 **Read the extract on page 147 quickly. Who is Carmen? What happens in the extract? Discuss in pairs.**

3 **Read the text again. Decide if statements 1–6 are true or false.**

1 ☐ Carmen visits her father's apartment downtown.
2 ☐ Her father kept his plans secret.
3 ☐ The woman and girl hug Carmen before she knows who they are.
4 ☐ Carmen's father called her 'bun' in front of the others.
5 ☐ Carmen is surprised that Lydia calls her father 'Albert'.
6 ☐ Carmen tells her father why she is upset with him.

4 **Complete the phrases which show how Carmen feels.**

1 excited: I can't w_________ to ...
2 confused: to be s_________; to have no i_________ what to do/say
3 nervous: she was holding her b_________

5 **Match words 1–6 with words or phrases a–f that have the same meaning.**

1 [c] **downtown** — **a** strange
2 ☐ **apartment** — **b** quietly
3 ☐ **in person** — **c** in the centre of the city
4 ☐ **weird** — **d** very excited and happy
5 ☐ **thrilled** — **e** flat
6 ☐ **faintly** — **f** face-to-face

6 ***4.23*** **Listen to two people discussing the film *The Sisterhood of the Travelling Pants* and match the characters to the information.**

1 ☐ Carmen — **a** feels depressed after a summer sports camp
2 ☐ Lena — **b** meets a young girl who is very ill
3 ☐ Tibby — **c** visits her father, he is getting married soon
4 ☐ Bridget — **d** goes to Greece and falls in love

7 **Listen again and complete the sentences with one word in each gap.**

1 The boy doesn't want to watch it because he thinks it will be about teenage girls' summer *romances*.
2 The girl thinks the boy will be interested in Carmen's story because her _________ with her family is similar to his.
3 The girl compares Lena's story with the story of _________ and _________.
4 After Tibby has her adventures, she becomes more _________.
5 The story about Bridget is not just about her time at camp but also shows how she _________ when she gets home.
6 The girl suggests watching part _________ of the story the following night.

8 **SPEAKING In pairs, discuss the questions.**

1 Carmen's father told his daughter about his new family when she arrived. Do you think he was right to wait with this news?
2 Do you find it difficult to tell family or friends about things which upset or annoy you? What are the advantages and disadvantages of not saying anything, like Carmen?

9 **WRITING TASK Imagine you are Carmen and that you are with your father and his new family. Write a letter to a friend describing how you feel and how you are getting on with Lydia and her children.**

FROM PAGE TO LIFE

There are two films about the stories in the books. The first came out in 2005 and the second came out in 2008. They were both so successful that a musical adaptation of the film is under development.

GLOSSARY

in person – face-to-face; not using a telephone or computer or other means
get settled – everything necessary to feel comfortable in a new situation; organise your clothes and cosmetics, wash, find out where things are, relax, etc.
inconsiderate – without thinking about another person's feelings
harsh – unpleasant, unkind
preparation – planning, getting ready for something

THE SISTERHOOD OF THE TRAVELLING PANTS

4.22

'I can't wait to see your place,' Carmen said. 'Isn't it pretty amazing that this is my first time here?'

Her father didn't say anything as they drove along small suburban streets until he slowed down and stopped in front of a cream-coloured house.

'Where's this?' Carmen asked.

'This is home.'

'I thought you lived in an apartment downtown.'

'I moved. Just last month.'

'You did? Why didn't you tell me on the phone?'

'Because ... there's a lot of big stuff, bun. Stuff I wanted to say in person,' he answered. 'Let's go inside, okay?'

Carmen had no idea where they were or what to expect. Her dad pushed open the door without knocking. Carmen realized she was holding her breath. Who would be here?

Within seconds a woman came into the room with a girl about Carmen's age. Carmen was very surprised as the woman and then the girl each hugged her. They were quickly followed by a tall young man, aged about eighteen.

'Lydia, Krista, Paul, this is my daughter, Carmen,' her dad said. Her name sounded weird in his voice. He always called her 'sweetheart' or 'baby' or 'bun'. He never called her 'Carmen'.

She had no idea what to say or do.

'Carmen, this is Lydia. My fiancée. And Krista and Paul, her children.'

Carmen closed her eyes and opened them again. 'When did you get a fiancée?' she asked in a near whisper.

Her father laughed. 'April twenty-fourth, to be exact,' he said.

'And you're getting married?'

'In August,' he said. 'The nineteenth.'

'Oh,' she said.

Lydia took one of her hands. 'Carmen, we are *so* happy to have you this summer. Why don't you come inside and relax? Albert will show you your room so you can get settled.'

Albert? Whoever called her father 'Albert'? She followed him upstairs to a bedroom facing the backyard. 'You get settled,' he said. 'I'll bring your suitcase up.'

He started for the door. 'Hey, Dad?'

He turned. He looked nervous.

She wanted to tell him it was pretty inconsiderate not to give her any warning. It was pretty harsh walking into this house full of strangers without any preparation.

'Nothing,' she said faintly.

She watched him go, realizing she was just like him. She also didn't like to say the difficult things.

LITERATURE SPOT 2 Tobermory

1 In groups, discuss the questions.

1 Have you seen these films? What do they have in common?

Alice in Wonderland   The Chronicles of Narnia   Garfield
The Jungle Book   Scooby Doo   The Guardians of the Galaxy

2 Would you like to have a pet that can talk? Say why.
3 What are the advantages and disadvantages of talking animals?
4 What do you think of the idea of teaching animals to talk? Is it ridiculous or realistic?

2 Read the Fact box and the text quickly. What do the people in the story want to do to Tobermory?

FACT BOX Hector Hugh Munro

Hector Hugh Munro (1870–1916), who wrote under the pen name 'Saki', was a British writer famous for his humorous short stories. As with most of Saki's short stories, *Tobermory* was first published in a newspaper. The story takes place during a party at Lord and Lady Blemley's posh country house. One of the guests, Cornelius Appin, has made an amazing scientific discovery about the Blemleys' cat, Tobermory.

3 Read the text again and decide if statements 1-7 are true or false

1 ☐ Mr Appin claims he has taught a cat to speak basic English.
2 ☐ The guests find it hard to believe Mr Appin's claim.
3 ☐ *Tobermory* is polite and respectful with the guests.
4 ☐ *Tobermory* felt embarrassed because he couldn't answer some questions.
5 ☐ The guests felt uncomfortable about the idea of animals talking about them.
6 ☐ Mr Appin agreed it was necessary to stop *Tobermory* from speaking.
7 ☐ Clovis didn't seem upset when he read about Appin's death.

4 Check you understand the highlighted adverbs in the text. Then, in pairs, choose the correct adverbs in sentences 1-6. Say if the sentences are true for you.

1 The kids in my school always talk *coldly* / *excitedly* until the teacher arrives.
2 I think it's *incredibly* / *nervously* difficult to pronounce English *perfectly* / *quietly*.
3 I spend a lot of time sitting at home *excitedly* / *quietly* and reading.
4 I laugh *nervously* / *patiently* and speak too incredibly / *quickly* whenever I meet someone new.
5 Even when I'm really hungry, I wait *patiently* / *quickly* for my family to sit down before I start eating.
6 When my sister's in a bad mood, she looks at me *coldly* / *perfectly* and says nothing.

5 *4.25* Listen to two students in an after school club talking about making a short film based on the story *Tobermory* and answer the questions.

1 What project do the students have to do?
2 When was *Tobermory* first published?
3 What does David think of the story?
4 What does Joyce think of the idea of a talking cat? Does David agree?
5 Has Joyce already read *Tobermory*?
6 Why does Joyce think *Tobermory* is not a good idea for a short film?

6 SPEAKING In pairs, discuss the questions.

1 How can animals communicate with people?
2 Which animals have people taught to talk?
3 Do you think that cats and dogs will be able to talk with us one day? Say why.

7 REFLECT | Values Do you think animals have the same feelings as humans? Should they have the same rights? Look at the list of things in the box and discuss in groups.

we eat animals and drink their milk
we make clothes from animals
we kill animals for sport
we test cosmetics on animals
we use animals in experiments
we make animals perform in circuses/shows/sports
we have animals beauty shows

8 WRITING TASK Imagine you meet a talking animal. Write a humorous conversation you have with it. Write about 100 words.

FROM PAGE TO LIFE

There have been several television adaptations of Saki's stories. The first *The Schartz-Metterklume Method* was an episode in the series 'Alfred Hitchcock Presents' in 1960. A BBC TV production in 2007 includes three of Saki's stories: *The Storyteller, The Lumber Room and Sredni Vashtar*. So far, no one has tried to make a film of *Tobermory* but there are many films and TV programmes with animals that can talk.

GLOSSARY

brainless – stupid
fall silent –become silent
gossip – talk about other people's private lives
ignore – pay no attention to something or someone
judge – decide, form an opinion
nod – to move your head up and down when you want to agree with someone
sceptical – doubtful, not convinced something is true

Tobermory
by Saki

4.24

'You claim,' Sir Wilfrid said, 'you can teach animals to speak, and that Tobermory is your first successful pupil?'

'Yes,' said Mr Appin, 'I've experimented with thousands of animals but Tobermory is an incredibly intelligent cat.'

'So Tobermory can say and understand short, easy words.'

'Tobermory,' said Appin patiently, 'can speak perfectly.'

The guests seemed sceptical.

'Perhaps we should invite the cat in so we can judge for ourselves?' suggested Lady Blemley.

Sir Wilfrid went to find the animal. After a minute he returned, his face white.

'It's true! I found Tobermory and told him to come and eat, and he replied that he'd come when he felt like it!'

They all began talking excitedly.

Tobermory entered the room. Everyone fell silent,

'Will you have some milk, Tobermory?' asked Lady Blemley.

'I don't mind if I do,' was the response.

Lady Blemley poured out the milk nervously.

'I'm afraid I've spilt some,' she apologised.

'So? It's not my carpet,' said Tobermory.

'Was it difficult to learn English?' asked Miss Resker.

Tobermory ignored her. It was clear he found the question boring.

'What do you think of human intelligence?' asked Mavis Pellington.

'Whose intelligence in particular?' asked Tobermory coldly.

'Well, mine for instance,' said Mavis.

'This is embarrassing,' said Tobermory, who didn't seem embarrassed at all. 'When Lady Blemley suggested inviting you, Sir Wilfrid said you're the most brainless woman he knows. Lady Blemley agreed but pointed out you're the only person idiotic enough to buy that old car they want to sell.'

As the conversation continued, the guests began to look worried.

Eventually, Tobermory saw another cat and quickly ran into the garden.

The anxious guests turned on Appin. Could Tobermory teach other cats to speak? This was terrible! Imagine a world where pets could gossip and share your secrets!

'I'm sure you agree,' Clovis said quietly, 'we must do something so that Tobermory can never speak again.' They all nodded.

'But my great discovery!' protested Appin, 'Years of research and experiment ...'

'You can experiment on cows or elephants. At least, they don't live in our houses and hear everything we say.'

That day Tobermory died in a fight with another cat.

Several weeks later an elephant in Dresden Zoo killed an Englishman. The victim's name was Appin.

'If he was teaching the poor animal German irregular verbs,' said Clovis, 'he deserved all he got.'

1 **SPEAKING In pairs, read the information in the Fact Box and answer the questions.**

1 Would you like to live on the Isle of Skye? Say why.
2 What do you/don't you like about life there?

FACT BOX *The Isle of Skye*

The Isle of Skye is an island on the west coast of Scotland. People have lots of space because only about 9,000 people live there. There is a bridge between the island and Scotland, but it is a two-hour trip to the small city of Inverness and four hours to the big city of Glasgow by car.

In the winter it often rains on Skye and it gets dark very early. But in the summer it gets dark later and people enjoy lots of outdoor activities. They go out in boats, go cycling, or go exploring nature on the beautiful island.

2 **2 Watch the video and decide if statements 1–5 are true, false, or doesn't say.**

1 ☐ Skye is not part of the UK.
2 ☐ There's peace and quiet on the island.
3 ☐ Tristan is sixteen years old.
4 ☐ He lives with his mum and dad, and a brother.
5 ☐ Tristan's friends don't like the island.

3 **2 Watch the video again and complete the profile about a teenager from Skye.**

Name: *Tristan*
Age: ________
Sport: ________
Where he practises: ________
Level: ________

4 **How do you usually spend your free time? Is it similar to what Tristan does? Say why.**

5 **Complete the summary with the verbs from the box.**

countryside freedom ~~island~~ lives loves quiet

What can you do on an [1]*island* like this when you are a teenager? Tristan is a teenager and he [2]________ on the Isle of Skye. He has kilometres of beautiful [3]________ all around him and he spends hours on his bike. He has the [4]________ to go everywhere he wants, explore and have fun. He doesn't want to change the way he lives – he [5]________ exploring the countryside. The Isle of Skye is a real paradise for those who want peace and [6]________.

6 **Match the words from the box with the definitions.**

adrenalin sport ~~adventurer~~ compete explore paradise woodland

1 A person that likes new and exciting experiences. *adventurer*
2 A beautiful and perfect place.
3 An area with trees in it.
4 A fast and dangerous activity.
5 Take part in a game or sport to win.
6 To discover new places.

7 **Choose the correct words to complete the sentences. Then, in pairs, say if the sentences are true for you.**

1 I'm a *freedom* / *nature* lover. I love the *free* / peace and quiet of the *country* / *playground*.
2 I love cycling up high *islands* / *mountains* and through *rivers* / *woodlands* with tall trees.
3 The *countryside* / *paradise* near my home is flat with lots of *oceans* / *open spaces*. It isn't very beautiful and there's nowhere special to *explore* / *practise*.

8 **SPEAKING Discuss the questions in groups. Then share your opinions with another group.**

1 What is good or bad about these things on Skye?

visiting other places spending free time having things to do hanging out with friends going shopping getting to and from school

2 What is good or bad about where you live? Look at the things in the box above and discuss.
3 Discuss the positives and negatives of teenage life in cities and teenage life in the countryside. Decide which you prefer. Use the expressions from the video to help you.

exciting free fun lucky perfect quiet

Teenage life in a city is fun because there are always new things to do.

But teenagers in the countryside are lucky because they can spend time outside.

9 **WRITING TASK Imagine Tristan is your friend. Write a profile about him for your school magazine. Use the information and the vocabulary from the video to help you.**

GLOSSARY

envy – to wish that you had someone else's possessions, abilities, etc.

jealous – feeling unhappy because someone has something that you would like to have

1 **SPEAKING In pairs, look at the photo and answer the questions.**

1 How many rooms do you think there are in this apartment?
2 Where can you find apartments like this?

2 **5 Watch the video and answer the questions.**

1 Why do people have micro apartments in big cities?
  a There aren't any big apartments. (**b**) They are cheap. **c** They are popular.
2 How many rooms do micro apartments have?
  a One **b** One or two **c** Two
3 Sean doesn't have many things in his apartment because he
  a doesn't need them. **b** hasn't got much money. **c** is never there.
4 Where do Andy and his wife live?
  a Vancouver **b** London **c** Hong Kong
5 What do they particularly like about their flat?
  a the wardrobe **b** the home cinema **c** the seats
6 Who is this type of living space good for?
  a families **b** old people **c** young people

3 **5 In pairs, check you understand the words in the box. Then watch the video again. Do they mention these things when talking about Sean's flat (A) or Andy's (B)?**

bed *A* bookcase __ extra chair __ coffee table __
home cinema __ kitchen table __ wardrobe __

4 **Would you like to live in a micro apartment? Say why.**

5 **Complete the text with the words and expressions from the box.**

cosy expensive micro apartments ~~move~~ solution space spend

A lot of people [1]*move* to big cities because there are more jobs there. But [2]__________ in these cities is a real problem. Vancouver and Hong Kong are popular and [3]__________ cities. So, it's very difficult to find somewhere to live. Luckily, there is a [4]__________ – going small. It seems that living in [5]__________ is the future for young people. They don't need a lot of space because they [6]__________ most of their time at work or out with friends. And small apartments can be very [7]__________ and comfortable places where you can create a real home.

6 **Replace the underlined words or phrases in sentences 1–6 with words with the same meaning from the box.**

seat surround-sound hidden doubles ~~bookcase~~

1 There's a place for books behind the door. *bookcase*
2 There is a bed that you can also use as a kitchen table.
3 Shelves that can become a chair.
4 There's a bed you can't see behind a sofa.
5 Andy and his wife have a home cinema system with noise all around you.

7 **SPEAKING Discuss the questions in groups. Then share your opinions with another group.**

1 Are there any rooms in your flat or house you don't use? Which rooms do you like most? Say why.
2 What do you think of the space-saving ideas in the two micro apartments? Which do you prefer? Can you think of any more?

a coffee table you can use as an extra chair
a bed that doubles as a kitchen table
shelves that can become a seat
a bed hidden behind a sofa
a wardrobe under the table
a bookcase behind a door
a home cinema inside a wall

3 Do you need all the things you have at home? List five things that are absolutely necessary for you and five things that you don't need. Compare in groups.
I don't really need a desk in my room because I can work on my laptop or in the library at school.

8 **WRITING TASK Write a description of one of the two micro apartments. Use the photo, the information, and the vocabulary from the video to help you.**

GLOSSARY

around the corner – near
honest – always telling the truth
two-tiered seating – having two parts or levels
unnecessary – something that you don't need

03 WATCH AND REFLECT

The Real Junk Food Project

1 SPEAKING **How can we stop food waste? Discuss in groups.**

2 ▷ *10* **Watch the video and choose the correct answers.**

1 The waste food comes from
a homes. b companies.
c both homes and companies

2 Adam Smith is from
a Leeds. b London. c Manchester.

3 He says that _________ are the reason why there is a lot of food waste.
a unhealthy food b bad containers c use-by dates

4 Customers at Adam's shop
a pay what they want. b get food for free.
c all pay the same amount.

5 An average family in the UK spends about _________ on food they throw away.
a £70 b £700 c £7,000

3 ▷ *10* **Watch the video again and complete the information about Adam Smith and his organisation.**

Adam Smith
Job: [1] *chef*
Organisation he runs: The Real [2] _________ Food Project
Sells food at his: [3] _________ and a café.
Only throws food away which looks or [4] _________ bad.
Gets about [5] _________ customers a day at his café.

4 **Would you like to eat at Adam's café? Say why?**

5 **Complete the text with the words from the box.**

afford banks bin price throw use-by ~~waste~~

Adam Smith gets [1] *waste* **food** from different places and sells it in his supermarket and café. Some of it comes from other shops or businesses and some comes from **food** [2] _________. These are places where poor people can get free food from. Why do shops [3] _________ food **away**? One reason is because it is past its [4] _________ **date**. Adam says that we can eat food after this date. We just have to use our noses to test that it's alright. Adam's food doesn't have a price. People pay what they **can**[5] _________. People who don't have a lot of money can **pay a low** [6] _________, or even nothing. Adam's organisation teaches people that when they **put food in the** [7] _________ they are throwing their own money away!

6 **Match the words from the box with the definitions.**

catering ~~ingredients~~ junk food recycling smell

1 All the different food items in a meal. *ingredients*
2 Using old materials, such as plastic, paper and glass again.
3 Food that is easy to cook but isn't healthy for us, like fast food.
4 Something you can sense with your nose.
5 The business of providing food and drinks for events, such as parties and meetings.

7 SPEAKING **Discuss the questions in pairs. Then share your opinions with another group.**

1 Do you worry about use-by dates on food? Do you throw food away which is one day older than its use-by date?
2 What do you think of having a shop and café with no prices and asking people to pay what they can? Are there any other businesses where this idea could work?
3 Look at the reasons below. Why do people in your family throw away food?

They buy special offers in supermarkets that they don't need.
They cook very big meals and throw away what they don't eat.
They make something new which the family doesn't like.
Sometimes people don't come home for dinner because they go out with friends.

8 WRITING TASK **Imagine you are from Leeds and often go to Adam's café with your friends. Write an email to a friend from a different town. Describe the café and the food and say why you like going there.**

GLOSSARY

available – to be there for us to use or have
average (UK home) – typical
environment – the air, land and sea
run an organisation – to be the boss of an organisation

1 **SPEAKING In pairs, look at the photo and answer the questions.**

1 Where are the students?
2 What are they doing?

2 **12 Watch the video and tick (✓) all the things you can learn at Gordonstoun School.**

☐ art ☐ camping ☐ climbing
☐ designing computer games ☐ drama ☐ hiking
☐ sailing ☐ team work

3 **12 Watch the video again and choose the correct answers.**

1 What are the students preparing for at the start of the video?
a entrance exams (b) final exams
c their holidays
2 What do the students learn apart from lessons and exams?
a business skills b practical skills c technical skills
3 How many days do the students spend on the boat?
a fifteen b ten c seven
4 What can they learn on their trip?
a How to live together. b How to live alone.
c How to live in the countryside.
5 How does the director describe the lessons learnt on 'Ocean Spirit'?
a easy b hard c strong
6 After the boat trip the students know more about
a nature. b sailing. c themselves.

4 **Decide if statements 1–6 are true or false. Correct the false ones.**

1 ☐ The boat belongs to Gordonstoun School.
2 ☐ The students do everything on the boat.
3 ☐ The sea is calm during the whole trip.
4 ☐ Some people don't feel well during the whole trip.
5 ☐ They learn to stay calm and help each other.
6 ☐ The students are happy to leave the boat.

5 **What activities do you do at your school that help you learn practical and teamwork skills?**

6 **Complete the text with the words from the box.**

calm challenge ~~exams~~ useful part responsible team

Students at Gordonstoun are studying hard for **final** [1] *exams*. But as well as lessons and exams, students **take** [2] ____ in many different activities during the school year.

These 15-year-old students in Year 10 face a **big** [3] ____: they are going to spend a week on the boat. The group is [4] ____ **for** everything on the boat. They also learn [5] ____ **lessons**: how to **stay** [6] ____ and help each other. After the week's journey the students know much more about themselves and [7] ____ **work**.

7 **SPEAKING Discuss the questions in groups. Then share your opinions with another group.**

1 In your opinion, what are the most important lessons the students learn on the boat? Put these in order: 1 (very important)–8 (not important).

☐ cleaning and tidying ☐ cooking
☐ helping each other ☐ learning about themselves
☐ living together in a small space ☐ sailing
☐ staying calm ☐ working together

2 Tell your group about a situation where you learnt important life lessons. What were they and how did you learn them?
3 How can young people learn about themselves and about team work? Do you think regular lessons or activities in school help you with this? Say why.
I think some activities in school teach you important lessons – for example sports and drama.

8 **WRITING TASK Write a post for an online school forum about your experiences of learning about yourself and learning to work as part of a team. Then compare your posts in groups.**

GLOSSARY

calm (sea) – no waves or bad weather
miserable – not happy
seasick – feeling ill on a boat
share – to do or divide things with other people

1 **SPEAKING In pairs, look at the photo and answer the questions.**

1 Can you guess what the video is about?
2 What are the people wearing? Do you know when in history the clothes are from?

2 **16 Watch the video and answer the questions.**

1 What is *Back in Time*?
2 What could the family experience in the programme?
3 What changed every week for the family?
4 What kind of lesson does Seth hope to get?
5 Who wanted the family to stop looking at their phones?
6 What could they do instead of looking at their phones?

3 **16 Watch the video again and match the phrases in the box with the two decades. A – 1950s or B – 1970s.**

[A] being overdressed [ ] camping holiday
[ ] colourful clothes [ ] darts and dancing
[ ] difficult housework [ ] DIY (Do It Yourself)
[ ] formal clothes [ ] fun hobbies
[ ] no vacuum cleaners
[ ] swingball, keyboards and computers

4 **Would you like to take part in the programme *Back in Time*? Say why.**

5 **Match the words from the box with the definitions.**

colourful formal overdressed ~~ridiculous~~ traditional typical

1 Silly or funny. *ridiculous*
2 Normal, not unusual.
3 Wearing a suit and tie, for example.
4 Not black and white.
5 Wearing a suit and tie to go to the supermarket.
6 Clothes people wore in the past.

6 **Complete the text with the words from the box.**

camping ~~decades~~ devices DIY formal fun past typical

The Ashby-Hawkins experienced life in different [1]*decades*. Changing their rooms, clothes and hobbies taught them about the [2]__________. They talked to each other instead of looking at their electronic [3]__________. They wore [4]__________ clothes from the 1950s but they all thought they were too [5]__________. There was lots of housework and [6]__________ to do, for example Dad made a chair. In the 1970s the clothes were colourful and the hobbies were [7]__________. The family enjoyed spending time together and went on a [8]__________ holiday!

7 **SPEAKING Discuss the questions in groups. Then share your opinions with another group.**

1 How did the family's life change between the two decades. Think about:

clothes free time hobbies housework holidays

The family had more free time in the 1970s.

2 What did the family learn from their experience?
3 Which decade would you like to travel back to? Say why.

8 **WRITING TASK Imagine you are Daisy or Seth. Write an email to your English-speaking friend about the experience of travelling back in time. In your email say:**

- what you liked
- what you didn't like
- what you learnt

GLOSSARY

bond – become good friends
century – a hundred years
DIY (Do It Yourself) – making things yourself
(electronic) devices – smartphones, tablets, etc.
overdressed – wearing formal clothes in a casual situation
vacuum cleaner – a machine that cleans floors

1 **SPEAKING In pairs, look at the photo and answer the questions.**

1 What are the people doing?
2 Do you think these performers are professionals? Say why.

2 **18 Watch the video and answer the questions.**

1 In which American state are students now working hard? *in Pennsylvania*
2 What are the prizes for high school musicals called?
3 Do students prefer being on or offstage? Why?
4 Who plays soccer and now loves drama?
5 How do the students feel on awards night?
6 Where are people watching the Freddy Awards?

3 **18 Watch the video again and complete the sentences with the missing information.**

All over [1]*Pennsylvania* high school students are working hard. They practise singing, acting, dancing and playing [2]__________. It takes a lot of time and effort but the students [3]__________ a lot. Amanda performs because she enjoys making others [4]__________. John has one of the starring roles in his school's [5]__________. Every time they practise, they get a bit [6]__________. The theatre is ready, and the [7]__________ is coming in. Each high school performs its musical for the [8]__________.

4 **Would you like to perform in a musical? Say why?**

5 **Match these words from the box with the definitions.**

audience musical note ~~offstage~~ stage star theatre

1 When you're not performing. *offstage*
2 You perform a show standing on this.
3 The people watching a show.
4 The activity of preparing and performing in a play.
5 A symbol or sound in music.
6 A play or film with singing and dancing.
7 A famous or talented person.

6 **Do you remember what some students said? Complete the sentences with the words from exercise 5.**

1 'It just feels natural for me to be on *stage*.'
2 'Because __________, like, you're vulnerable.'
3 'I love to have that connection with the __________.'
4 'I can just take them away from all their troubles just because I'm singing a __________.'"
5 'I was always a soccer __________, not a drama.'
6 'People don't realise that __________ is a team sport.'
7 A team trying to make a beautiful __________.'

7 **SPEAKING Discuss the questions in groups. Then share your opinions with another group.**

1 What did students learn performing in the musical?
2 Does theatre help the young people in the video to feel better about themselves and with the others? Say why.
3 'These are the people that are going to take care of this theatre, this town, this world. That's wonderful!' What abilities and talents does this speaker admire so much in the young people?
I think she admires the way they work in a team.
Yes, I agree. And the fact that all the actors are important.

8 **WRITING TASK Write a review of a live show. Use the words and expressions from the video to help you. In your review include:**

- general information
- information about the characters and story
- your opinion
- if you recommend the show

GLOSSARY

confused – not able to think clearly
effort – the time and energy put into an activity
highlight – best thing/moment/person
judges – people who choose the winner of a competition
soccer – football
starring role – the most important character in the cast
vulnerable – a vulnerable person can be easily hurt or attacked

07 WATCH AND REFLECT Sydney – the perfect city?

1 SPEAKING **In pairs, look at the photo and answer the questions. Then read the Fact Box to check.**

1 What is the man in the photo doing?
2 What do you know about Sydney?

2 ▷ 22 **Watch the video and answer the questions.**

1 What is Morgan Burnett's job?
He's a cameraman and a presenter.
2 Where does Morgan work?
3 Where is he from?
4 How does he travel to Sydney?
5 What does he think of Sydney?
6 Where is he going to drive?

3 ▷ 22 **Watch the video again. Decide if statements 1–6 are true or false. Correct the false ones.**

1 ☐ Sydney has an opera house.
2 ☐ There are lots of restaurants and places to shop.
3 ☐ There are ten beaches in Sydney.
4 ☐ Nowra has a beautiful forest.
5 ☐ Morgan is staying in a hotel in Nowra.
6 ☐ He goes paddleboarding in the sea.

4 **Would you like to visit Sydney? Say why.**

5 **Complete the text with the correct words and expressions from the box.**

being on holiday drive south famous landmarks own city starting the journey too far away from ~~travels the world~~

Morgan Burnett [1]*travels the world* and films different places for TV shows. Today he is going to visit his [2]____________: Sydney, in Australia. He's [3]____________ in Sydney. And then he's going to [4]____________ to visit some beautiful places that aren't [5]____________ the city. Morgan thinks that living in this city is a bit like [6]____________ because it has beautiful views. Sydney is a great place for sightseeing because there are lots of [7]____________, like the Opera House and the Harbour Bridge.

FACT BOX Sydney

Sydney is a city on the east coast of Australia. It isn't the capital city, but it is the biggest city in Australia, and over four million people live there. It's a great city for tourists because there are lots of things to do there. You can go sightseeing and visit its many famous buildings, like the Sydney Harbour Bridge or the Sydney Opera House. But you can also go to the beautiful national parks and beaches – Bondi beach is the most famous.

6 **Replace the underlined parts of the sentences with the words and expressions from the box.**

(his) accommodatio ~~cameraman~~ connection to go paddleboarding paradise spectacular

1 Morgan Burnett is a person that films things and a presenter. *cameraman*
2 He says: 'I'm living in a beautiful place where everyday's a holiday.'
3 One of the greatest things about Sydney is the city's links with water.
4 It's got a beautiful and dramatic coastline, countless beaches and a big, beautiful harbour.
5 In Nowra, the place where Morgan stays isn't a hotel but a huge tent in the forest.
6 He can surf on a board on the river.

7 SPEAKING **Discuss the questions in groups. Then share your opinions with another group.**

1 What can tourists do in your favourite town or city? Think about:

activities famous sights how to get around the city things to visit

2 What is important for local residents in a city?
3 What makes a perfect city? Say why.
I don't think our city is perfect because there is too much traffic and it is very dirty and noisy.
Yes, but there are lots of things to do here like ...

8 WRITING TASK **Write a short message to an English-speaking friend, inviting him or her to join you on a sightseeing tour of a town or city. In your message:**

- ask them if they are free
- tell them when and where you are meeting
- say what you're going to visit/do

GLOSSARY

coastline – area of land near the sea
crowded – full of people
harbour – where people leave small boats
landmark – a well-known place people know
view – the whole area that you can

1 SPEAKING **In pairs, look at the photo and answer the questions.**

1 Where are the men?
2 What do you think is happening in the photo?

2 ▷ *25* **Watch the video and answer the questions.**

1 In which country are people using microchips when travelling by train? *In Sweden.*
2 Where is Stephan Ray's microchip?
3 What information does it contain?
4 Where else are people using microchip implants?
5 What aspects of microchipping do people worry about?

3 ▷ *25* **Watch the video again and match the two parts of the sentences.**

1 [*d*] 'Chipped' passengers have a tiny microchip implanted
2 [ ] The conductor can scan the implant,
3 [ ] Patrick Mesterton introduced optional microchipping
4 [ ] Putting a piece of technology into your body
5 [ ] Microchip implants will be able to collect a lot of data
6 [ ] It's not certain who will have access

a to the personal data stored in microchip implants.
b to make people's lives easier.
c is an extreme thing to do.
d into their hand.
e and access their ticket information online.
f about our daily activities.

4 **Would you like to have a microchip implant in your hand? Say why.**

5 **Complete the text with the words and expressions from the box.**

airline fares   data   gym   implant   keys   ~~microchip~~   printers   unique

This man has got his ticket stored in his hand on a [1]*microchip* implant. This tiny piece contains their [2]__________ customer number. The conductor can scan the [3]__________, and access their ticket information online. Train tickets aren't the only [4]__________ we can store on a microchip. Workers can use their microchip implants to open doors, use [5]__________, and buy food and drinks.

You don't have to have [6]__________, you don't have to use tags or anything else. You can also pay for [7]__________ with it, or go to your local [8]__________.

GLOSSARY

conductor – a person who checks tickets on a train or bus
optional – you don't have to do it
privacy – to be free from other people's attention
tags – electronic devices you can wear that make things work or open
simplify – make things easier
unique – only one

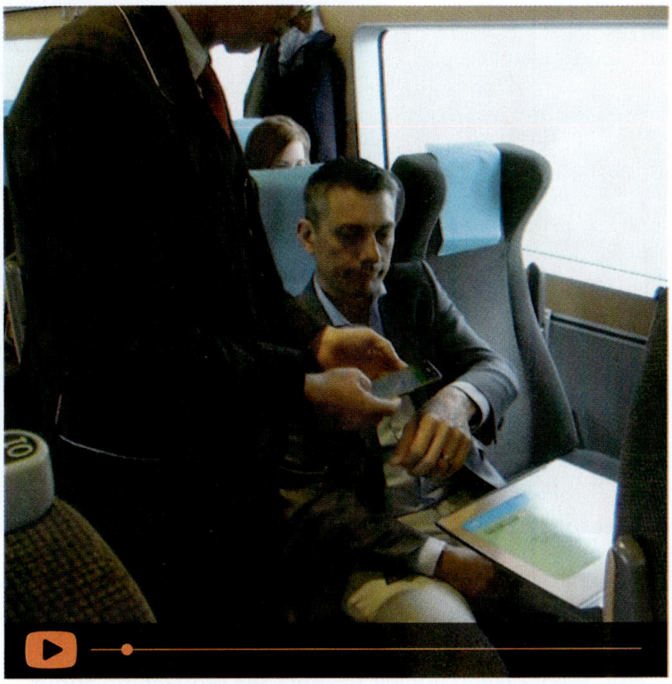

6 **Replace the underlined words and phrases with the phrases from the box with the same meaning.**

~~data~~   experts   have access to   health   microbiologist   your whereabouts

1 They will be able to collect a lot of facts about our daily activities. *data*
2 So some people who know a lot about it are worried about our privacy.
3 Ben Libberton, a person studying very small living things, is worried about this technology.
4 It's not certain who will be able to see the personal data.
5 You could get data about your physical condition.
6 You could get data about where you are.

7 SPEAKING **Discuss the questions in groups. Then share your opinions with another group.**

1 In what situations and where will we use microchip implants in the future?
We will use them to buy things online.
2 The narrator says: 'Putting a piece of technology into your body is an extreme thing to do.' Do you agree? Say why.
3 Read these questions and give your opinions: 'Are microchip implants something to be happy, or worried about? How will we use them?'
We are happy about using microchip implants as they will make our lives easier. We'll be able to ...
We are worried about using microchip implants because we won't have privacy in the future ...

8 WRITING TASK **You work for a company selling microchip implants. Write a short advert for your product. In your advert you should:**

- describe the product
- explain how it will change customers' lives
- say how cheap and easy it is to implant it

1 SPEAKING **In pairs, look at the photo and answer the questions.**

1 What is the astronaut doing in the photo?
2 What do you think is the best and worst thing about living in space?

2 28 **Watch the video and answers the questions.**

1 Where does the International Space Station travel? *Around Earth*
2 How long does each astronaut work and live there?
3 What do they have to build and do?
4 What happens to water in space?
5 Who fixes problems on the space station?
6 What does Karen like doing every day and how does she do it?
7 Why are simple activities difficult in space?
8 How do astronauts return to Earth?

3 28 **Watch the video again. Put a tick (✓) next to what astronauts do and a (✗) next to what they don't do.**

☑ build parts of the space station ☐ cook their food
☐ do exercise ☐ do tests and experiments
☐ eat dry food ☐ eat lots of vitamins and nutrients
☐ go home after 6 months
☐ go outside to fix problems ☐ wash their hair
☐ go out without their spacesuits
☐ sleep connected to the wall ☐ sleep on a bed

4 **Which of the activities in exercise 3 would you like to do or wouldn't you like to do in space?**

5 **Match the words and phrases from the box with the definitions.**

astronaut ~~Earth~~ gravity International Space Station space spacesuits zero

1 The planet we live on. *Earth*
2 When there is no force that pulls you to the ground.
3 Astronauts' clothes.
4 Everything outside the Earth's atmosphere.
5 A place where astronaut go to study space.
6 A person trained to travel in space.

6 **Complete the sentences with the correct words.**

blood bones hair healthy heart muscles nutrients ~~vitamins~~

1 Food should have lots of *vitamins* and __________ so that the astronauts stay healthy in space.
2 They must do exercise every day to keep fit and __________ on the space station.
3 'We exercise to keep our __________ and our __________ strong.'
4 Karen uses her arms, legs and __________ to push __________ around her body.
5 How do you think astronauts wash their __________ in space?

7 SPEAKING **Discuss the questions in groups. Then share your opinions with another group.**

1 What are the things you have to do and things you don't have to do in space?
2 Imagine you are going to live on the Space Station for six months. List five personal objects you want to take with you and say why you need them.
3 Which aspects of life in a space station can be the most difficult/most interesting?
Keeping fit can be the most difficult because you have to stay inside and there's not much space.
Understanding how things work in zero gravity can be the most interesting.

8 WRITING TASK **You are an astronaut on the International Space Station. On an online health and fitness forum post a problem you are having in space and ask for some advice.**

GLOSSARY

cabin – a small room in a ship/spaceship
capsule – a small vehicle for travelling through space
floating – moving freely in liquid or air
no rinse (shampoo) – you don't have to wash it out
secure – attach, connect

1 **SPEAKING In pairs, look at the photos and answer the questions.**

1 What are these people doing?
2 Why do you think they are doing it?

2 **30 Watch the video and answer the questions.**

1 What do volunteers do on Cape Cod? *They help save turtles.*
2 Why do they have to do this?
3 What do the volunteers do with the turtles they find?
4 Which animals do Susan and Jim look after?
5 When did they start looking after them?
6 How do Jim and Susan see the animals?

3 **30 Watch the video again and complete the profiles about the two wildlife projects.**

Species: Kemp Ridley [1]*turtles*
Location: Wellfleet Bay [2]_______ Sanctuary, Cape Cod
People involved: [3]_______
Problem: in danger of [4]_______
Number rescued: [5]_______ every year
Project aim: To return them to the [6]_______.

Species: Kodiak bears
Location: Animal [7]_______ for bears in New York.
People involved: Susan and [8]_______
Problem: the bears lost their [9]_______
Number rescued: [10]_______
Project aim: To [11]_______ them.

4 **Which of the two wildlife projects would you like to volunteer for? Say why.**

5 **Complete the sentences with the correct words from the box.**

alive ~~environment~~ help in danger sanctuary volunteers

1 All around the world there are people who care about animals and the *environment*.
2 Some people love to _________ wild animals.
3 This species is _________ of disappearing.
4 But luckily, these _________ are ready to help.
5 They make the turtles healthy at the _________.
6 There are more Kemp's turtles _________ today.

6 **Choose the correct words to complete the sentences.**

1 Susan and Jim (*run*) / *walk* an animal sanctuary for bears.
2 They look *after* / *for* eleven bears.
3 Living with the bears is *dangerous* / *safe* because they are very *strong* / *weak* animals.
4 Kodiak bears are one of the *largest* / *smallest* species in the world.
5 They can weigh up to 1,400 lbs! A lot *more* / *less* than Susan and Jim.
6 But Jim and Susan have developed a *close* / *closed* relationship with the furry animals.
7 These people show us that we can *do* / *make* a difference.

7 **SPEAKING Discuss the questions in groups. Then share your opinions with another group.**

1 Are there similar wildlife projects in your country? Who runs them? What do they do?
2 Which of the two projects in the video is the most effective in your opinion and why?
3 Read these sentences from the video and give your opinions.
... Many animal species are still disappearing every year. Can we still save them, or is it too late?
I think we can still save lots of animal species, but we need to protect the environment where they live.
Yes, but some species, like the black rhino, are almost extinct so it's too late for them!

8 **WRITING TASK Write an article about a species in danger of disappearing in your country. In your article you should give information about:**

- the species
- where it usually lives
- why it is in danger
- what people can do to save it

GLOSSARY

alive – not dead
get stuck – can't move
species – a group of animals whose members are similar

0A Subject pronouns, *to be*

Subject pronouns	
I'm a student.	**We**'re from Spain.
You are in my class.	**You**'re sixteen.
He's a teacher. **She**'s a new student. **It** is black.	**They**'re French.

Subject pronouns replace nouns:
*Jo is seventeen. = **He**'s seventeen.*
*Are Marie and Pierre from France? = Are **they** from France?*

To be

Affirmative			Negative		
I	**am ('m)**	French.	**I**	**am not ('m not)**	from India.
You/We/ They	**are ('re)**		**You/We/ They**	**are not (aren't)**	
He/She/It	**is ('s)**		**He/She/It**	**is not (isn't)**	

Questions			Short answers
Am	I	16?	Yes, I **am**. No, I **am not** (**'m not**).
Are	you/we/ they		Yes, you/we/they **are**. No, you/we/they **are not** (**aren't**).
Is	he/she/ it		Yes, he/she/it **is**. No, he/she/it **is not** (**isn't**).

Wh- questions		
What	**is ('s)**	your email address?

0B Plural nouns, articles, this/that/these/ those

Plural nouns

	Singular	Plural
most nouns	tablet	tablet**s**
nouns ending in *-sh*, *-ch*, *-s* , *-x*, *-z* and some ending in *-o*	watch box class	watch**es** box**es** class**es**
nouns ending in a consonant and *-y*	family diary	famil**ies** diar**ies**
irregular nouns	child person sheep wife woman	**children** **people** **sheep** **wives** **women**

Articles (*a*, *an*, *the*, no article)

We use the indefinite article *a* or *an* to talk about single countable nouns when:

- the thing or person we are talking about is one of many similar people or things:
  *It's **an** old house.*
- we mention a person or thing for the first time:
  *There's **a** new restaurant on this street.*

We use the definite article *the* with singular and plural countable nouns and with uncountable nouns to talk about:

- something specific or unique:
  *Look at **the** sky!*
- something we have mentioned before:
  *There is a new café on this street. **The** café is very good.*

We don't use an article when we are talking about something in general:
Chocolate isn't healthy.

This/That/These/Those

We use *this* (singular) and *these* (plural) to talk about people or objects close to us:
***This** is my new house. **These** are my keys.*

We use *that* (singular) and *those* (plural) to talk about people and things further away from us:
***That** is my school. **Those** are my neighbours.*

0C Possessive adjectives, possessive 's, *have got*

Possessive adjectives

My brother is 6 years old.
Your friend is very nice.
His bike is cool.
Her mum is a nurse.
This bag is great. **Its** colour is orange.
Our neighbours are French.
Your cousins are in the garden.
Their car is fantastic.

We use possessive adjectives to say who has something or to talk about family members and friends.
*These are **our** best friends, Jake and Thomas.*

Possessive 's

We use the possessive 's to say who has something:
*Whose bag is it? It's my friend**'s** bag.*

We add:
's to singular nouns:
*He's Sally**'s** boyfriend.*
' to regular plural nouns:
*They're the boys**'** bags.*
's to irregular plural nouns:
*The children**'s** room is over there.*

Have got

Affirmative			Negative		
I/You/ We/ They	**have got ('ve got)**	a dog.	I/You/We/ They	**have not got (haven't got)**	a dog.
He/ She/It	**has got ('s got)**		He/ She/It	**has not got (hasn't got)**	

Yes/No questions				Short answers
Have	I/you/we/ they	**got**	cool toys?	Yes, I/you/we/they **have**. No, I/you/we/they **haven't**.
Has	he/she/it			Yes, he/she/it **has**. No, he/she/it **hasn't**.

Wh- questions			
How many cameras	**have** **has**	I/you/we/they he/she/it	**got**?

We use *have got* to talk about possessions (things and people):
I ***have got*** *a big family.*
Has *he* ***got*** *two sisters?*
We ***haven't got*** *cats.*

0D Imperatives, object pronouns

Imperatives

We use the infinitive or *don't/do not* + infinitive to give instructions or orders:
Listen *to the teacher.*
Don't forget *to check the spelling.*

Object pronouns

Tell ***me****.*
Talk to ***him****.*
Listen to ***her****.*
Don't forget ***it****.*
Help ***us****.*
See ***you*** *tomorrow.*
Don't use ***them*** *(mobile phones).*

Object pronouns:

- go after the verb if they are direct:
  Help ***me****. Tell* ***him****.*
- go after a preposition *to* if they are indirect:
  Talk ***to me****. Listen* ***to her****.*

1 **0A Choose the correct verbs.**

1 I *'m / 're* Canadian from Montreal.
2 They *isn't / aren't* from China. They 's / 're Japanese.
3 We *'s / 're* school friends.
4 She *'s / 're* our English teacher.
5 *'Am / Are* I in your class?' 'Yes, you is / are.'
6 *'Is / Are* Alex Hungarian?' 'No, he isn't / aren't. He 's / aren't Romanian.'
7 *Am / Are* I in Class 1A?
8 She *'s / am* a young woman.

2 **0B Write the sentences in the plural form.**

1 This is a photo of our family.
2 This is Helen's secret diary.
3 Look at that man with sunglasses and a gold watch!
4 How old is this boy?
5 Is that student from Spain?

3 **0B Complete the text with *a/an/the* or no article.**

Welcome to [1]________ my new home! It's [2]________ old house, but it isn't in [3]________ expensive area. It's [4]________ cool place. [5]________ people in [6]________ houses in my street are very nice!

4 **0B Write *this*, *that*, *these*, or *those*.**

1 ________ is a big dog over there!

2 ________ are very small sheep!

3 ________ is an expensive watch!

4 ________ are cool sunglasses!

5 **0C Complete the conversation with the correct possessive pronoun or *whose*.**

Rick Hi, I'm Rick and this is [1]*my* brother. [2]________ name's John.
John Hi, girls! What are [3]________ names?
Sarah Hi Rick! Hi John! [4]________ names are Sarah and Jill. We're twins.
John So [5]________ name is Sarah, right?
Jill No, it's Jill. [6]________ name is Sarah!
John Hey Rick, these girls are twins and [7]________ names are ...
Rick I've got it! And [8]________ is this dog?
Sarah He's my dog! [9]________ name is Rufus!

6 **0C Write *'s* or *s'*.**

1 My mum*'s* name is Elena.
2 Dan____ skateboard is really cool!
3 Our cousin____ names are Ivan and Marianne.
4 'What's your English teacher____ name?' Sam.
5 'Whose bags are those?' 'They're the children____ bags.'
6 These are my grandparent____ favourite objects.

7 **0C Complete the sentences with the correct form of *have got*.**

1 *Has* Rick *got* a brother? Yes, he ________.
2 John ________ a sister, but he ________ a brother. His name is Rick.
3 Jill and Sarah are twin sisters, but they ________ brothers.
4 ________ you ________ a dog? No, I ________.
5 ________ your brother ________ a job? Yes, he ________. He's a vet.
6 ________ your dog ________ a toy? Yes, it ________.

8 **0D Complete the sentences with the correct form of the verbs from the box. Then rewrite the sentences changing the underlined words into the correct object pronouns.**

~~give~~ listen start talk tell write

1 *Give* the dictionary to Chloe. *Give it to her.*
2 ________ me and your dad about your new bicycle.
3 Class, please ________ to what I say.
4 ________ the test before the teacher tells you to.
5 ________ the answers in your exercise book.
6 ________ to your friends during the test!

1A Present Simple: affirmative and negative

Present Simple				
Affirmative		**Negative**		
I/You/We/They	**eat**.	I/You/We/They	**do not** (**don't**)	**eat**.
He/She/It	**eats**.	He/She/It	**does not** (**doesn't**)	

We use the *Present Simple* to talk about:

- regular/repeated actions or activities:
  *I **start** each day with some exercise.*
- facts:
  *We **live** in the south of Spain.*

Spelling rules for third person singular:

- general rule: infinitive + *s*, e.g. *start – start**s**, drive – drive**s***
- verbs ending in *-o*, *-ch*, *-sh*, *-s*, *-x*: *+es*, e.g. *go – go**es**, watch – watch**es**, wash – wash**es***
- verbs ending in a consonant and *-y*: *-y +ies*, e.g. *try – tr**ies***

1C Adverbs of frequency and Present Simple questions

Adverbs of frequency

never < hardly ever < sometimes < often < usually < always
0% 100%

The battery **always** dies before the end of the day.

They **never** leave their phones at home.

We put adverbs of frequency after the verb be and before other main verbs:

*She **is always** busy at the weekends.*

*I **often do** sport.*

We use frequency expressions to talk about how often we do things:

*John goes to the cinema **once a month**.*

*My parents have a big party **twice a year**.*

Present Simple: questions			
***Yes/No* questions**			**Answers**
Do	I/you/we/they	**take** photos?	Yes, I/you/we/ they **do**. No, I/you/we/ they **do not** (**don't**).
Does	he/she/it		Yes, he/she/it **does**. No, he/she/it **doesn't**.
***Wh-* questions**			
How often	**do**	you	**check** messages on your phone?
Where	**do**	your parents	**work**?
What time	**does**	school?	**start**?

1 1A **Complete the sentences with the correct form of the verb in brackets.**

1. She *doesn't like* (not like) her school uniform.
2. School __________ (start) at 8.30 and __________ (finish) at 3.30 p.m.
3. Lucy and her friends often __________ (study) in a homework club after school.
4. Her parents __________ (work) in the city and they __________ (not get) home before 7 p.m.
5. My dad always __________ (read) a newspaper before breakfast.
6. Some teenagers __________ (not do) any exercise.
7. Kevin __________ (not get up) before 9 a.m. at the weekends.

2 1C **Put the words in the correct order.**

1. do / park / you / how / go / the / often / to / ?
   How often do you go to the park?
2. favourite / activities / are / your / what / free-time / ?
3. play / you / sport / when / do / ?
4. your / check / do / often / phone / you / ?
5. friends / you / with / where / hang out / your / do ?
6. shopping / you / do / often / go / how / ?
7. films/ you/ like /what / do / watching / ?

2A *There is/There are* with *some* and *any*

There is/There are with *some* and *any*			
Affirmative		**Negative**	
There is (**'s**)	a picture on the wall.	**There is not** (**isn't**)	a picture on the wall.
There are (**'re**)	**some** pictures on the wall.	**There are not** (**aren't**)	**any** pictures on the wall.
***Yes/No* questions**		**Short answers**	
Is there	a picture on the wall?	Yes, **there is**. No, **there isn't**.	
Are there	**any** pictures on the wall?	Yes, **there are** (**some**). No, **there aren't** (**any**).	

We use *there is/there are* to say where things are:
***There is** a big window in the living room.*
***There isn't** a fireplace in this house.*
***There are** a lot of photographs on the wall.*
***There aren't** many houses in this street.*

We use *some* in affirmative sentences:
*There are **some** beautiful plants in the garden.*

We use *any* in negative sentences or questions:
*Are there **any** mirrors here?*
*There aren't **any** chairs in the kitchen yet.*

2C Can/can't

Can/can't					
Affirmative			**Negative**		
I/You/She/He/It/ We/You/They	**can**	swim.	I/You/He/She/ It/We/You/ They	**can't**	swim.

***Yes/No* questions**			**Short answers**
Can	I/you/he/ she/it/ we/you/ they	swim?	Yes, I/you/he/she/it/we/you/ they **can**. No, I/you/he/she/it/we/you/ they **can't**.

***Wh-* questions**			
What	**can**	I/you/he/ she/it/we/ you/they	do well?

We use *can* and *can't* to talk about ability:
Matt **can** vacuum the carpets very quickly.
I simply **can't** keep my room tidy.
Can you iron your shirts and not burn them?
What **can** she cook very well?

1 **2A Choose the correct words.**

1. Are there *any* / *some* windows in the room? No, there aren't / isn't.
2. Is there *a* / *any* picture on the wall? Yes, there is / are one.
3. *Are there any* / *Is there a* light in the room? Yes, there are / is.
4. *Is there* / *Are there* any doors in the room? No, there aren't *any* / *some*.
5. Are there *any* / *some* things on the shelves? Yes, there are *any* / *some* books.
6. Are there some /any new carpets in the house? Yes, there is / are some.

2 **2C Complete the sentences with *can* or *can't*.**

1. Can't you cook? No, I _________ but I _________ use a microwave!
2. I _________ wash clothes, but I really _________ iron very well!
3. 'Anybody _________ do the washing up!' 'Freddy _________!'
4. My parents _________ take good photos, but they _________ paint very well.
5. '_________ your brother drive a car?' 'No, he _________. He's only 12!'
6. 'What _________ you do well?' 'I _________ play football.'
7. I don't want to be in the band. I _________ play any instrument!

3A Countable and uncountable nouns with *some/any/no*

Countable and uncountable nouns with *some/any/no*	
Countable nouns	**Uncountable nouns**
I always have **an egg** for breakfast. I usually take **some bananas** with me.	I sometimes have **some bread** too.
There isn't **a can** of coke in the fridge. There aren't **any crisps** in this packet./ There are **no crisps** in the packet.	There isn't **any milk** in the fridge./There is **no milk** in the fridge.
Have you got a **sandwich** for lunch? Are there **any cakes** for desert?	Do you eat **any pasta** in your diet?
How many snacks do you eat between meals?	**How much** chocolate do you eat every day?

Countable nouns:

- name things we can count: *There is* ***an apple*** *on the table.*
- have singular and plural forms: *This* ***tomato*** *is very sweet. These* ***tomatoes*** *are big.*

Uncountable nouns:

- name things we cannot count: *I often drink* ***tea****.*
- do not have a plural form: *Vegetarians don't eat* ***meat****.*

We use *some* with plural countable or uncountable nouns:
There are ***some*** *eggs in the fridge.*
Can I have ***some*** *water, please?*
We use *any* in questions and in negative sentences with uncountable nouns and plural countable nouns:
Are there ***any*** *potatoes in this salad?*
I'm sorry, we haven't got ***any*** *ice cream.*
We can use *no* in affirmative sentences to replace not any.
There isn't ***any*** *tea in the cupboard = There is* ***no*** *tea.*

1 **3A Complete the sentences with *a/an*, *some*, *any* or *no*.**

1. There is no flour in this cake. I made it with ice cream!
2. 'Are there _________ biscuits?' 'Yes, please have _________.'
3. I have _________ snack on my way to school. I usually have _________ apple.
4. I don't drink _________ sugary drinks because they are bad for your health.
5. 'Do you need _________ butter for the cake?' 'No, thanks. _________.'

2 **3A Match the questions with the answers.**

1. How much coffee do you drink?
2. How many packets of crisps do you eat?
3. How much pasta do you eat?
4. How many meals do you have?

a. Three: breakfast, lunch and dinner.
b. I don't drink any. I prefer tea.
c. I eat two packets a week.
d. I eat it every day.

3D Quantifiers: *a lot of, too many, too much, a few, a little, not many, not much*

Quantifiers: *a lot of, too many, too much, a few, a little, not many, not much*	
Plural countable nouns	**Uncountable nouns**
There are **a lot of** tomatoes on this pizza!	There's **a lot of** cheese on this pizza.
Don't eat **too many** sweets because they're bad for you!	Don't use **too much** sugar because it is bad for you!
There are **a few** biscuits in the packet – eat them!	There's **a little** coffee in the pot – drink it!
There are **not many** tins in the cupboard! Do people eat **many** potatoes in your country?	There is **not much** mayonnaise in this jar! Do people eat **much** bread in the UK?

We use *a lot of* to talk about big amounts of countable or uncountable nouns:

*I try to eat **a lot of** vegetables every day.*

We use *too many* to talk about countable nouns when we have more than we need:

*Eating **too many** crisps isn't good for you.*

We use *too much* to talk about uncountable nouns when we have more than we need:

*There's **too much** salt in this soup.*

We use *a few* to talk about small amounts of countable nouns:

*Can I have **a few** bananas?*

We use *a little* to talk about small amounts of uncountable nouns:

*Add **a little** olive oil to the sauce.*

We use *not many* to talk about small amounts of countable nouns:

*There are **not many** vegetarian dishes on the menu.*

We use *not much* to talk about small amounts of uncountable nouns:

*There's **not much** carrot cake left.*

1 **3D Choose the correct words to complete the conversations.**

1

A There is a *lot of* / *many* salt in this dish!

B I agree! There's too *much* / *many*!

2

A How *much* / *many* food do you waste?

B We don't waste *much* / *many* things.

3

A Do you want a *few* / *little* sugar in your tea?

B No, I try not to eat too *much* / *many* sugar.

4

A Are there *much* / *many* ingredients in this recipe?

B No, only a *few* / *little*.

4A Present Continuous

Present Continuous					
Affirmative			**Negative**		
I	**am** (**'m**)	**eating**.	I	**am not** (**'m not**)	**eating**.
You/We/They	**are** (**'re**)		You/We/They	**are not** (**aren't**)	
He/She/It	**is** (**'s**)		He/She/It	**is not** (**isn't**)	

***Yes/No* questions**			**Short answers**
Am	I	**eating**?	Yes, I **am**. No, I**'m not**.
Are	you/we/they		Yes, you/we/they **are**. No, you/we/they **are not** (**aren't**).
Is	it		Yes, he/she/it **is**. No, he/she/it **is** (**isn't**).

***Wh-* questions**			
What	**am** **are** **is**	I you/we/they he/she/it	**talking** about?

We use the Present Continuous:

- to talk about actions that are happening now at the moment of speaking:
  *Listen! Peter **is playing** the piano.*
  *I can't talk now. I**'m sitting** in the library.*
- to talk about temporary situations:
  *This term we **are learning** to write essays.*

Spelling rules: -ing form

General rule: infinitive + *-ing*, e.g. *go* – ***going***, *play* – ***playing***

Verbs ending in a consonant + *-e*: -e *-ing*, e.g. *make* – ***making***, *use* – ***using***

One-syllable verbs ending in one vowel + one consonant: double the consonant + *-ing*, e.g. *sit* – ***sitting***, *run* – ***running***

Time expressions we use with the Present Continuous:

at the moment, now, at present

4C Present Simple and Present Continuous

Present Simple

We use the Present Simple to talk about:

- regular activities:
  *I often **listen** to music on my way to school.*
- states and permanent situations:
  *We **live** near the mountains.*
- preferences, with verbs like like, love, hate, prefer:
  *Children **love** water.*

Time expressions we use with the Present Simple:

always, often, never, sometimes, usually, every day/evening/week/winter, on Sundays, once a week

Present Continuous

We use the Present Continuous to talk about:

- activities and events taking place at the moment of speaking:
  *Listen! Peter **is playing** the piano.*
- temporary situations:
  *We **are learning** to write emails now.*

Time expressions we use with the Present Continuous:
at the moment/right now, now, today, this morning/evening, this month, this summer

1 4A **Complete the sentences with the correct Present Continuous form of the verb in brackets.**

A Where's Tom?
B *He's shopping* (He/shop).
A Really? What [1]_________ (He/buy)?
B Well, [2]_________ (he/try) to buy a present for his sister.

A Where are Paul and Ed? [3]_________ (they/work) on the art project?
B No, [4]_________ (they/not). Their posters are here. I think [5]_________ (they/study) in the library.
A Really? [6]_________ (they/try) to prepare for the exams?
B Yes, they want to get good grades this year.

A [7]_________ (you/listen) to me, John?
B Yes, sir.
A Have you got a mobile phone under the desk?
B Er, yes sir but [8]_________ (I/not) using it.
A Good, so you can give it to me until the end of the lesson, right?

2 4A **Complete the sentences with the correct form of the Present Continuous.**

1. Why aren't you *wearing* your school uniform?
2. Sh! I _________ trying to sleep!
3. 'Where's Hannah?' 'She's just _________ a shower.'
4. '_________ you listening to me?' 'Yes, of course I _________!'
5. 'What's Dad _________ for dinner?' 'Paella!'
6. Stop! Where _________ you going?

3 4C **Complete the sentences with the correct Present Simple or Present Continuous form of the verbs in brackets.**

Stacy What [1]*are you doing* (you/do)?
Gary [2]_________ (I/start) a blog.
Stacy What [3]_________ (it/be) about?
Gary It's about the subjects [4]_________ (we/do) at school at the moment.
Stacy That's a good idea. [5]_________ (I/write) a blog too.
Gary Really? What [6]_________ (you/do) right now? Can you help me get started?
Stacy Sorry! [7]_________ (I/study) for our English test tomorrow!

5A Past Simple: *to be*, *can* and affirmative of regular and irregular verbs

Past simple: *to be*

Affirmative			Negative		
I/He/She/It	**was**	at school.	I/He/She/It	**was not (wasn't)**	at school.
You/We/They	**were**		You/We/They	**were not (weren't)**	

Yes/No questions			Short answers
Was	I/he/she/it	at school?	Yes, I/he/she/it **was**. No, I/he/she/it **was not** (**wasn't**).
Were	you/we/they		Yes, you/we/they **were**. No, you/we/they **were not** (**weren't**).

Wh- questions		
Where	**was**	I/he/she/it?
	were	you/we/they?

Past simple: *can*

Affirmative			Negative		
I/You/He/She/It/We/They	**could**	sing.	I/You/He/She/It/We/they	**could not (couldn't)**	sing.

Wh- questions			
What	**could**	I/you/he/she/it/we/they	sing?

We use the *Past Simple* to talk about events that started and ended in the past.

The Past Simple form of the verb to be is *was/were*:

*They **were** both amazing artists.*
***Was** she a famous writer?*
*He **wasn't** confident at the beginning of his career.*

The past form of the verb *can* is *could*.

We use *could* and *couldn't* to talk about ability in the past:

*I **could** sing well but I **couldn't** dance when I was a child.*
*He **could** sing a lot of songs when he was a child.*
*I **couldn't** dance very well at school.*

Past Simple: affirmative

Regular verbs		Irregular verbs	
I/You/He/She/It/We/They	**watched** TV.	I/You/He/She/It/We/They	**went** to the cinema.

We use the Past Simple to talk about actions and situations that started and finished in the past or happened at a specific time in the past:

*Jason **watched** the match yesterday.*
*Last year we **went** to Majorca.*
*I **started** boxing in the 1980s.*

Time expressions we use with the Past Simple:
yesterday, last weekend/year, ten days/a minute ago, in 1969/the 1980s/July.

Spelling rules

Regular verbs:

- infinitive: + *-ed*, e.g. *start* – ***started***, *ask* – ***asked***
- verbs ending in *-e*: + *-d*, e.g. *move* – ***moved***
- verbs ending in a consonant + *-y*: *-y* + *-ied*, e.g. *study* – ***studied***
- verbs ending in one vowel + one consonant: double the consonant + *-ed*, e.g. *stop* – ***stopped***

Irregular verbs

For a list of irregular verbs, see page 171.

5D Past simple: negative and question forms

Past simple: negative and question forms				
Affirmative		**Negative**		
I/You/He/She/It/We/They	**watched** TV and **went** to the cinema.	I/You/He/She/It/We/They	**did not** (**didn't**)	**watch** TV and **go** to the cinema.

***Yes/No* questions**			**Short answers**
Did	I/you/she/he/it/we/they	**watch** TV and **go** to the cinema?	Yes, I/you/she/he/it/we/they **did**. No, I/you/she/he/it/we/they **didn't**.

***Wh-* questions**			
What	**did**	I/you/she/she/it/we/they	**watch**?

We use the *Past Simple* to talk about events and finished situations from the past.

We use *didn't + infinitive* to make negative sentences in the Past Simple:

*We **didn't see** this movie.*

We use did to make questions:

***Did** you work long yesterday?*

1 5A **Choose the correct form of the verb to complete the sentences.**

Cal Where [1]*were* you last night? Dan and I [2]_________ at your house.
Jen I [3]_________ at home all night!
Cal No, you [4]_________! There [5]_________ no answer at the door.
Jen What time [6]_________ it? Maybe I [7]_________ asleep.
Cal It [8]_________ very late, about 8 p.m.
Jen Ah! I [9]_________ at the park with my dog.

2 5A **Choose the correct form of the verb.**

1 '*Could / Couldn't* you see us at the airport with the big 'Welcome home' sign?' 'Yes!'
2 I *could / couldn't* swim when I was young, but I'm really good now.
3 All the Jackson Five brothers *could / couldn't* sing and dance from a young age. They were amazing.
4 I *could / couldn't* play the piano well so I joined the football team instead.
5 Were you good at Art? Yes, I *could / couldn't* paint or draw almost anything.

3 5D **Complete the text with the correct Past Simple form of the verbs in brackets.**

BIOGRAPHIES Winnie Mandela

Winnie Mandela (be) [1]*was* born in South Africa in 1936. She (marry) [2]_________ Nelson Mandela in 1957 and they (have) [3]_________ two children together. Winnie (go) [4]_________ to prison many times, but unlike Nelson she (not stay) [5]_________ there for twenty-seven years. She and Nelson (get) [6]_________ divorced in 1996, a few years after Nelson (come) [7]_________ out of prison. A lot of people (not like) [8]_________ Winnie Mandela because of things she (do) [9]_________, but she (fight) [10]_________ for black rights all her life. She (die) [11]_________ in 2018 at 81.

4 5D **Make questions for the sentences below. Ask about the underlined part.**

1 Paul went to <u>the cinema</u> on Sunday.
Where *did Paul go on Sunday*?
2 Susan gave me <u>a present</u>.
What _____________?
3 We visited that museum <u>five years ago</u>.
When _____________?
4 Kate met <u>her cousin</u> at the concert yesterday.
Who _____________?
5 They came back home early <u>because they were tired</u>.
Why _____________?
6 Peter played football <u>three times a week</u> when he was in primary school.
How often _____________?
7 My grandparents lived <u>in a little town in Scotland</u>.
Where _____________?
8 She went to bed <u>at 10 o'clock</u> yesterday.
What time _____________?

6A Comparative and superlative adjectives

Comparative and superlative adjectives			
	Adjective	**Comparative**	**Superlative**
one-syllable	high	high**er**	**the** high**est**
one-syllable ends in *-e*	large	larg**er**	**the** larg**est**
one-syllable ends vowel + consonant	hot	hot**ter**	**the** hot**test**
two syllables, ends in *-y*	scary	scar**ier**	**the** scar**iest**
two or more syllables	expensive	**more** expensive	**the most** expensive
irregular	good bad	**better** **worse**	**the best** **the worst**

We use comparative adjectives to compare two people or things:

*Films are **more exciting than** books.*

We use superlative adjectives to say that someone or something has the highest degree of a certain quality (when compared with at least two other people or things):

*Bollywood films are **the longest** of all.*

We can also use (not) as + adjective + as to compare two things:

*'The Dark Side of the Moon' (Pink Floyd) wasn't **as successful as** Thriller (Michael Jackson).*

*The film Titanic is **as long as** Godfather II.*

6D Too, (*not*) *enough*

Too and (*not*) *enough*

We use *too* + adjective when something is more than you need or want:

*That film was **too short**.*

We use adjective + *enough* when something is suitable for what you need or want:

*I think that plot was **interesting enough**.*

We use *not* + adjective + *enough* when something is less than you need or want:

*That comedy was just **not funny enough**.*

1 6A **Complete the sentences with the correct form of the adjectives in brackets.**

1. I heard the (funny) *funniest* joke the other day!
2. That's the (bad) _________ TV programme ever!
3. Which is (interesting) _________: the British Museum or the National Gallery?
4. The garden looks (big) _________ than usual in this photo because I used a (wide) _________ panoramic camera view.

2 6D **Complete the book review with *too* or *enough*.**

The novel was [1]*too* long and the plot [2]_________ slow, I just wasn't patient [3]_________ to read it. The characters were realistic [4]_________, but the narrator was [5]_________ boring. Overall, for a first novel, it was good [6]_________, I suppose, but I wouldn't read it again!

7A *Going to*

Going to					
Affirmative			**Negative**		
I	**am** (**'m**)	**going to** study.	I	**'m not** (**am not**)	**going to** study.
You/ We/ They	**are** (**'re**)		You/ We/ They	**aren't** (**are not**)	
He/ She/ It	**is** (**'s**)		He/ She/ It	**isn't** (**is not**)	

***Yes/No* questions**			**Short answers**
Am	I	**going to** study?	Yes, I **am**. No, I**'m not**.
Are	you/we/they		Yes, you/we/they **are**. No, you/we/they **aren't**.
Is	he/she/it		Yes, he/she/it **is**. No, he/she/it **isn't**.

***Wh-* questions**				
What	**are**	you	**going to**	visit in New York?

We use *going to* to talk about future intentions and plans which may change:

*I'm **going to** take some driving lessons.*

*Is Amanda **going to** buy a flat?*

7D Present Continuous for future arrangements

We use the Present Continuous for near future plans that are fixed because we made an arrangement, with another person, by paying money, etc:

***I'm visiting** my friends in London this weekend.* (That's my plan – I made an arrangement and bought my train ticket.)

*Josh **is having** an appointment at the dentist tomorrow.*

Time expressions:

next weekend/month, on Friday, in the morning/afternoon, at 3 p.m., tomorrow

1 7A **Complete the conversation with the correct form of *going to*.**

Jen What [1]*are you going to* do next weekend?
Sam I [2]_________ play video games. You?
Jen My parents [3]_________ have a barbecue in their garden.
Sam That sounds like fun. [4]_________ your brother [5]_________ be there?
Jen No, he [6]_________. He [7]_________ study.

2 7D **Use the prompts to write about future plans in the Present Continuous.**

1. I/have/lunch/Nando's/tomorrow
   I'm having lunch at Nando's tomorrow.
2. We/fly/Miami/Friday
3. She/not work/next weekend
4. They/come/to/UK/this summer?
5. I/take/my younger brother/to/cinema/Sunday

8A *Will*

Will					
Affirmative			**Negative**		
I/You/He/ She/It We/They	**will** ('ll)	buy things online.	I/You/He/ She/It We/They	**will not (won't)**	**buy** things online.

***Yes/No* questions**			**Short answers**
Will	I/you/he/ she/it we/they	**buy** things online?	Yes, I/you/he/she/it/we/they **will**. No, I/you/he/she/it/we/they **won't**.

***Wh-* questions**			
How long	**will**	I/you/he/she/it/ we/they	**live** in the future?

We use *will/won't* to make predictions based on our opinions, feelings or experiences:
*I think in the future people **will work** from home.*
***Will** robots **become** our family members?*
***We won't buy** things in shops, we **will buy** everything online.*

Time expressions we use with will:
in (the) future, in two months/years, next month/year, by 2030/March

We use will to make personal predictions about the future, based on our opinion or experience:
*In 20 years, I **will have** children and at least two dogs.*
*In the future, people **won't work** in offices.*

We often use expressions like *I think*, *In my opinion* or *I'm sure* before will:
***I don't think** space flights **will be** possible in the near future.*
***I'm sure** robots **will become** our family members.*

When we talk about ability in the future we use *be able to*, not *can*:
Present: *Drones **can** take aerial pictures.*
Future: *Drones **will be able to** deliver things to us in less than half an hour.*

8C Adverbs of manner

Adverbs of manners	
Affirmative	**Negative**
slow loud	slow**ly** loud**ly**
careful hopeful	careful**ly** hopeful**ly**
healthy easy	health**ily** eas**ily**
good fast hard	**well** **fast** **hard**

An adverb describes a verb and tells you how something happens:
*He ate his sandwich **quickly**.*

To form an adverb, we add *-ly* to most adjectives:
quick – **quickly**, careful – **carefully**

For adjectives ending in *-y*, we change *y* to *i* and add *-ly*:
happy – **happily**, angry – **angrily**

We often put adverbs at the end of a sentence:
*She can dance **well**.*
*He doesn't drive very **carefully**.*

The adjectives *good* (**well**), *fast* (***fast***) and *hard* (***hard***) are irregular.

1 8A **Complete the sentences with will and the verbs in brackets.**

1 Children *won't go* (go) to school because there __________ (be) only virtual schools in the future.
2 We__________(buy) any food in the supermarkets. Drones__________ (deliver) it to our homes.
3 We__________ (live) longer than 120 years in the future.
4 There__________ (be) any cinemas – we__________ (watch) all films at home.
5 Robots__________ (do) all household chores for us.

2 8A **Match 1–6 to a–f to make future predictions.**

1 ☐ We'll all walk or travel
2 ☐ People will live
3 ☐ School will be
4 ☐ Chinese will be
5 ☐ We won't be able to go outside
6 ☐ We won't need any money

a because we will pay for everything with cards.
b in driverless cars.
c in summer because of global warming.
d on the moon.
e the most important language.
f virtual not real.

3 8C **Complete the sentences with the correct adverbs.**

1 You can run very *fast* (fast)!
2 It's important to talk to people __________ (polite).
3 I'll __________ (happy) wait in the car while you go to the shop.
4 My fitness tracker tells me when I swim __________ (good).
5 Shout __________ (loud) if you want any help.
6 Tell me __________ (quick) how to install this app.
7 Can you give me his phone number? I need to call him (urgent).
8 Listen __________ (careful)! I won't repeat it again!

9A Must/mustn't/have to/don't have to

Have to

Affirmative			Negative		
I/You/ We/They	**have to**	practise every day.	I/You/ We/ They	**don't**	practise every day.
He/She/It	**has to**		He/She/ It	**doesn't**	

Yes/No questions				Short answers
Do	I/you/ we/they	**have to**	practise every day?	Yes, I/you/we/they **do**. No, I/you/we/they **don't**.
Does	he/she/ it			Yes, he/she/it **does**. No, he/she/it **doesn't**.

Wh- questions				
How often	**do** **does**	I/you/we/they he/she/it	**have to**	practise?

Must/mustn't

Affirmative		
I/You He/She/It We/They	**must**	**practise** a lot.
Negative		
I/You/ He/She/It We/They	**mustn't**	**touch** the ball.

To talk about obligation and necessity we use *must* and *have to*:
You ***must*** *use the right equipment.*
I ***have to*** *wear a helmet when I go cycling.*
He ***doesn't have to*** *bring any equipment.*

To say what is not allowed we use mustn't:
You ***mustn't*** *cross the line.*

To say there is no necessity…
Players ***mustn't*** *use their hands.*

To say there is no necessity or obligation, we use *don't have to*, not *mustn't*:
You ***don't have to*** *wear special shoes.*

He ***doesn't have to*** *practise every day.*
Like all modal verbs, *must/mustn't* have the same form for every person:
I/you/he/she/it/we/they ***must*** *work hard.*
I/you/he/she/it/we/they ***mustn't*** *drink so much coffee.*

1 9A **Choose the correct verbs to complete the notice.**

Welcome to the Yogarama studio!
You [1]*don't have to / have to be* an experienced Yogi to practise yoga, but you [2]*must / mustn't* only do what your body is ready for.
You [3]*don't have to / must* take your shoes off before you enter the studio. You can leave them by the door.
You [4]*don't have to / mustn't* wear any special clothes, but you [5]*have to / mustn't* be able to move around freely.
You [6]*don't have to / must* practise every day, but you will become stronger if you do. Enjoy the class.

9D Should/shouldn't

Should/shouldn't

Affirmative			Negative		
I/You/He/ She/It We/They	**should**	**eat** less sugar.	I/You/He/ She/It We/They	**should not (shouldn't)**	**eat** less sugar.

Yes/No questions			Short answers
Should	I/you/he/ she/it we/they	**eat** less sugar?	Yes, I/you/he/she/it/we/they **should**. No, I/you/he/she/it/we/they **shouldn't**.

Wh- questions			
Why	**should**	I/you/he/she we/you/they	**eat** less sugar?

We use *should/shouldn't* to say something is a good idea and to give advice:
You ***should*** *sleep more.*
Sarah ***shouldn't*** *eat so much sugar.*
The boys ***should*** *spend more time outside.*
How many meals a day ***should*** *we eat?*

1 9D **Complete the conversation with *should* or *shouldn't*.**

Kate Hey! Are you eating chocolate again? You [1]*shouldn't* eat a lot of chocolate!
Alan But I'm hungry! I keep thinking about food. What [2]_________ I do?
Kate I don't know, maybe you [3]_________ eat something healthy, like an apple.
Alan I know! [4]_________, but I really hate apples and most of the fruit!
Kate Well it says online that people [5]_________ eat healthy snacks and meals.
Alan [6]_________ I have some vegetables then? I like those.
Kate Yes, you [7]_________!

10A Present Perfect with *ever* and *never*

Present Perfect with *ever* and *never*					
Affirmative			**Negative**		
I/You/We/ They	**have** ('**ve**)	**lived** abroad.	I/You/We/ They	**have not** (**haven't**)	**lived** abroad.
He/She/It	**has** ('**s**)		He/She/It	**has not** (**hasn't**)	

***Yes/No* questions**			**Short answers**
Have	I/you/ we/they	**lived** abroad?	Yes, I/you/we/they **have**. No, I/you/we/they **haven't**.
Has	he/she/it		Yes, he/she/it **has**. No, he/she/it **hasn't**.

***Wh-* questions**			
Which countries	**have**	you	**visited**?

We use the Present Perfect to talk about actions and events which ended in the past but we don't know or it's not important when exactly they happened:
*Kate **has worked** part time in a zoo.*
***Have** you ever **volunteered** on a wildlife project?*

Time expressions we use with the Present Perfect:
ever (= at any time) in questions:
***Have you ever lived** in another country?*
never (instead of not) in negative sentences:
*Tobias **has never played** chess.*

Spelling rules: past participles
Regular verbs:
The past participles of regular verbs are the same as the Past Simple form of a verb and end in *-ed*, e.g. *work – worked – **worked***.
Irregular verbs:
See the list of irregular past participles on page 171.

10C Present Perfect with *just, already* and *yet*

We use the Present Perfect to talk about things that happened in the past but are still important now.
*I **have decided** to stop wasting water at home.*
*Our teacher **has taught** us a lot about the environment.*
We often use the Present Perfect with *just*, *already* and *yet*:
- We use *just* in affirmative sentences, between *have* and the past participle, for things that happened a short time ago:
  *We**'ve just finished** the test.*
- We use *already* in affirmative sentences, between *have* and the past participle, to say something happened earlier than we expected:
  *We**'ve already cleaned** out room.*
- We use yet at the end of negative sentences and questions to talk about something we expect to happen:
  *I **haven't sent** my application **yet**.*
  ***Has** he **collected** all the signatures **yet**?*

The past participles of the verb go is gone or been:
*She's **gone** to Paris.* (= She is in Paris or travelling there now)
*She's **been** to Paris.* (= She went to Paris and she returned)

1 **10A Complete the sentences with the correct Present Perfect form of the verb in brackets.**

1 Look! Somebody ***has cleaned*** (clean) the park and the playground.
2 'Can I borrow this book from you?' 'Yes, sure. I [1]__________ (finish) reading it.'
3 'Are you going to volunteer on this project?' 'I [2]__________ (not decide) yet.'
4 I don't know that man. I [3]__________ never __________ (see) him before.
5 I [4]__________ (find) these keys in front of the house. Are they yours?
6 It's my first trip to France. I [5]__________ never __________ (be) abroad.
7 [6]__________ you ever __________ (be) in a very difficult situation?

2 **10A Use the words to write sentences and questions in the Present Perfect.**

1 Have/you/ever/volunteer abroad?
Have you ever volunteered abroad?
2 Lisa/never/have problems/with homesickness
3 John/go/gap year/with friends
4 I/go/Thailand/twice
5 your cat/ever/catch/a mouse?
6 My little brothers/never/swim/sea
7 Where/your parents/live and work?
8 What's/strangest animal/you/ever/see?

3 **10C Rewrite the sentences with *just*, *already* or *yet*.**

1 I've come back from a month in South Africa.
I've just come back from a month in South Africa.
2 'Have your parents been on holiday this year?' 'No, they haven't.'
3 Don't worry, you're not late – the party hasn't really started!
4 'We have met! We volunteered together last summer, remember?
5 Join us for dinner – we've started.
6 I can't lend you this book. I haven't finished reading it.
7 You can't be hungry. You've eaten a big sandwich!

5.71

Verb	Past Simple	Past Participle
be	was/were	been
beat	beat	beaten
become	became	become
begin	began	begun
break	broke	broken
bring	brought	brought
build	built	built
buy	bought	bought
can	could	been able to
catch	caught	caught
choose	chose	chosen
come	came	come
cost	cost	cost
cut	cut	cut
do	did	done
drink	drank	drunk
drive	drove	driven
eat	ate	eaten
feel	felt	felt
fight	fought	fought
find	found	found
fly	flew	flown
forget	forgot	forgotten
get	got	got
give	gave	given
go	went	gone/been
grow	grew	grown
have	had	had
hear	heard	heard
hold	held	held
keep	kept	kept
know	knew	known
learn	learned/learnt	learned/learnt
leave	left	left
lose	lost	lost
make	made	made
mean	meant	meant
meet	met	met
pay	paid	paid
put	put	put
read /ri:d/	read /red/	read /red/
ride	rode	ridden
run	ran	run
say	said	said
see	saw	seen

Verb	Past Simple	Past Participle
sell	sold	sold
send	sent	sent
show	showed	shown
sing	sang	sung
sit	sat	sat
sleep	slept	slept
speak	spoke	spoken
spend	spent	spent
stand	stood	stood
swim	swam	swum
take	took	taken
teach	taught	taught
tell	told	told
think	thought	thought
throw	threw	thrown
understand	understood	understood
wake	woke	woken
wear	wore	worn
win	won	won
write	wrote	written

Unit 1

Choose the correct words a–c to complete the texts.

1

Do you want to ____ with your friends? Then join our local youth club.

a go **b** hang out **c** go to

2

Do you need help at home to do ____? Contact *Canton Cleaners*.

a housework **b** homework **c** exercises

3

New fitness class on Monday mornings – get ____ early and have energy all day!

a dressed **b** home **c** up

4

Would you like to help us write the school blog? We meet three ____ a month.

a twice **b** once **c** times

Unit 2

Choose the correct words a–c to complete the text.

There [1]*is* a modern flat to rent for £600 [2]__ Birmingham. It is in a quiet area [3]__ the city centre. It's on the first [4]__ and there is a double [5]__, a bathroom and a kitchen-dining area. There is also a [6]__, so you [7]__ have dinner outside in the summer. The flat is very [8]__, so don't miss out!

1 **a** are **b** be **c** is
2 **a** at **b** in **c** on
3 **a** between **b** near **c** under
4 **a** floor **b** ground **c** stage
5 **a** bath **b** furniture **c** bedroom
6 **a** attic **b** balcony **c** cellar
7 **a** can **b** can't **c** do
8 **a** noisy **b** comfortable **c** messy

Unit 3

Complete the text with one word in each gap.

You can cook [1]*an* omelette with only a [2]_________ things: [3]_________ cheese, a carton [4]_________ eggs and [5]_________ onion. To give your omelette flavor, you can use some salt and pepper but not [6]_________ - they're not very healthy.

Unit 4

Complete the text with the correct words of the words in bold.

Life skills

Young people work hard to get the right [1]*qualifications* (**QUALIFY**) at school. But what about [2]_________ (**USE**) life skills they learn outside the classroom through things like part-time jobs, sports or [3]_________ (**INTEREST**) hobbies? [4]_________ (**STUDY**) are getting experience of life through these activities. And this can help them get a good [5]_________ (**EDUCATE**) or find good jobs in the future. It can also help them with life's many [6]_________ (**CHALLENGE**).

Unit 5

Complete the second sentence using the word in bold so that it means the same as the first one. Use no more than three words including the word in bold.

1. Phil's not very funny - he never smiles. **SERIOUS**
   Phil's *a serious person* - he never smiles.
2. Are those trousers the right size? **FIT**
   Do _________ you?
3. Those shoes aren't the same colour. **MATCH**
   Those shoes _________ - they're different colours.
4. Were these your everyday clothes when you were twenty? **WEAR**
   _________ these clothes every day when you were twenty?
5. **A** Can I help you? **B** Yes, please. I need a red hoody. **FOR**
   A Can I help you? **B** Yes, please. I _________ a red hoody.

Unit 6

1 **Complete the second sentence using the word in bold so that it means the same as the first one. Use no more than three words including the word in bold.**

1. Modern thrillers aren't scarier than older films. **AS**
   Older films are *as scary as* modern thrillers.
2. Gauguin wasn't as good a painter as Picasso. **THAN**
   Picasso was a _________ Gaugin.
3. All other cinemas are smaller than the Odeon. **BIG**
   There isn't a cinema _________ the Odeon.
4. In this museum there isn't a more famous painting than 'Swans'. **FAMOUS**
   'Swans' is _________ painting in this museum.
5. We haven't got many parks in our city. **ENOUGH**
   There _________ parks in our city.

2 **Choose the correct words a-c to complete the texts.**

1

City of stars is one of ____ songs from the musical called *La La Land*.

a the most popular **b** the more popular **c** most popular

2

Conceptual art and photography is an exhibition at the Richard Saltoun ____.

a cinema **b** gallery **c** theatre

3

South West Four, London's ____ music festival, returns for an epic weekend.

a dance **b** dancer **c** choreography

4

The Importance of being Earnest is a new version of the ____ Oscar Wilde's play.

a composer **b** sculptor **c** writer

Unit 7

1 **Complete the text with the correct words of the words**

Explore Edinburgh's Old Town and New Town

This tour is ideal for first-time [1]*visitors* (**VISIT**) to the city. The tour begins in the Old Town with its narrow streets and [2]________ (**HISTORY**) squares. Then it goes up to Edinburgh Castle, St Giles' Cathedral and the [3]________ (**NATION**) Museum of Scotland. In August you can watch the many street [4]________ (**PERFORM**) at the Edinburgh Festival. New Town is [5]________ (**DIFFER**) from Old Town. It has [6]________ (**WIDE**) streets and buildings with Georgian architecture.

2 **Complete the second sentence using the word in bold so that it means the same as the first one. Use no more than three words including the word in bold.**

1. The city centre isn't far. Let's walk. **ON**
   The city centre isn't far. Let's *go on foot*.
2. Where do I get on the train? **BOARD**
   At which station ________ the train?
3. It's better to take a taxi if you want to be on time. **BY**
   It's better ________ taxi if you want to be on time.
4. Sorry, can you tell me the way to the park? **HOW**
   Excuse me, ________ get to the park?
5. I'm going to live in local people's home when I'm in Australia. **STAY**
   I'm going to ________ a host family when I'm in Australia.

Unit 8

Choose the correct words a-c to complete the text.

FOR SALE

[1]*Fitness tracker* £50 – with heart rate monitor (install [2]________ and use it on your smartphone or [3]________).

[4]________ keyboard and mouse £30 (AA [5]________ included) compatible with most personal [6]________

	a	b	c
1	fitness tracker	smart fork	website
2	a film	an application	memory
3	tablet	mouse	charger
4	digital	portable	wireless
5	speakers	batteries	lamps
6	computers	trackers	speakers

Unit 9

Complete the second sentence so that it means the same as the first one. Use no more than three words in each gap.

1. They have to keep their feet on the ground.
   They *mustn't take* their feet off the ground.
2. Your head feels very hot – you're not well!
   You've ________ – you're not well.
3. In rugby you're not allowed to throw the ball forward.
   You ________ the ball forward in rugby.
4. It's not necessary to practise every day.
   You ________ to practise every day.
5. Don't go to school if you're ill.
   You ________ home if you're ill.

Unit 10

Complete the text with the correct words of the words in bold.

COMMUNITY GARDEN [1]*competition* (**COMPETE**)

This is your chance to win a special makeover for your community garden. Recent [2]________ (**SEARCH**) has found that spending just ten minutes in a [3]________ (**NATURE**) environment is good for us. And creating city gardens is good for people too.

People who live near gardens are [4]________ (**HEALTHY**) and feel [5]________ (**RELAX**). It also reduces air [6]________ (**POLLUTE**) and makes life in a city more [7]________ (**PLEASURE**). Send us your project today to enter!

Unit 1

Read *Active Vocabulary*. Then study the word list on page 21 and choose six words that are new to you. Prepare flashcards for these words.

ACTIVE VOCABULARY | Flashcards

We usually remember new things better when we write them down and come back to our lists many times. For example, you could write a new word on the front of a paper card and its definition or translation on the back. Then you can test yourself and check how many words you remember.

Unit 2

Read Active Vocabulary in Unit 1 again. Choose six words from the word list on page 33 and prepare a flashcard for each word. Then, in pairs, swap your flashcards and guess the words based on the information on the back of the card.

Unit 3

Read *Active Vocabulary*. Then study the word list on page 47 and add more sub-categories and words to the map below.

ACTIVE VOCABULARY | Vocabulary maps

Vocabulary maps are a visual way of recording and remembering new vocabulary. They let you group vocabulary by certain criteria, but connected to the same topic e.g.

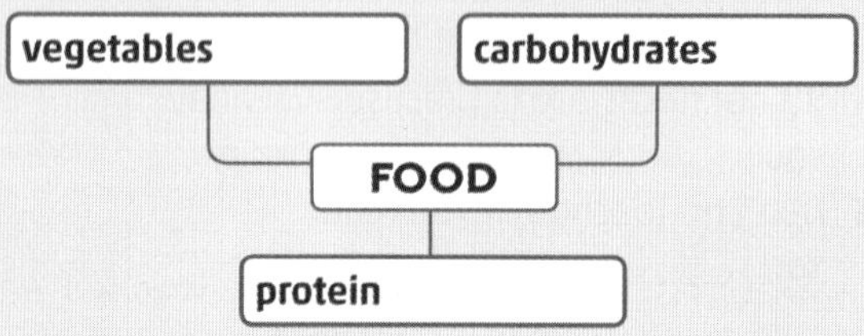

Unit 4

Read *Active Vocabulary*. Then study the word list on page 59 and draw a vocabulary map. Put SCHOOL in the middle. In pairs, compare your maps and answer the questions:

- Are your categories the same?
- Who has more words in their vocabulary map?
- Can you add any more words to your maps?

Unit 5

Read *Active Vocabulary*. Then find the antonyms of the words below in the word list on page 73.

1 different from ________ **2** funny ________
3 long ________ **4** small________ **5** young ________

ACTIVE VOCABULARY | Synonyms and antonyms

Synonyms are words that have the same or a very similar meaning. Antonyms are words with an opposite meaning. When you meet a new word, it's a good idea to look it up in a dictionary and record its synonyms and antonyms.

Unit 6

Read *Active Vocabulary* in Unit 5 again. Then write synonyms of the words below using the word list on page 85.

1 film ________ **2** awful ________ **3** artist ________
4 love story________ **5** suggest ________

Unit 7

Read Active Vocabulary and find the words in the word list on page 99 that collocate with *take* and *visit*. Then complete the sentences with these collocations.

A take: *a trip*, ________, ________, ________, ________
B visit: ________, ________, ________, ________

1. On the first day of our trip, we will ________ tour of the city.
2. Tomorrow we're visiting a ________ in the city centre. There's a modern art exhibition.
3. You need to ________ a water taxi to get to the island.
4. Every time I visit a ________, such as London or Rome, I like to eat in local restaurants.

ACTIVE VOCABULARY | Collocations

Collocations are words that often go together. For example, you say *have a party* NOT ~~*take a party*~~. Learning collocations will make your English sound more natural. When you learn new vocabulary, always record collocations.

Unit 8

Read *Active Vocabulary* in Unit 7 again and find five collocations in the word list on page 111. Then, in pairs, use these collocations to write sentences with gaps and give them to your partner. Can you guess your partner's missing words?

Unit 9

Read *Active Vocabulary* and study the words in the box below. In pairs, discuss how you could categorise them.

aerobics analyse discover racket tech-free sad urgently scared

ACTIVE VOCABULARY | Categorising

Categorising helps to remember groups of words better. You can categorise vocabulary by type (e.g. verbs, nouns, adjectives), negative or positive (e.g. happy – sad), etc.

Unit 10

Read *Active Vocabulary* in Unit 9 again. Then study the word list on page 137 and complete the table.

Nouns	Verbs	Adjectives	Positive	Negative
lion	*spread*	*sharp*	*good news*	*bad weather*

STUDENT A

2B Exercise 6, page 26

Follow the instructions.

Draw five cats in your picture. Don't show your picture to your partner!

In pairs, ask and answer questions to find the cats in your partner's picture. You can only ask 15 questions. Use the prepositions from the box to ask and answer questions.

behind between on next to under

A *Is there a cat under the chair?*
B *Yes, there is. No, there isn't.*

2F Exercise 5, page 31

Follow the instructions. Use the notes below and the phrases in the Speaking box on page 31 to role play the situation.

You see this advert online. Call Student B to find out more information:

- Extra beds? Bathrooms? How many?
- Shower or bath?
- Wi-Fi?
- Parking space?

3B Exercise 6, page 40

Follow the instructions. Then change roles.

1 You are the customer. Read your shopping list and ask the shop assistant if he/she has got these things. Don't forget to ask about the prices!

Shopping list
- two bags of pasta
- one bottle of oil
- four cartons of juice
- one jar of coffee
- two tins of tomatoes
- one packet of biscuits

A *Have you got any pasta?*
B *Yes, I have. How much do you want?*
A *How much is it?*
B *99p for a bag.*
A *I'd like two bags, please.*

2 You are the shop assistant. Look at the table and serve your customer with the items you have got.

PRODUCT	PRICE	NOTES
milk	£1 (a bottle)	lots of bottles
eggs	£1.62 (a carton)	lots of cartons
butter	£1.18 (a pack)	lots of packs
potatoes	95p (a bag)	0
tuna	£1.89 (a tin)	0
mayonnaise	£2.49 (a jar)	1

3C Exercise 8, page 41

Follow the instructions. Use the menu on page 40 and the Speaking Box on page 41 to help you.

You are the customer in a café. Think about these questions.
- Do you eat meat and fish? Or are you a vegetarian?
- Are you really hungry?
- How much money do you want to spend?

4F Exercise 7, page 57

Follow the instructions. Use the Speaking Box on page 57 to help you. Then change roles.

You are student A's mum/dad. Your son or daughter asks your permission to do the things below. If you say 'no', give a reason.

- Invite some friends to your house
- Go to the shopping centre
- Borrow some money
- Get back home after midnight

5C Exercise 7, page 67

Follow the instructions. Use the Speaking Box on page 67 to help you. Then change roles.

You are the shop assistant in a clothes shop.
- Offer to help the customer.
- Find the sizes of clothes the customer wants.
- Answer any other questions the customer has.

6F Exercise 8, page 83

Follow the instructions. Use the Speaking Box on page 83 to help you. Try to agree on something to do.

1 It's hot. You're bored. You want to do something outside. Phone student A and make some suggestions.

2 It's Student B's birthday tomorrow and there is a surprise party at his/her house at 6.30 p.m. Respond to Student B's suggestions appropriately.

9E Exercise 6, page 121

Follow the instructions. Use the Speaking Box on page 121 to help you. Then change roles.

- Your friend (Student B) looks sick.
- Ask about his/her health.
- Show sympathy.
- Offer some advice.

STUDENT B

2B Exercise 6, page 26

Follow the instructions.

Draw five cats in your picture. Don't show your picture to your partner!
In pairs, ask and answer questions to find the cats in your partner's picture. You can only ask fifteen questions. Use the prepositions from the box to ask and answer questions.

behind between on next to under

A *Is there a cat on the shelf?*
B *Yes, there is. No, there isn't.*

2F Exercise 5, page 31

Follow the instructions. Use the Speaking box on page 31 to help you.

You rent a house online. Student A calls you to find out more information. Read the description below and answer Student A's questions.

It's a beautiful 3-bedroom house in central Edinburgh, suitable for 6–8 guests. There are two bathrooms: one with a bath and the other with a shower. There are two extra beds, Wi-Fi and parking space in the street.

3B Exercise 6, page 40

Follow the instructions. Then change roles.

1 You are the shop assistant. Look at the table and serve your customer with the items you have got.

PRODUCT	PRICE	NOTES
pasta	99p (a bag)	lots of bags
oil	£3.60 (a bottle)	lots of bottles
tomatoes	85p (a tin)	lots of tins
juice	£1.34 (a carton)	2
coffee	£2.70 (a jar)	0
biscuits	£4.20 (a box)	0

2 You are the customer. Read your shopping list and ask the shop assistant if he/she has got these items. Don't forget to ask about the prices!

Shopping list
- one bag of potatoes
- two bottles of milk
- one box of eggs
- one packet of butter
- three tins of tuna
- one jar of mayonnaise

A *Have you got any potatoes?*
A *No, sorry we haven't got any!*
B *Okay. How much is the milk?*
A *It's one pound for a two litre bottle.*
B *OK, can I have two bottles, please?*

3C Exercise 8, page 41

Follow the instructions. Use the café menu and the Speaking box on page 41 to help you.

You are the server in a café. Think which things on the menu are available today.

A *Are you ready to order?*
B *Yes, please. I'd like ...*

4F Exercise 7, page 57

Follow the instructions. Use the Speaking box on page 57 to help you.

You're talking to your mum/dad. You want permission to do the things below. Ask questions.

- Invite some friends to your house.
- Go to the mall.
- Borrow some money.
- Get back home after midnight.

5C Exercise 7, page 67

Follow the instructions. Use the Speaking box on page 67 to help you. Then change roles.

You are the customer in a clothes shop.
- Think of three items of clothing you need.
- Ask the assistant for the sizes you need.
- Ask to try the clothes on and decide if you want to buy them.

6F Exercise 8, page 83

Role play the situations. Use the Speaking box on page 83 to help you. Try to agree on something to do.

1 You're busy at home. You're happy to do something with Student A but you don't want to go out. Respond to Student A's suggestions appropriately.

2 It's your birthday tomorrow and you want to do something interesting after school. Phone student A and make some suggestions.

9E Exercise 6, page 121

Follow the instructions. Use the Speaking box on page 121 to help you. Then change roles.

- You are not feeling well.
- Describe your problems/symptoms.
- Say when it started.
- Thank Student A for their advice.

ALL STUDENTS

6E Exercise 1, page 82

Answers to the quiz: 1 a, **2** a

9B Exercise 2, page 118

Answers to the quiz: 1 91,4 cm **2** A lawyer and president of FIFA **3** A bat: baseball, cricket; A racket: table tennis, tennis, badminton **4** A goalkeeper **5** 7.3 m **6** climbing, cycling, horse riding, kayaking, mountain biking, skateboarding **7** We think the Persians first used swimming goggles in the 14th century when they were diving for pearls. **8** Orange